ST. ANSELM OF CANTERBURY

A CHAPTER IN THE HISTORY OF RELIGION

ST. ANSELM

OF CANTERBURY

A CHAPTER IN THE HISTORY OF RELIGION

BY

J. M. RIGG

OF LINCOLN'S INN, BARRISTER-AT-LAW

Wipf & Stock
PUBLISHERS
Eugene, Oregon

Wipf and Stock Publishers
199 West 8th Avenue, Suite 3
Eugene, Oregon 97401

St. Anselm of Canterbury
A Chapter in the History of Religion
By Rigg, J.M.
ISBN: 1-59244-667-1
Publication date 4/21/2004
Previously published by Methuen and Company, 1896

PREFACE

THE Church has reason to be thankful that in his secretary, Eadmer of Canterbury, St. Anselm found a chronicler of his public and private life, whose impartiality may of course be questioned, but whose general sobriety and conscientiousness are universally acknowledged; and Eadmer may be congratulated on the scholarly edition of his *Historia Novorum in Anglia* and *De Vita et Conversatione Anselmi*, contributed by Mr. Martin Rule to the Rolls Series of our national chronicles and memorials. These works, with Anselm's voluminous correspondence (Migne, *Patrolog.* clviii., clix.), the few extant letters of his suffragan, Herbert Losinga and Osbert of Clare (Caxton Soc., 1846), the Lives of the Abbots of Le Bec, by Gilbert and Miles Crispin, edited by Giles in *Patres Ecclesiae Anglicanae*, Oxford, 1845, the anonymous but contemporary Life of Gundulf of Rochester (Migne, *Patrolog.* clix.), the *Anglo-Saxon Chronicle* (Rolls Series), the Chronicle of Florence of Worcester (Eng. Hist. Soc.), Henry of Huntingdon's *Historia Anglorum* (Rolls Series), William of Malmesbury's *De Gestis Pontificum Anglorum* and *De Gestis Regum Anglorum* (Rolls Series), the *Historia Ecclesiastica* of Ordericus Vitalis, edited by Le Prevost for the Société de l'Histoire de

France, Paris, 1838–1855, the Jumièges Chronicle (Migne, *Patrolog*. cxlix.), the *Chronique de Robert de Torigni* and the *Chronique du Bec*, edited by M. Léopold Delisle and the Abbé Porée respectively for the Société de l'Histoire de Normandie, Rouen, 1872 and 1883, the *Chronicon Beccense*, edited by Giles (Pat. Eccl. Angl., *Lanfranc*), the Life of St. Anselm by John of Salisbury, also edited by Giles, and the St. Albans Chronicles (Rolls Series) are the principal sources for the history of the life and times of the saint.

They are by no means in all cases of equal or independent authority, but the order of enumeration is, roughly speaking, the order of their value. The St. Albans Chronicles, by reason of their late date, are of quite secondary importance.

In the present work I have used them all as best I could, supplementing them by Mansi's *Concilia* and Martène's *De Antiquis Ecclesiae Ritibus*. The historical background, so to speak, I have studied from the *Annales Ecclesiastici* of Baronius, Milman's *Latin Christianity*, Gregorovius's *Geschichte der Stadt Rom im Mittlelalter*, Giesebrecht's *Geschichte der Deutschen Kaiserzeit*, Freeman's *Norman Conquest* and *Reign of William Rufus*, the Abbé Delarc's *Histoire de Grégoire VII.*, and other historical works. I have also consulted, with more or less, and sometimes with no little, profit, the Lives or Studies of St. Anselm by Möhler, Montalembert, Rémusat, Charma, Church, Croset-Mouchet, Mr. Martin Rule, and Père Ragey. To the two last named writers I have especial reason to acknowledge my obligations.

CONTENTS

CONTENTS

ST. ANSELM OF CANTERBURY

CHAPTER I.

CHURCH AND STATE

NO epoch in the long and chequered history of the Catholic Church is of more absorbing interest, none exhibits more signally the marvellous vigour of her vitality, than that which marks her first encounter with the organised feudal power. During the three centuries of turmoil which intervened between the collapse of the Western Empire under Augustulus, and its revival under Charlemagne, amid the fitful rise and fall of temporal powers and principalities—Visigothic, Burgundian, Suevian, Ostrogothic, Lombardic—the Church silently and, as it were, by instinct, maintained, consolidated, and, where possible, extended her œcumenical polity. By her were preserved, not only what remained of art, letters, and the traditions of civilised life, but the coherent and symmetrical structure of the Roman law, which was to mould the nascent institutions of the Empire, the monarchies, the republics of the new age. Without her to interpret and administer, Theodoric and Justinian would have legislated in vain; her part in shaping subsequent secular legislation was by no means unimportant, especially in Spain, to say nothing of her own creation, the necessary but abused system of canon law; and even parliamentary government is but an offshoot of her conciliar system.

Towards the close of that eventful period she saw herself menaced with the odious domination of the Arian, or, at least, semi-Arian, Lombard, appealed to Pepin for deliverance, hailed his donation of the Exarchate of Ravenna as a gift of God, and requited its confirmation by Charlemagne with the crown of the Caesars. Thereby she gained, with enormous prestige, temporal security, and compromised her spiritual independence.

Pepin's donation, though the most important, was, indeed, by no means the first, as it was also far from being the last, of its kind. The greater sees and monasteries had long held extensive domains, and their endowments were lavishly augmented by Charlemagne and his successors. These grants were commonly made in frankalmoign; *i.e.* without express reservation of military service; but, in course of time, such service came to be ordinarily rendered, and, *pari passu*, the minor benefices were converted into military fiefs. The priest was not indeed bound to bear arms himself, though he frequently did so; but he took the oath of fealty to his lord, and became responsible to him for a prescribed quota of armed retainers. Thus the Church became an integral part of the vast secular polity known as the feudal system, with the result that while she did not, as, indeed, she could not, abandon or abate her claim to spiritual autonomy and supremacy, she was, nevertheless, in her character of temporal power, dependent upon her feudal superiors. It was natural, it was inevitable, that they should claim the right, should usurp the function, of legislating in her behalf, even in matters not of purely temporal concern—of reforming her, of limiting her freedom in a variety of ways. So Pepin's dowry brought in its train the tutelage, if not the servitude, of the Bride of Christ. Thenceforth, busy and supple fingers were ever at work weaving imperceptibly around her the fine fibres of precedent, custom, law. She has parted with her freedom, and she will have to suffer and contend long and sorely before she regain it. The relations of Church and State remained, indeed, long ill-defined, for fine juristic theories, like those evolved from the two lights of Genesis, the two swords of St. Peter, the supposed donation of Constantine, the supposed concession of Hadrian I., are not woven in a day, but are the slow product of time and events.[1] But as often as a see fell vacant, the two powers came into close contact, if not collision.

In prefeudal times bishops had been elected by the joint vote of the clergy and laity, and once duly elected, nothing more than consecration was needed to confer the pastoral office; and the form, at least, of popular election survived in the Western Church far into the feudal period. In course of time, however, the general body of the laity ceased to exercise their franchise, while the vote of the clergy came, in many instances, to be little more than a form for giving effect to the will of the emperor, king, or other secular prince. This practice established, it was but a logical corollary that, upon his consecration, the bishop should receive, not merely his temporalities,

[1] *Cf.* DANTE, *De Monarchia*, lib. iii. cc. 4–12.

but the insignia of his spiritual office, his ring and crosier, from the prince who, in truth, made him. To this usurpation, which may be roughly dated from the ninth century, a certain counterpoise was found in the stricter enforcement of the canon which required metropolitans to sue at Rome for the *pallium*, or sacred stole of office, within a prescribed period from their consecration, on pain of forfeiting their authority.[1]

Meanwhile, the independence of the Holy See was threatened by the pretensions of the Emperors to confirm the election of the Popes, which still rested nominally in the suffrages of the clergy and people of the city of Rome, and the open violence or covert intrigues by which lesser potentates sought to compass the election of their own nominees. No wonder, then, that the hard bestead Popes of that stormy period looked none too critically at decretals which purported to have been compiled by Isidore of Seville. The marvel is, not that they should sometimes have clutched eagerly at doubtful expedients for sustaining their tottering power, but that they should have preserved any sense whatever of the sacredness of their office, any regard whatever for the common maxims of morals.

From their seat, by the tomb of St. Peter, the Popes of the ninth century looked out upon a world which seemed to be fast reeling into chaos. While rival pretenders were parting, in arms, the heritage of Charlemagne, the heathen Northmen carried havoc and desolation to every coast, up every navigable river; wherever, in short, their long-beaked galleys could

[1] No distinction was made between England and the continent. From Augustine to Lanfranc a long line of English primates either received the pallium from Rome, or went to Rome to receive it. Will. Malmes. *De Gest. Pontif.* (Rolls Ser.) passim.

penetrate. In the east, even before the Photian schism, the authority of the Holy See had faded almost to a shadow. In Spain, in Sicily, the Saracen was supreme. Taranto, Brindisi, Bari, knew his rovers only too well. He gained a footing in the Duchy of Benevento; he sailed up the Tiber, and looted the churches of St. Peter and St. Paul (846); he established a permanent camp on the Garigliano, and harried the Campagna at his pleasure.

In the succeeding age the meteoric irruptions of the heathen Magyars bade fair for a time to complete the ruin of Christendom. In the second quarter of the tenth century they traversed South Germany, overran Southern Gaul, passed the Alps, menaced Rome (936), and then returned to Germany, there to meet, at last, their match in Otto the Great.

Meanwhile, under the nominal sway of a succession of feeble or ferocious, dissolute or rapacious puppet-pontiffs, foes hardly less formidable than the Saracen or the Magyar occupied and desolated the Holy City. Her annals during this period present a motley pageant of license, sedition, anarchy, civil strife, culminating from time to time in the domination of some master of the robes to one of the said puppets; or some military adventurer from the Marches, prototype of the *condottieri* of later days; or some turbulent Roman baron, or Tuscan marquis or count, masquerading in the antique titles of consul or patricius, senator or prefect of the Romans; or, worst of all, some able and intriguing Roman dame, who found in her fatal beauty and easy virtue the means wherewith to gratify an inordinate ambition. Wounded in her head, and bruised in every member, the Church seemed languishing unto death. Beyond the Alps, the impulse given to learning by the schools of Charlemagne, and to speculation by the genius of Scotus Erigena, had spent itself. Even theology had hushed her strident voice, as if foreboding that her doom was nigh at hand. By the middle of the tenth century, what of letters and science remained in Europe was almost confined to the Saracens and Greeks. Discipline was scandalously lax. The clergy, regular and secular alike, and almost without distinction of rank or rule, were tainted with simony, and sunk in sloth and licentiousness. Here and there, indeed, as at Cluny and Glastonbury, noble souls were struggling to realise a higher ideal; and a new era may well have seemed to be dawning when Gerbert (Silvester II.) carried the lore of the schools of Spain to Reims, and across the Rhine to Ravenna, and to Rome. But Gerbert owed his tiara to imperial influence; clergy, nobles, and populace alike viewed him with suspicion, and he fell a victim to Roman pestilence, or poison, before he had so much as essayed the mighty task of reforming the Church. The Tusculan dynasty which followed ruled at best as secular princes, at the worst as licentious and ferocious despots.[1] Nevertheless, jealousy of transalpine intervention kept Rome passive under their tyranny, until the enormities of Benedict IX. provoked a revolution; nor was it until three pretenders had partitioned the vicegerency of Christ, that the city sullenly acquiesced in the consecration of the imperial nominee, Suidger, Bishop of Bamberg, who ruled for a space as Clement II. (25 Dec., 1046–9 Oct., 1047). It redounds to the credit of Clement, and through

[1] The only possible exception would be Benedict VIII., who made some faint and ineffective tentatives towards reform.

him of the German people, that his brief pontificate saw the first step taken, though it was but a short one, towards the suppression of the all but universal practice of simony. At the Council of Rome (1047) a decree was passed that whoso should knowingly receive ordination from a simoniacal bishop should do penance for forty days, and meanwhile be suspended from the exercise of his ministry. More was accomplished by Leo IX., the saintly Bruno, Bishop of Toul. At the councils held by him, in 1049, at Rome, at Pavia, at Reims, at Mainz, simoniacs were degraded, and the authority of the ancient disciplinary canons of the Church reasserted in its full vigour. But however excellent were Leo's intentions, his methods were not calculated to eradicate the cancer which was eating out the life of the Church. The true cause of simony, and not of simony only, but of the general and deplorable relaxation of clerical morals, lay in the secularisation of the hierarchy, which had resulted from its virtual incorporation into the feudal system. As long as the right of granting investiture of sees and benefices remained with the laity, it was not in human nature that the grant should ordinarily be made without what lawyers term a consideration; or, the venal practice once established, that the clergy should retain unimpaired either their ideal of sanctity or their sense of independence. Leo allowed his attention to be diverted from ecclesiastical reform by his ill conceived and worse executed schemes for the expulsion of the Normans from Italy. He died, 19 April, 1054, without effecting more than a temporary and trifling amelioration of the condition of the Church. His successor, Victor II. (Gebhard of Eichstädt), had larger and bolder views. By prohibiting the alienation of the Church's lands to the laity he did something to retard her further secularisation; nay, he even compelled the restitution of certain of the already secularised fiefs. His pontificate, however, lasted little more than two years; and that of his successor, Stephen IX., hardly eight months. It was for an ecclesiastic of the true Italian type, wise as a serpent, if hardly as harmless as a dove; austere as an anchorite, yet accomplished in worldly affairs; proud by nature as a fallen archangel, yet humbly self-forgetting in the service of the Church; sharp-eyed as a lynx; stealthy-footed as a panther; patient, unerring as a sleuth-hound; staunch and tenacious as a Spanish bulldog—it was for Hildebrand of Sovana, for all his northern name and Cluniac training a Tuscan of Tuscans, and moreover a man of the people,[1] that it was reserved to initiate, and for a quarter of a century to control, the only policy that could redeem the Church from her secular bondage.

Subdeacon to Gregory VI. and Leo IX., also Abbot of St. Paul's at Rome, legate to the Imperial Court on the death of Leo IX. in 1054, legate of his successor, Victor II., at the Councils of Lyon and Tours (against simony and the heresy of Berengar) in the following year, legate again in Germany in 1057, Hildebrand had seen much, meditated deeply, and already matured his plans, when the death of Stephen IX. (1058) gave him the long-looked-for opportunity of putting them in execution. By an adroit stroke he united both the Empress Agnes and her mortal enemy, Godfrey of Lorraine, Marquis of Tuscany, against the Roman

[1] His descent from the aristocratic Aldobrandeschi is merely an etymological fable.

baronial faction, which in haste, in arms, and at dead of night had intruded the Cardinal-bishop of Velletri, John Mincio, a scion of the consular Crescentian House, into the chair of St. Peter, drove him from Rome, and set in his place one whom he knew he could control, Gerard, Bishop of Florence, who took the style of Nicolas II.

Under Hildebrand's inspiration, Nicolas inaugurated his pontificate by the memorable decree (passed at a council held in the Lateran, in April, 1059) by which the right of voting at papal elections was restricted to the cardinal-bishops. The general body of the clergy and people of Rome were thus deprived of their ancient and long-abused franchise; for, though their right of approbation was expressly reserved, this was as far as possible from carrying with it the power of veto. The "honour" due to the Emperor also received verbal recognition, but in effect was reduced to a mere form. Henceforth he had no colour of constitutional right to influence the deliberations of the Sacred College, or overrule its choice. For the rest, the Pope was, if possible, to be chosen from the bosom (e gremio) of the Roman Church, but need not be elected within the walls of the city. The future independence of the Holy See thus secured, so far as decree and anathema could secure it, against secular dictation or influence, the Pope provided for his own security by an alliance with the Norman masters of Southern Italy, whose lances formed his bodyguard. By this bold and astute policy Hildebrand laid the basis of that future exaltation of the Papacy by which, and which alone, the Church was enabled to fulfil her mission of guardian of the liberties, and nurse of the renascent intellectual and spiritual life of Europe.

ST. ANSELM OF CANTERBURY

For the dark age, having reached its darkest, was now passing away. The heathen inundation had spent its strength: the hordes of grim warriors from the far north, lately the terror, were now the bulwark of the Church; and a new and nobler spirit, born of long centuries of strife, suffering, agony, was stirring the mind of Western Christendom to its inmost depths. The monasteries were throwing off their sloth, new religious houses were being founded, especially in Normandy, already distinguished by that devoutness which it has retained to our own day. The Abbeys of Jumièges, of Conches, of Fécamp, of Mont St. Michel, of St. Wandrille at Fontanelle on the Seine, near Rouen, of St. Amand within, of Ste. Catherine or La Trinité du Mont, and St. Ouen, without the walls of that famous city, of Grestain, near Lisieux, of Le Bec, Bernay and Cormeilles, between Rouen and Lisieux, of St. Evroult, between Laigle and Argentan, of St. Leufroy, between Evreux and Gaillon, of St. Pierre sur Dives, near Troarn, were all restored, reformed, or founded during the latter half of the tenth, or the first half of the eleventh century. And with the revival of religion came also the intellectual renaissance. From Pavia Lanfranc carried to Avranches, and thence to Le Bec, a mind disciplined by the exact study of the civil law and the Latin classics, to find many an eager and apt pupil among the northern barbarians. At Tours, the spirit of Scotus Erigena lived again in the hardy rationalism of Berengar, which spared not even the profound mystery of the Blessed Sacrament. In France, in Burgundy, in Aquitaine, schools of learning sprang up as if by magic.

CHAPTER II.

THE ABBEY OF STE. MARIE DU BEC

THE Abbey of Ste. Marie du Bec (St. Mary of the Stream) owed its origin to the piety of a Norman knight of high degree and distinguished prowess—Herlwin, son of Ansgot. On the father's side he boasted descent from the first Danish settlers in the duchy; through his mother, Eloisa, he was closely related to the Counts of Flanders. In grateful recognition of a signal deliverance from imminent peril of death on the field of battle, he had made a vow, while yet in the prime of life, to devote the rest of his days to religion, and having, not without difficulty, obtained the consent of his immediate feudal superior, Count Gilbert of Brionne, had built, on his own upland estate of Burneville, now Bonneville-Appetot, a few miles north-east of Brionne, a lowly house for monks of the order of St. Benedict. The house was dedicated to the Blessed Virgin in 1034, by Herbert, Bishop of Lisieux; and there Herlwin, with his brother-in-law, Baldric of Servaville, and a few more of his old companions-in-arms, took the cowl and set up his rest. In 1037 he received priest's orders, and the style and title of abbot.

The site of the monastery was ill-chosen, for the upland was dry as a desert, and some miles distant from the nearest river, the gentle Rille, which, after washing Brionne, winds its meandering course by Pont Authou, Montfort, and Pont Audemer to the sea near Honfleur. Near Pont Authou the Rille is joined, on the right bank, by a tiny tributary, which purls pleasantly between two uplands clad with spruce and larch from its source at St. Martin du Parc, a few miles to the south-east; and, by reason of its insignificance, has received no other than the common appellative of Le Bec (beck, or brook). For all its insignificance, however, the beck has had its history, and one which is not likely to be forgotten. For when Herlwin and his monks, tired at last of living on such scanty provender, mostly vegetarian, as could be wrung from their inhospitable domain, and of fetching their daily supply of water from a distant spring, began to think of shifting their quarters, they pitched, as if beguiled by the cruel spite of some malicious fairy, but, in fact, for the very prosaic reason that no better site was available, on some land belonging to Herlwin on the right bank of the Bec, hard by its confluence with the Rille. By so doing they exchanged a desert for a swamp. Nothing daunted, however, the sturdy Normans plied their rude mason's craft with strong hands and willing hearts, and in the early spring of 1040 took possession of their new Abbey of St. Mary of the Stream, a quadrangular structure of mud and flint, extremely primitive, but containing within its circuit provision for the needs, spiritual and temporal, of some three score souls.

To the north and south-east of the abbey rose the two uplands which enclose the little gorge of the Bec; to the west, beyond the Rille towards Lisieux, stretched a dense forest infested by bears, wolves, and marauders, but of these the stout Norman monks had probably little fear; and on one occasion the outlaws did them unwittingly a signal service. It chanced that, in 1042, Lanfranc was on his way from Avranches to Rouen, when one of these gangs surprised him as he drew near Le Bec, robbed him of all he had, tied his hands behind his back, drew his hood over his eyes, thrust him into a dense thicket, and there abandoned him to his fate. Night fell, and he would fain have broken the awful silence with a chant; but, rack his memory as he might, not a canticle, not a verse, could he recall. Conscience-stricken that, in his pursuit of secular learning, he should so shamefully have neglected his Maker, he vowed thenceforth to devote himself, body and soul, to His service for the rest of his life, should life be spared him.

So passed the night, and the freshening breeze of the early dawn bore with it the glad sound of human voices. Lanfranc made himself heard, and was released by the wayfarers, who, in response to his request to be shown the way to the lowliest house of prayer in the neighbourhood, guided his steps to the Abbey of St. Mary of the Stream. There, after a rigorous novitiate of three years passed in almost total silence, he took the cowl, and soon afterwards was made prior. Concerning Lanfranc's life at Le Bec we have little authentic information, and it is idle to attempt to supply the void by conjecture. But it must have been there that he meditated the argument for transubstantiation (afterwards developed in his *Liber de Corpore et Sanguine Domini*) with which, at the Councils of Rome and Vercelli (1050), he crushed for the nonce the incipient heresy of Berengar, and established his reputation as the champion of Catholic orthodoxy; and we know that there and at the larger house, which was afterwards built higher up the stream, he gathered about him from near and far such a goodly band of scholars as, with the *élite* of the monks, transformed the abbey into a seat of learning and an arena of intellectual gymnastics. Conspicuous among these early *alumni* of Le Bec are his nephew and namesake, his and Herlwin's devoted friends Roger and William, the future Abbots of Saint Wandrille, Lessay and Cormeilles, Paul, his kinsman, and Henry, who will carry the light of sound learning and true religion, the one to St. Albans, to live in the pages of Matthew Paris, the other to Canterbury and Battle; Yves of Beauvais, Latinist and civilian, Abbot of St. Quentin and Bishop of Chartres that is to be; Ernost, Gundulf, and Ralph, destined each in turn to wear the mitre at Rochester, the last also at Canterbury; Gilbert Crispin, in whom Herlwin will find a biographer, and Westminster an abbot, William Bonne Ame, the future Archbishop of Rouen, and Guitmund, champion of orthodoxy no less stout than Lanfranc, who will shepherd unruly sheep in the new Normandy carved out by the sword of Rainulf beyond the Garigliano:[1] also a keen-witted Milanese, Anselm of Baggio, who will live to wear the tiara, but not to forget his old master;[2] and another and much younger Anselm, who, when Lanfranc took the cowl, was still being painfully

[1] Author of a treatise *De Corporis et Sanguinis Christi Veritate in Eucharistia;* afterwards Bishop of Aversa.

[2] Anselm of Baggio, Bishop of Lucca, succeeded Nicolas II. in 1061, and assumed the title of Alexander II. He was still Pope when, ten years later, Lanfranc, as Archbishop-elect of Canterbury, came to sue for the pallium. Alexander received him standing, honouring thereby, as he

initiated in the mysteries of the *trivium* in secluded Val d'Aosta, little dreaming that he would one day be the pupil and friend of the great Pavian in the distant Norman abbey, and later on his successor in the chair of St. Augustine.

In course of time it became evident that the little abbey must be replaced by a more capacious structure. A new site, bequeathed by Count Gilbert of Brionne, about a mile higher up the valley and on the same bank of the stream, was in every way eligible, being provided in the rear with a goodly extent of woodland or park, and sheltered by the uplands of the narrowing gorge; and there in the spring of 1058 was founded, with no little pomp and ceremony, the historic Abbey of Le Bec, destined to grow in after years into one of the stateliest and wealthiest of the religious houses of the West. It took some three years to make it even habitable; for Lanfranc's taste, as became a Pavian, was for the majestic and magnificent; and the spacious and beautiful church was not completed till 1074. The solemn function of its dedication to our Blessed Lady was performed by Lanfranc, then Archbishop of Canterbury, assisted by Odo, Bishop of Bayeux, and the Bishops of Lisieux, Evreux, Séez, and Le Mans, and in presence of a vast concourse of Norman nobility, on 23 Oct., 1077.

The abbey was endowed by Herlwin with the third part of the manors of Burneville, Quevilly, and Surcy, and the entire manor of Cernay sur Orbec and its dependencies; and by degrees other domains were

graciously observed, not the archbishop, but the master, at whose feet he had sat, and to whom he owed what he had of learning. He then gave Lanfranc two pallia, one as the symbol of investiture, the other that which he was himself accustomed to wear in saying mass, as a token of regard; and at the same time named him Primate of all Britain.

added with rights of lordship and patronage over parishes too numerous to detail. The abbey also put forth not a few offshoots, dependent priories, or cells, not only in Normandy and France, as those of St. Pierre de Cauchy in the diocese of Amiens, Ste. Honorine de Conflans in the diocese of Paris, and St. Pierre de Pontoise; but also in England, at Okeburn and Brixton Deverill, in Wiltshire; at Ruislip, in Middlesex; at Dunton, in Essex; at Balham, Streatham, Tooting Bec, in Surrey; at Great Blakenham and Stoke by Clare, in Suffolk; at Hoo and Preston Beckhelwyne, in Sussex; at Steventon, in Berkshire; at Winchcombe, in Oxfordshire; at St. Neot's, in Huntingdonshire; at Povington, in Dorset; at Weedon-on-the-Street, Northamptonshire; at Chester (St. Werburg); and at Wivelsford, in Lincolnshire.[1]

The jingling refrain, long current in Normandy—

> "De quelque part que le vent vente
> L'Abbaye du Bec a rente,"

attests the impression made on the popular imagination by these widely-extended seigneurial rights. Most of these estates continued attached to the abbey until the suppression of alien priories in 1414.

The abbey had also not a few illustrious benefactors, among them William the Conqueror's Queen Matilda; his nephew, William of Mortain; and the Empress Maud, who found her last earthly resting-place in the sanctuary of its church (Sept., 1167).

At Le Bec the monks wore a white habit; but except in this and a few other minor particulars, noted in Martène's monumental work, *De Antiquis Ritibus Ecclesiae* (ed. 1788), their rule did not deviate from

[1] DUGDALE, *Monasticon*, ed. 1830, vi. 1067.

the ordinary Benedictine type.[1] The following sketch of the constitution and customs of the abbey may therefore be hazarded, without risk of serious error.

The constitution was essentially feudal; the abbot, though in the first instance he derived his authority from the consent of the community, became upon election and consecration as absolute lord and master in the house as any baron in his castle. None might sit in his presence except by his express permission. If during the day he chanced to nod, none might wake him except in case of urgent need. His word was law, his hint a command. His very mistakes in grammar or quantity were privileged from correction even by his prior, though he were the greatest scholar of the age. If, *e.g.*, Herlwin took Lanfranc to task for pronouncing the verb docere with the second *e* long, alleging that it should be short, Lanfranc would not dream of disputing the point, but would bow his head, and accommodate his pronunciation to the ignorance of his superior.

When a postulant for reception into the fraternity presented himself, the monks assembled in the chapter-house, under the presidency of the abbot, of whom the postulant, standing near the door and bowing low, craved pardon (venia) for his intrusion. Then ensued a brief dramatic dialogue, as follows:—

Abbot. Quid dicis? What have you to say?

Postulant. Dei misericordiam et vestram miserationem

[1] Only a few fragments of the archives of the abbey survived its sack, and almost total demolition, during the first French Revolution. The ruins have been converted into cavalry barracks. *Cf.* the *History of the Royal Abbey of Bec, near Rouen, in Normandy*, translated from the French of BOURGET by J. Nichols, London, 1779, 8vo; and the ABBÉ PORÉE's *L'Abbaye du Bec et ses Ecoles*, Evreux, 1892, 8vo.

vestramque societatem volo habere. I crave the mercy of God, and your compassion, and association with you.

Abbot. Noster Dominus det tibi societatem electorum suorum. Our Lord grant you association with His elect.

The Monks. Amen.

The postulant would then throw himself at the abbot's feet, rise and retire to his former position at the entrance of the chapter-house, where the rule would be read to him, and its rigour duly explained, that he might know exactly what the vow he proposed to take would involve.

On his promising obedience, the abbot would say to him, "Deus sic in te quod promittis perficiat ut ad aeternam vitam pervenire merearis"; and the monks would respond, "Amen."

The postulant would then make another obeisance, be conducted to the church, and after kneeling for a time at one of the altars, be duly shaven and arrayed in the white robe of a novice. At the close of his period of probation, if he desired, and was thought worthy to be "professed," he would be conducted by the master of the novices, chanting the *Miserere mei*, and attended by a brother bearing a cowl and hood, to the church during the office of tierce, the congregation joining in the *Miserere mei*, while the novice approached the gospel side of the altar, and there prostrated himself. At the conclusion of the psalm he would rise, make his profession in an audible voice, and lay it in writing upon the altar. He would then say thrice, "Suscipe me, Domine, secundum eloquium tuum, et vivam, et non confundas me ab expectatione mea"; accompanying the words with a deep genuflexion, which done he would again prostrate himself. A special office would then follow, concluding with the chanting of the *Veni Creator Spiritus;* during which the novice would rise, be sprinkled with holy water, habited with cowl and hood, and blessed and kissed by the abbot. He would then set the seal on his profession by the reception of the Blessed Sacrament.

The staff of the monastery was marshalled under two priors, major and minor, who, as the abbot's lieutenant and sublieutenant, had command of the circumitores, a sort of domestic police, at whose head they patrolled the buildings and demesne, and who were primarily responsible for the security of the house and the maintenance of order and discipline. Next below them ranked the cantor, or precentor, who acted as dean and librarian—the library at Le Bec, at the beginning of the twelfth century, contained between one and two hundred volumes, comprising not only the principal works of the great Fathers and canonists of the Western Church, but some at least of the masterpieces of classical Latinity. Then came the sacristan, who had charge of all that specially appertained to the church and the sacred offices; the camerarius, or chamberlain, and the cellarius, who presided respectively over the dormitory and refectory; the latter a functionary whose importance was evidently felt to be out of all proportion to his rank, for St. Benedict's rule expressly provides that he is to be "discreet, of formed character, not much given to eating, sober, of a quiet, peaceable disposition, neither chary nor lavish, but a God-fearing man, and, as it were, a father to the entire community."

Finally, there was a magister puerorum, who had charge of the youth who were sent to the monastery to be taught the rudiments of learning, besides several minor officials, as the infirmarius, almoner, and ostiarius, whose names sufficiently indicate their functions.

The routine of the day was distributed into periods of about three hours each by the recitation of the canonical offices, consisting of psalms, lections, and prayers, beginning with matins in the small hours of the morning, and ending at midnight with nocturns. The intermediate offices were distinguished as prime (after sunrise), tierce (the third hour from sunrise), sext (noon), none (3 p.m.), and vespers (before sunset), followed, after a short interval, by compline. Mass was said twice daily, after prime and tierce. After the first mass in summer, during the rest of the year after the second, the monks assembled in the chapter-house, to hear a lecture on some portion of the rule of St. Benedict or Holy Scripture, and dispose of any case of discipline that might have arisen. The rest of the forenoon was divided between the hard manual labour which formed an integral part of the rule, and study. Breakfast (prandium), which none were permitted to anticipate, was taken at sext in the summer; during the rest of the year was deferred until none. In the summer also the community took a brief afternoon siesta in the dormitory, during which such as were not inclined for sleep might read. Dinner (coena) was taken between vespers and compline. During both breakfast and dinner silence was preserved, broken only by the voice of one of the monks, who read a passage from some edifying work. All otherwise unoccupied intervals in the day were devoted to lectures, private study, and the transcription or correction of MSS. in the cloister or chapter-house, according to the season. After compline the monks, in strict silence, filed off to the dormitory, to rest until summoned to the church for nocturns; which ended, they returned to sleep the sleep of the just, until roused by the matin-bell for the prayer and labour of the ensuing day.

In ordinary, though frivolous talk was discouraged, silence was not obligatory, and conversation was probably pretty lively after meals in the refectory or cloister. For the rest, the monks, in the strongest possible sense, had all things in common, even the least trifle which any of them might find vesting at once in the community. They could not quit the precincts of the abbey without leave; they were bound to yield implicit obedience to superior orders, unless (*absit omen!*) manifestly contrary to the law of God, in which case they were equally bound to disobey them at all costs; they were bound to confess to their superiors, and to no one else; to assist with due decorum at all canonical offices and masses; to observe the canonical feasts and fasts; to be diligent in all matters of obligation; and to practise the virtue of humility in all its degrees. Discipline was rigorously enforced by corporal punishment in the chapter-house, in the presence of the entire community; by excommunication in very grave cases; and, in the event of obdurate contumacy, by expulsion.

Cook there was none, nor need for any. The staff of life, washed down with a little thin wine, or more probably Normandy cider, and supplemented by a few *pulmentaria*—apparently omelettes—prepared by the monks in turn, constituted their ordinary diet.

When one of the monks fell ill, he was removed to the infirmary, to be there tended with such rude skill as the brother in charge could command. When death became imminent, and the last sacraments had been administered, the last kiss of peace given and received, a mat of hair cloth was laid on the floor, upon which the outline of the cross was traced with ashes. The dying man was then laid thereon, while the monks, obedient to the urgent summons of the gong, gathered from near and far around him, chanting in low tones the Nicene Creed, that, fortified by their countenance and prayers, their brother might depart in peace. When life was extinct, the corpse was carefully washed, incensed, sprinkled with holy water, reclothed in the habit it had worn in life, and buried with great solemnity in the church. For thirty days after the funeral mass was said daily for the repose of the soul of the deceased.

Besides the *trivium* and *quadrivium*, or seven liberal arts—*i.e.* grammar, or the whole mystery of reading and writing as taught by Priscian and Donatus; rhetoric, as expounded by Cicero and Quinctilian; logic, or dialectic, in which the great authorities were Boethius and Porphyry on the *Organon and Categories of Aristotle* and the *Topics of Cicero;* music, *i.e.* the traditional and fanciful harmonics of the period; and arithmetic, plain geometry and astronomy, with Isidore of Seville, Gerbert, and the elder Pliny for guides—the studies of the monks included a systematic course of *literae humaniores* and theology, based upon the Latin classics and the works of St. Augustine and Alcuin, with the rudiments, though probably no more than the rudiments, of Greek, canon and civil law, and medicine. No wonder, then, that the fame of Lanfranc and his "profound sophists" and "egregious doctors" spread far and wide, until Le Bec became the veritable focus of the renascent energies of Western Christendom.

CHAPTER III.

ST. ANSELM—EARLY YEARS IN VAL D'AOSTA

THE year which saw the foundation of the lowly retreat at Burneville, which was to prove the nidus of the famous Abbey of Le Bec, saw also the birth, in the ancient city of Aosta, in the heart of the Graian Alps, of a child who was destined in after-life to link his fortunes with those both of Herlwin and of Lanfranc, and to make good a threefold title to immortality as saint, sage, and victor in one of the most memorable of the conflicts recorded in the stormy history of the Church. He came into the world at the close of a period of widespread grievous dearth, and amid the mustering of hosts, if not the clash of arms; for in 1034, Val d'Aosta, which had long been a veritable no man's land, or land of all men—a bone of interminable contention between the German Emperors, the Kings of Italy and Transjuran Burgundy, and the fierce Saracenic hordes which, in the tenth century, penetrated even into the fastnesses of the Alps, became the theatre of a sanguinary struggle between Odo of Champagne and Humbert the White-handed, and by the victory of the latter passed definitively under the dominion of the House of Savoy. This child, with whose history we shall now be principally concerned, was Anselm—the name is said to signify *God's helm*—only son of Gundulf, a Lombard, by his wife Ermenberg. His birth took place at some date not precisely determinable, between 21 April, 1033, and 21 April, 1034. Of the lineage and social condition of his parents little is known, except that both were of gentle birth (*nobiliter nati*) and good substance. In after-years, Anselm was acknowledged as a blood relation by Humbert II., Count of Maurienne, a descendant of Humbert the White-handed, who, by his marriage with Anchilia, sister of Udelrico II., Count of the Valais, had acquired fiefs in Val d'Aosta. There also Ermenberg held fiefs in her own right, including, in all probability, the manor of Gressan, at the foot of the Becca di Nona, where a massive keep, which may or may not date from the eleventh century, is still known as the Tower of St. Anselm.[1] It is, therefore, not unlikely that Ermenberg belonged to a branch of the House of Valais. She had two brothers, Lambert and Folcerad, both *reverendi domini*, canons in all probability of St. Ours, in Aosta; and, as names run in families, it may be presumed that Bishop Anselm, of Aosta, who died in 1025, was also related to her.

The clue to Gundulf's family connections has yet to be discovered.[2] But, whoever he was, it is evident that

[1] That this was not Anselm's birthplace is, however, certain. Eadmer states explicitly that he was born in the city of Aosta, which, by the utmost latitude of interpretation, could not include the manor of Gressan. Equally untrustworthy is the tradition which assigns the house No. 4, Via S. Anselmo, in the Borgo S. Orso, as the place in which he first saw the light. (*Cf.* RULE, *Life and Times of St. Anselm*, i. 4.)

[2] The pedigrees constructed for Gundulf and Ermenberg by the Abbé Croset-Mouchet, *S. Anselme d'Aoste Archevêque de Cantorbéry*, Paris, 1859, and Mr. MARTIN RULE, *Life and Times of St. Anselm*, London, 1883, are more ingenious than plausible. *Cf. Il Conte Umberto I. e il Re Ardoino*, by DOMENICO CARUTTI, Rome, 1888.

he was Ermenberg's equal in wealth and social status, a prosperous Lombard gentleman, large-hearted, and open-handed almost to a fault, with a fund of shrewd worldly sense and a strong will. Ermenberg was a faithful wife, a thrifty housewife, and a model of all the Christian virtues and graces. Besides Anselm, this worthy pair had one other child, a daughter named Richera, Anselm's junior by some years. When we add that Anselm had two cousins, Peter and Folcerad, nephews of Ermenberg, and two consanguinei, Aimon and Rainald, probably nephews of Gundulf, we exhaust all that is positively known about his kith and kin.

The Benedictine Abbey of Fructuaria, in Piedmont, had established early in the eleventh century a dependent priory at Aosta, and this we conjecture to have been the place of Anselm's early education. There he would be grounded, probably not without much suffering, in the three liberal arts of grammar, rhetoric, and dialectic. What more he may have learned we know not; but in these, his subsequent eminence, both as a Latinist and a logician, attests the soundness of the instruction he received.

The want of fraternal companionship and rivalry was, doubtless, not without its influence in moulding Anselm's character. From the first he appears to have been a shy, recluse child, caring little for play, an apt scholar, and much given to dreaming about mysteries beyond his years. From Ermenberg's lips he early heard so much of the sublime verities of religion as was suited to his apprehension; and in his childlike faith he supposed that the heaven of which she spoke to him must surely lie somewhere above the fantastically-domed and pinnacled Alpine walls of his native valley

—perhaps beyond the rent ice-fretted bastions of Valgrisanche, where nightly, in weird splendour, the sun makes his pavilion; so that could he but climb so high, he might even find his way to the palace of the Great King. And so full was his mind of this quest, that one night he dreamed that he made the ascent, and actually found the palace, and the King there alone with His chief butler; for it was autumn, and He had sent His servants out to gather in the harvest. And the King called him, and he went and sat down at His feet; and the King talked with him graciously and familiarly, and bade the chief butler bring the whitest of bread, so that he ate and was refreshed in His presence.

This dream made a lasting impression on Anselm's mind; and before he was fifteen he felt that he had a vocation to the religious life, and opened the matter to a friendly abbot. The idea, however, was extremely distasteful to Gundulf, and the abbot dared not countenance the boy in thwarting his father's wishes. In his distress Anselm prayed for ill-health, that Gundulf might concede to his infirmity what he refused to his devotion. He fell ill, but recovered; and Gundulf remained as obdurate as before. Years passed, Ermenberg died, Anselm became a man, and his religious fervour, which had doubtless been fed by his mother, languished for a time, to revive in greater intensity than ever, and to encounter from Gundulf a still more determined opposition. At last it became evident to him that he must act for himself. So in the early summer, probably, of 1057, with a single clerk for his companion and servant, and an ass to carry the few necessaries for the journey, he bade adieu to Aosta, with the intention of placing the great barrier of the Alps between himself and his past. Instead, however, of taking the direct route into Burgundy by the Little St. Bernard, or crossing into the Rhone valley by the Great St. Bernard, the fugitives, for some unexplained reason, bent their steps towards the Mont Cenis. This, unless Anselm were a much better mountaineer than his cloistered education renders at all likely, involved a descent into Italy as far as Ivrea, if not Turin ; and by the time our adventurers reached the top of the pass, their stock of provisions was, as they supposed, exhausted. Worn out with fatigue, faint with hunger, and mad with thirst, Anselm threw himself on the snow, and thrust some handfuls of it into his mouth. His servant, meanwhile, made a last despairing scrutiny of the provision wallet, when lo ! to his unbounded surprise, what was it that gleamed from its inmost recess but a loaf of the whitest wheaten bread, which happy accident—or, as perhaps simple faith suggested, providential interposition—had placed there as in fulfilment of Anselm's early dream, that, therewith refreshed, he might pursue his journey towards the spiritual Canaan of which he was in search ?

CHAPTER IV.

ANSELM AT LE BEC—HIS RELATIONS WITH LANFRANC

OF Anselm's movements we have now for nearly three years no detailed record. He lived, apparently, the life of the roving scholar so dear to the adventurous spirits of the Middle Ages. How precious would have been a journal of these *Wanderjahre*—Anselm's own carelessly-jotted notes of a journey through Burgundy, France, and Normandy, in the years of grace 1057–9, showing how he got his bread, the hostelries and monasteries at which he slept, the adventures he met with, the manifold and ever-changing incidents of a life entirely strange to him. But, alas! we are left to our own poor guesses, or those of our predecessors, without so much as a bare itinerary to guide us. That he visited Lyon we may take for granted; for it is morally certain that his first destination was Cluny, then in the height of its fame; and no traveller from Aosta to Cluny by the Mont Cenis could well avoid passing through Lyon. We may conjecture also, with Mr. Rule, that after admiring the pristine severity of the monastic life as lived at Cluny, he passed to contemplate the still more rigorous austerities practised by the monks of St. Benignus at Dijon; nor can we readily suppose that he failed to visit Paris. All that is recorded, however, is that by a devious route through Burgundy and France he made his way to the scene of Lanfranc's earlier labours, Avranches, on the confines of Normandy and Brittany; where, doubtless, he laid the basis of the close and enduring friendship with its young Count, Hugh the Wolf, afterwards Earl of Chester, which was to exert a determining influence in the most critical epoch of his subsequent career; and that from Avranches, probably in the autumn of 1059, he passed to Le Bec to seek and gain admission as one of Lanfranc's pupils.

Lanfranc was then nearing the zenith of his fame.

Loyal and devout Normandy was overjoyed at his recent return from Rome with the dispensation needful to release her from the interdict which the uncanonical marriage of her Duke had brought upon her.[1]

Duke William will soon be King, and Matilda Queen, of England, and Lanfranc, Abbot of the noble monastery of St. Stephen, which their penitence will found at Caen, whence he will pass to Canterbury. It is not given to Anselm to foreshorten the future; but of the canonical impediment to the union of the Duke and Duchess;

[1] The theory adopted by Freeman (*Norman Conquest*, iii. 85), that the impediment in the way of William's marriage with Matilda was no less than that she was the wife of another man, was eventually abandoned by him. (*Engl. Hist. Rev.*, Oct. 18, '88.) The spuriousness of the charters in which William of Warenne describes Matilda as his wife's mother, and William the Conqueror recognises Gundrada as his daughter, is now generally acknowledged. William was in the fifth degree of descent from Rollo, from whom it is probable that Matilda was also descended within the prohibited degrees of consanguinity.

of the interdict; of Lanfranc's mission to Rome to sue for its removal; of his success—of all this he has heard, for it is matter of common notoriety in Normandy. Doubtless, also, he has heard of Lanfranc's dialectical triumphs over Berengar at Vercelli, Rome, and Tours, and of the vast stores of erudition which he is reported to have brought with him from Pavia. It is therefore, we may suppose, with no small trepidation that he stands in presence of the great master in the hall of the stately abbey which has risen, as if by magic, by the side of the little Norman stream.

He has little real cause for fear, however; for Lanfranc is too good a judge of character to be blind to the fine qualities, mental and spiritual, of his new pupil. Moreover, they are both strangers in these northern wilds; to both the Latin speech, the traditions of Latin culture, are native. Neither can fail to feel a certain instinctive contempt, tempered only by fine Italian courtesy, for the barbarians among whom his lot is cast. No wonder, then, that, notwithstanding their disparity in age and learning, an unusual degree of sympathy bound the two men together from the first. Months passed, months of true guidance on Lanfranc's part, and on Anselm's of loving obedience, intense study, rigorous asceticism, profound meditation, earnest prayer. Then came tidings of Gundulf's death, and Anselm felt that he must now make the decisive act of will on which the tenor of his future life depended. He had thoughts of returning to Aosta, there to live on his patrimony, in the world yet not of it, devoted to good works; thoughts also of secluding himself in a hermitage. On the other hand, ambition prompted him to take the cowl at some house where his learning might show to better advantage than at Le Bec; while humility bade him remain where he was, eclipsed by the lustre of Lanfranc's fame. In his perplexity he naturally had recourse to Lanfranc, and Lanfranc referred the difficult case of conscience to the decision of the venerable Maurille, Archbishop of Rouen. The archbishop pronounced emphatically in favour of the monastic life, and, humility having triumphed over ambition, Anselm, in the year 1060, entered upon his novitiate at Le Bec, and soon afterwards took the irrevocable vow.

Two years later Lanfranc quitted Le Bec to take charge of the Abbey of St. Stephen, recently founded at Caen by Duke William, in pursuance of the pledge given on occasion of the recognition of his marriage by the Holy See, and Anselm thereupon succeeded to the vacant priorate.

His elevation was ill-received by not a few of the monks, and it needed all the address, graciousness, and firmness of which he was capable, to establish his ascendancy over them. He succeeded, however, in the end, not merely in gaining their respect, but in completely winning their affection, nay, devotion; and, on the death of Herlwin, 26 August, 1078, yielded, with unfeigned reluctance, to the unanimous and reiterated vote of the fraternity, and was installed abbot in his room.

He was consecrated by Gilbert, Bishop of Evreux, on the Feast of St. Peter's Chair at Antioch, 22 February, 1078–9, having first received investiture of the temporalities from William the Conqueror, at Brionne, by the delivery of the crosier.

His ascendancy was but the natural result of the singular fascination of his character — a fascination which subdued even the Conqueror—the charm of a personality in which sanctity and sagacity, sweetness and light, gentleness and strength, were harmoniously blended, and which wrought like a spell upon all who came in contact with it, from the raw lad whom he initiated in the mysteries of the Latin grammar, or the novice fighting his first battle with the flesh, to the oldest and most opinionative brother in the house. In sickness he nursed them with the tenderness of a mother; on all occasions of doubt, difficulty, or distress, he was their unfailing counsellor and guide; while the example of his own life of stern self-discipline and ceaseless activity, spoke to them more eloquently than words. Day and night he was ever occupied—teaching, reproving, exhorting, studying, expounding the Holy Scriptures or the Fathers, administering the temporal affairs of the monastery, giving counsel, or correcting manuscripts.

No wonder, then, that Anselm came to be regarded by not a few of his subordinates—rude, half-tamed Northmen as most of them were—as almost a being of another sphere, and that signs and wonders attended him in all he did. As he stood in prayer in the dark chapter-house before the ordinary hour of vigil, a mystic light was observed to play around him. As he lay sleepless in bed, pondering how the prophets discerned the future as if it were present, lo! through the wall which divided the dormitory from the oratory, he saw the brothers going to and fro about the altar lighting the candles, and otherwise making ready for matins, and ceased to marvel how He who had made the solid wall transparent should also make the future present. His clairvoyance extended to matters of creature comfort, things evidently by no means despised by the good monks of Le Bec. Belated in the woods with one of the brothers, and no better provision for supper than a little bread and cheese, he had but to give the word, and forthwith a trout, of such dimensions as had not been seen in those parts for twenty years, was taken in the neighbouring stream. On another occasion, when fish ran short at Walter Tirrel's table, Anselm met his host's apologies with the assurance that a sturgeon was even then on its way to the castle; and the words had hardly left his lips when two men appeared, bearing as fine and fresh a sturgeon as had ever swum in the Autie.

His courage and sanctity were more than a match for the Prince of Darkness himself. Once, during the midday siesta, when all was silent in the house, a sick brother was heard to cry out that two immense wolves had him in their grip, and were throttling him. Anselm, who was correcting manuscripts in the cloister, was at once sent for, and the timid monks shrank behind him, as, with raised hand, making the sign of the cross, he entered the infirmary and pronounced the formula of exorcism, In nomine Patris et Filii et Spiritus Sancti. As he did so the sick man saw a forked flame dart from his lips and light upon the wolves, which straightway vanished into air.

Side by side with these stories, which hardly purport to be more than the gossip of the cloister, occur two which Eadmer places in another category. He adduces the testimony of two monks of Le Bec, men of good repute (non ignobilis famæ) and acknowledged veracity, to the healing of a nobleman from the Flemish marches by the drinking of a few drops of the water in which Anselm had washed his hands during mass ; and that of the venerable Abbot Helias, of La Trinité du Mont, near Rouen, to the instantaneous and complete disappearance of a swelling in the knee, which had long defied medical skill, upon occasion of his ordination by Anselm.

To himself, meanwhile, the saint was as far as possible from seeming what he was. No man ever was more thoroughly penetrated by the sense of his own unworthiness in the sight of God, his own dependence upon Him, his utter impotence without Him. No man ever had less of ambition, less of the love of spiritual ascendancy, or secular authority. Again and again during his priorate he thought of abandoning the position, of taking refuge in some remote hermitage. Once he even went so far as to consult Maurille on the matter. As abbot of the monastery of Sta. Maria, at Florence, Maurille had had ample experience of the heavy burden of care and constant harass incident to the direction of a great religious house, but he had not shrunk from it himself, and he was not prevented, by his sympathy with Anselm, from laying upon him his positive and peremptory injunction to remain where God had placed him. The death of Maurille, in 1067, and the translation of Lanfranc from Caen to Canterbury, in 1070, deprived him of the two counsellors on whom he could best rely. Lanfranc's journey to Rome for his *pallium* afforded him, however, the opportunity of paying Anselm a visit at Le Bec, and he was there again in the autumn of 1077, when he consecrated the new church. After his election to the abbacy Anselm was compelled, more than once, to cross the Channel for the purpose of inspecting the English domains of the abbey, and was thus able to return Lanfranc's visits at Canterbury.

In the meantime he kept up a regular correspondence not only with Lanfranc, but also with Gundulf, Henry, and Maurice, who either accompanied Lanfranc to England or joined him there. Maurice was evidently his favourite pupil, Gundulf his *alter ego.* There is also one letter to Ernost, whom Gundulf succeeded in the See of Rochester, and another to Paul, upon his preferment to the Abbey of St. Albans. The correspondence attests the close and cordial relations which subsisted between the writers, but sheds no light upon the great public events of the period. Of the dubious and bloody contest with the imperialist Antipope Cadalus of Parma, which occupied the earlier years of the pontificate of Alexander II.; of the long and embittered strife on the question of clerical celibacy which followed; of the election, on Alexander's death, of Hildebrand, Pope's lord so long, now at length (22 April, 1073), "by the will of St. Peter," and amid the universal acclaim of the Roman clergy and people, Pope Gregory VII.; of his crusades against the Spanish Saracens, against simony, and the marriage of the clergy; of his schemes for another crusade; of his theocratic aims and claims; of his prohibition of lay investiture at the Council of Rome, in February, 1075; of that wild scene in the crypt of Sta. Maria Maggiore, when the Christmas-eve vigil was broken by the clash of arms, and the Pope, stunned and bleeding, was hauled by the hair of his head from the sanctuary, hurried across the silent city to a dungeon in the Parione, to be delivered thence, on the morrow, by the infuriated citizens, to stand in the spirit of a primitive Christian between their vengeance and his persecutors, and to finish the mass with all the impassive dignity of an ancient Roman; of his citation of the King of the Romans to Rome, to answer for his simoniacal practices and other misfeasances; of his "deposition" by Henry and his hireling synod at Worms (24 January, 1076); of his counter-deposition and excommunication of the king; of the gradual but steady defection of the king's adherents; of his penitence, self-abasement, and submission at Canossa; of all this, with which, during the fifteen years of Anselm's priorate, all Christendom was ringing, in Anselm's correspondence not a word. Not a word either of Lanfranc's heroic efforts to revivify the torpid religious life of England, and in particular to reform the monasteries on the model of Le Bec; not a word of the rebuilding of St. Albans Abbey, of Rochester and Canterbury Cathedrals; of the vindication of the ancient rights and franchises of the archbishopric against the usurpations of the Conqueror's brother Odo, Bishop of Bayeux; of the Conqueror's ecclesiastical policy not a word.

The last matter, however, must have caused grave anxiety to both Lanfranc and Anselm. William's piety was doubtless sincere, but it was the piety of a nature essentially despotic. He was not negligent of the outward observances of religion; he was lavish of gifts to pious uses; he abhorred simony; and, provided they were Normans, he preferred that the

Church should be served by devout and able men. But from the first he was determined to rule as absolutely, not in temporal matters only, but also in spiritual, in the rich heritage which his sword had won, as in his Duchy of Normandy; and no sooner did he feel himself secure in his new dominion than he gave practical effect to his will.

He prohibited recourse to, or communication with, the Holy See without his express consent; deprived the synods of their legislative power; and to a large extent the ecclesiastical courts of their independent initiative. Henceforth no Pope was to be recognised, no excommunication decree or canon to have effect, no ecclesiastical cause, in which any of the king's barons or servants were concerned, to be tried in England without a royal license. These decrees were probably passed before 1073, when Lanfranc was constrained to decline an invitation to spend Christmas at Rome, with which Alexander II. had honoured him. Their tendency was to rend the English Church from the unity of Christendom. Lanfranc was, or conceived himself to be, powerless to arrest the schism, and it was not until after the event of Canossa that Gregory VII. had leisure to intervene. He then did so with characteristic vigour.

In 1079 his subdeacon, Cardinal Hubert, visited England as legate, cited two bishops from every diocese to Rome, and demanded of the king prompt payment of the Peter-pence, which had fallen into arrear, and an acknowledgment of fealty in redemption of the pledge which he had given to Alexander, when on the eve of the invasion of England he had sought and obtained the Papal blessing on his enterprise, and which was represented as amounting to a promise to hold the country "of God and the Apostle." Gregory at the same time wrote to Lanfranc, urging him to do all in his power to secure the success of the mission.

That Lanfranc loyally obeyed his instructions there is no reason to doubt; but his fine diplomacy was thrown away upon the king. "In concert with your legate," he wrote to the Pope, "I commended your propositions to my lord the king; I tendered my advice, but I did not succeed in getting it accepted. (Suasi sed non persuasi.)"

Except in the matter of the Peter-pence, which William readily promised to make good, the mission proved an entire failure. The King of England retained no recollection of the promise of fealty which the Duke of Normandy was said to have made to Alexander II.; and Lanfranc was unable to refresh his memory. The Norman prelates were by no means to be induced to quit the realm without his permission, and that permission was not given. Mistaking the man with whom he had to deal, Gregory imputed the failure of the mission to Lanfranc, reproached him with lack of zeal, and cited him to Rome. But Lanfranc either dared not or would not defy the king; and, turning a deaf ear to the Pope's reproaches, he remained at Canterbury.

It was at this juncture that Abbot Anselm—he was consecrated, it will be remembered, on the Feast of St. Peter's chair at Antioch, 22 February, 1079—paid in the course of the same year his first visit to England. He landed at Lympne, then a seaport, and rode to Lyminge, where he was received by Lanfranc.

There he wrote the following letter, which the piety

of the good brethren of Le Bec has happily preserved for us:—

"To his honourable and most dear brothers, who serve God in the Monastery of Le Bec, their servant and fellow-servant Anselm. May they ever live holily, and attain the reward of holy living. Knowing—and the knowledge is of a truth most sweet to me—that your love toward me makes you desire with your whole hearts intelligence of my safety and well-being, I could not bear to occasion you the distress of the least delay. Know, then, that the same day on which at prime Dom Gerard left me on shipboard, the Divine protection, in answer to your prayers, brought me at none to the English shore after a good passage, and with none of that trouble from which many who fare by sea are wont to suffer, and permitted me to reach our lord and father, Archbishop Lanfranc, at eventide, and to be received by him with joy at his manor, which is named Lyminge. This I write on the morrow, that I may satisfy your desire aforesaid, and remind you of your holy intent to be ever fervent in zeal, and more and more assiduous in good works. As a brother, therefore, I pray you; as a father, I exhort you, that you study so to live in peace and piety, as becomes good monks, that both you may reap in beatification the reward of your diligence, and I may one day participate in your joy. May the Lord Almighty defend you from all adversity, and show you His mercy by continuing to you health and happiness of mind and body. Let our mother and Lady Eva know what, with no less anxiety than you, she craves to hear concerning her eldest son; and bid her pray that, as her prayers and yours have obtained for me a prosperous commencement of the journey you so much dreaded, so they may secure for me a joyous restoration to you in joy.[1]

From Lyminge to Canterbury is no long ride; and, in all probability, the same day on which these lines were written saw Anselm installed in the rooms at Christ Church, which Prior Henry had placed at his disposal. He was received by the brotherhood with the utmost distinction; and to evince his gratitude, took an early opportunity of calling them together to listen to a little homily on the familiar text, "It is more blessed to give than to receive."

Among his auditors was a young Englishman, by name Eadmer, afterwards his secretary and biographer, who noted down the substance of his discourse, which was as follows:—

"Whoso," he said, "has charity, has that whereby he earns the gratitude of God; not so he who is its object. For what gratitude does God owe me, if I am loved by you, or anyone else? But it is better to have that whereby one earns the gratitude of God, than that whereby one does not earn it; and since God is grateful for charity bestowed, not for charity received, it follows that whoso bestows charity on another has something better than he on whom it is bestowed. Furthermore, he who is beholden to another's love is but the passive recipient of a favour, *e.g.* a benefice, an office of dignity, a dinner, or some similar good office. But he who has bestowed the favour has it still for himself. Whereof, most holy brothers, you may see a present example in my case and yours. You have done me a good office; you have done me, I say, an office of charity, and from

[1] *Epp.* ii. 9.

me it has already passed away; but the charity which is grateful to God remains with you. Do you not esteem a permanent good better than a transient one? Add to this, that if by your good office aught of charity has been engendered in me towards you, this also will be but an addition to your reward, inasmuch as it is you who have occasioned the growth of so good a thing in me. In any case, while the good office which you have done me has now passed entirely from me, your charity remains yours. If, then, we only consider these matters, we shall clearly perceive that we have greater cause for joy if we love others, than if we are loved by them. And it is because not everybody does so, that many prefer to be loved by others than to love."

At the conclusion of this gracious little address, Anselm was received into the confraternity. Eadmer adds that he spent some days at Christ Church, during which he spoke much, both in public and in private, discoursing both of the duties of the monastic life, and the mysteries of the faith, with great eloquence and subtlety.

Of his converse with Lanfranc, Eadmer has preserved one fragment, which, though relating to a matter in itself of no very great importance, is not without interest as indicative of the large and liberal spirit in which Anselm dealt with ethical problems. And the story is told by Eadmer with so much freshness and vivacity, that it would be a pity to condense or paraphrase his narrative.

"Lanfranc," he says, "was still but little of an Englishman (quasi rudis Anglus), and was not yet thoroughly used to the institutions which he found in

England. Hence, while he made some innovations with good reason, he made other changes upon his own mere and sole authority. So while occupied with these reforms, and thinking to have the concurrence of his friend and brother Anselm, he addressed him one day familiarly as follows:—"These English, among whom we dwell, have taken upon themselves to make certain whom they venerate into saints. But when I cast about in my mind to determine what manner of men these were, according to the account of them which the English themselves give, I am not able to refrain from doubts as to their sanctity. See, here is one of them, who now, by the blessing of God, rests in this holy see over which I now preside, Ælfeg by name, a good man undoubtedly, and who in his time held this same archbishopric. Him they reckon, not only among the saints, but among the martyrs too, though they admit that he was slain, not for confessing the name of Christ, but for refusing to ransom his life with money. For when—to tell the story in their own words—the pagans, in their spite towards him and enmity towards God, had taken him prisoner, yet from reverence for his person, had conceded him the right of purchasing his liberty; they demanded by way of ransom an immense sum of money; and as he could in no other way raise it than by despoiling his own people, and reducing some of them, perhaps, to abject beggary, he preferred rather to lose his life than to preserve it on such terms. This, then, is the case upon which I crave to hear Your Fraternity's opinion."

With excellent good sense, Anselm resolved the doubt in favour of the English and their grand Gothic saint.

"It is manifest," he said, "that he who does not hesitate to die rather than commit even a slight sin against God, would, *a fortiori*, not hesitate to die, rather than offend God by a grave sin. And certainly it seems to be a graver sin to deny Christ than, being an earthly lord, to lay a certain burden on one's people for the ransom of one's life. But this lesser sin it was which Ælfeg refused to commit. *A fortiori*, then, he would not have denied Christ had the raging adversaries sought to constrain him thereto by menace of death. Whence one can perceive that justice must have had a prodigious mastery over his soul, since he preferred to surrender his life rather than, doing despite to charity, to give occasion of stumbling to his neighbours. Far indeed, then, from him was that, too, which is denounced by the Lord against him by whom offence comes. Nor unworthily, I think, is he reckoned among martyrs, whose voluntary endurance of death is truly attributable to so high a sense of justice. For even Blessed John the Baptist, who is deemed in the front rank of martyrs, and is venerated by the entire Church of God, was slain—not for refusing to deny Christ, but for refusing to suppress the truth. And what distinction is there between dying for justice and dying for truth? Moreover, since by the witness of holy writ, as Your Paternity knows very well, Christ is truth and justice, he who dies for truth and justice dies for Christ. But whoso dies for Christ, by the witness of the Church, is esteemed a martyr. Now, Blessed Ælfeg died for justice, as Blessed John died for truth. Why, then, rather of the one than of the other should we doubt whether he be a true and holy martyr, seeing that a like cause kept both constant in the suffering of death? This, reverend Father, as far as I can see, is what reason itself approves. But to your wisdom it belongs, if otherwise minded, to correct and recall me from my error, and to show by the teaching of the Church what, in a matter of such importance, ought to be believed."

This argument prevailed. Lanfranc confessed himself convinced by "the perspicacious subtlety" of Anselm's reasoning, and promised thenceforth to venerate Blessed Ælfeg as "a great and glorious martyr of Christ."

So Anselm's finer reason justified the instinctive wisdom of the rude, but not ignoble, barbarians; and the name of Blessed Ælfeg was suffered to retain its place in the roll of those confessors who have sealed their testimony with their blood; and Lanfranc, Eadmer tells us, conceived an altogether peculiar veneration for the saint, and had his life written by Osbern, one of Anselm's pupils, who did the work "nobly," as was fitting; nay, had it set to music, and chanted in church for the edification of the faithful.[1]

[1] St. Ælpheg's day is 19 April. A fragment of the mass anciently proper to that day, and not improbably written by Lanfranc himself, has been discovered by Mr. Martin Rule in the Vatican Library. It is as follows:

"Custodiat. per Dominum.

"*Praefatio.*

"Eterne Deus. In cujus amoris virtute beatissimus martyr Elfegus hostem derisit, tormenta sustinuit, mortem suscepit. Quique ab ecclesia tua tanto gloriosior praedicatur quanto [per] sui devotionem officii bino moderamine effulsit. Ut in uno creditum sibi populum tibi Domino Deo conciliaret, in altero semetipsum in odorem suavi[ta]tis sacrificium offerret, in utroque Filii tui Domini nostri Jesu Christi fidelis imitator existeret. Qui pro omnium salute tibi eterno Patri suo preces effudit, et peccati typographum quod antiquus hostis contra nos tenuit proprii sanguinis effusione delevit. Et ideo.

Eadmer, who evidently accompanied Anselm as he visited the several estates which the Abbey of Le Bec already held in England,[1] is copious in praise of the tact which he displayed in his intercourse with our countrymen, and which ensured him a hearty welcome and a reluctant adieu wherever he went. Following apostolic precedent, he made himself (without offence) all things to all men. Layman and clerk, gentle and simple, alike felt the charm of his gracious manner and engaging conversation. Earls and countesses vied in doing him honour, and even the grim Conqueror relaxed somewhat of his habitual sternness in his presence.

Of Anselm's later visits to England, which, it is plain from Eadmer, were not infrequent—" England," he says " became henceforth quite familiar to him, being visited by him as diversity of occasion required"—we have no

"*Postcommunio.*

"Grata tibi sint, omnipotens Deus, nostrae servitutis obsequia, ut illius interventu nobis salutaria reddantur pro cujus immarcessibili gloria exhibentur. Per."

[1] What these were, besides the manors of Streatham and Tooting Bec (both given by Richard Fitz-Gilbert, Earl of Clare, and his Countess Rohais), and the Priory of St. Neot's in Huntingdonshire, which, after some years of abeyance, had recently been converted into a cell of Le Bec, we cannot say for certain. The manors of Winchcombe in Oxfordshire, Brixton Deverill in Wiltshire, and Atherstone in Warwickshire—the last the gift of Hugh the Wolf—may, or may not, have been held of the abbey at this time. In any case it is unlikely that the proud and passionate, but generous and devout, seigneur of Avranches, now Earl of Chester, whom Anselm had fascinated twenty years before, would suffer him to pay his first visit to England without tasting the hospitality of his county Palatine. It is matter of regret that Eadmer did not preserve an itinerary of the tour: his language implies a long journey, but, of course, it does not follow that the Le Bec estates were numerous. The jawbone of St. Neot, long preserved at Le Bec, was probably removed thither by by Anselm himself on his return to Normandy.—GORHAM'S *History of Eynesbury and St. Neots*, i. 61.

detailed record; and his letters during this period, though some of them bear internal evidence of having been written in England, while another refers to a sojourn in Caen,[1] shed, on the whole, but little light on his movements. On the other hand, they are invaluable for the insight they afford into the monastic life of the time. Even at this date, the greater religious houses maintained, it is evident, regular relations with one another, notwithstanding their separation by distances which, in view of the imperfect means of locomotion, and the insecurity of the roads, may justly be considered enormous. Anselm has correspondents not only at Canterbury and Rochester and throughout Normandy, but in Burgundy, in Auvergne, even in Southern Germany. To Lanzo, a novice at Cluny, afterwards Prior of St. Pancras', Lewes, in Sussex, he addresses more than one letter full of wise counsel and gentle admonition.[2] From Robert, a monk of Mont St. Michel, he hears of a noble stranger from Venice, lately arrived at the Monastery of the Mount, who bears a Greek name, Anastasius, and is learned in the Greek tongue; and he writes praying that so rare an acquisition may be spared awhile for the delectation and instruction of the brotherhood of Le Bec.[3] In the heart of Auvergne, Abbot Durand, of Chaise Dien, has heard of the prayers and devout meditations which Anselm has composed—has even seen some of them—and writes with much deference to his saintship, to beg that what may be wanting to his collection may be forthwith sent to him. Anselm replies with due

[1] *Epp.* ii. 9, 14, 18, 26, 27.
[2] *Epp.* i. 2 and 29.
[3] *Epp.* i. 3.

humility, disclaiming all pretensions to sanctity; but at the same time, does not presume to refuse "His Paternity's" request.[1] But it is in his relations with the saintly William, Abbot of the famous monastery of Hirsau, near Stuttgart, that the extent of his fame and influence is most signally apparent. As the builder of seven monasteries, the restorer of sundry others, the vigilant censor of the morals of the clergy, the friend and confidant of Hildebrand, Abbot William of Hirsau was the very life and soul of the religious revival of Southern Germany. Yet we find him appealing to Anselm—not yet apparently abbot—for his counsel in certain grave cases of discipline, and Anselm replying in a tone which shows that he was by no means surprised to receive such a communication even from the saintly Abbot of Hirsau.[2]

For the rest, his letters shew him to us as the experienced director of souls, profoundly versed in Holy Scripture and the human heart; as the firm yet gentle disciplinarian, intent on the reformation of tipsy chamberlains and renegade or refractory monks; as the careful administrator, sorely tried by want of means, and much beholden for timely subsidies to Lanfranc, or Gundulf, or the Countess Ida,[3] or his especial patronesses and "dearest mothers" the Ladies Eva and Basilia, who, it would seem, with their husbands, William Crispin, Viscount of the Vexin, and Hugh Lord of Gournay, on

[1] *Epp.* i. 61, 62.

[2] *Epp.* i. 56. William's letter is not extant, and Anselm's reply is undated; but as he describes himself simply as "frater Anselmus," it is probably referable to the period of his priorate. William became Abbot of Hirsau in 1070, and died in 1091.

[3] Wife of Eustace II., Count of Bouillon, and mother of Godfrey of Bouillon.

the confines of Normandy and the Beauvoisin, had formed a retreat in the vicinity of the abbey, and there lived devoted to the service of God and man. Nor does this intense ascetic and shy recluse, who luxuriates in the holy calm of the cloister, and shuns, as far as possible, even casual contact with the outer world, fail now and again to disclose another man, tender, sympathetic, warm-hearted, who casts fond backward glances towards distant Aosta and his "dearest uncles," Lambert and Folcerad, and is inconsolable as, one by one, the companions of his early manhood are reft from him, and are replaced by "new men, strange faces, other minds."

CHAPTER V.

ANSELM AS TEACHER AND THINKER—THE MONOLOGION AND PROSLOGION

ONE day the abbot of a neighbouring monastery, perhaps St. Evroult, perhaps Fontanelle, fairly at his wits' end to know how to deal with the stiffnecked Norman youth, whose unmanageable disposition sadly belied their character of oblates, came to Le Bec to seek Anselm's counsel; charging the poor lads with incorrigible perversity, because, under the Spartan discipline of rigorous constraint and daily and nightly castigation, so far from mending their ways, they only grew more idle and refractory, and in the end turned out more like beasts than men. Anselm listened patiently to this woful tale, and then by a few apt analogies hinted to the good abbot, that perhaps, without giving rein to license, he might find a somewhat less harsh and more generous treatment more effectual in the nurture of those who were as saplings in the garden of the Church, there to grow and fructify unto the Lord, or as silver and gold in the workshop of the smith, needing not merely to be rudely hammered, but also to be gently wrought and moulded into shape. At the close of this little homily the abbot, says Eadmer, confessed that he had gravely erred in his disciplinary methods, and throwing himself in shame and confusion at Anselm's feet, craved absolution for his past misdeeds, and promised amendment for the future. So we may surmise that the lot of many a young barbarian in fair Normandy was rendered more tolerable by the word in season spoken in his behalf by the gentle Abbot of Le Bec.

With such an ideal of the duty of the "magister puerorum," an ideal which he could not fail to inculcate upon the brother who had charge of the oblates of Le Bec, it would not be Anselm's fault if the boys, as they grew up, looked back, as many, both before and since his day, have looked back, upon their schooldays as the least profitable and most painful period of their lives; and we can readily infer that his relations with his own pupils, the chosen few of the novices and younger monks, and the roving scholars who were from time to time drawn to the abbey by the fame of his lectures, must have been unusually intimate and sympathetic; nor are hints and glimpses wanting—slight indeed, but significant—which serve to corroborate our conjecture.

Among the stranger-scholars who studied under Anselm at Le Bec, is probably to be ranked his namesake, known as Anselm of Laon, from the famous school of learning which he founded in that city, and whose reputation has, perhaps, suffered unduly at the hands of his illustrious pupil, Abelard. It is also probable, though positive proof is wanting, that Gaunilon of Marmoutier, and Roscellin of Compiègne, with both of whom we shall see Anselm in controversy, were of the number of his pupils, though certainly neither was professed at Le Bec. Among the oblates was one who was especially endeared to Anselm by his quick and keen intelligence and unusual seriousness—Guibert by name, a scion of one of the great houses of the Beauvoisin. And when he had returned to his own land, and had taken the cowl at St. Germer, Anselm did not fail from time to time to find or make occasion for a visit to St. Germer, to enjoy a *causerie* with his former pupil, and drop by the way some of his golden words of gentle admonition and wise instruction. He thus imbued Guibert with his own passionate love of Holy Scripture, and taught him to apply thereto the exegetical methods of St. Gregory the Great. These studies bore fruit in the commentaries which won for Guibert a place of honour among the doctors of the mediæval Church; nor when, in old age, Guibert, as Abbot of Nogent sur Coucy (diocese of Laon), wrote his autobiography, did he fail to acknowledge the debt he owed to Anselm's wise counsel and encouragement.†

Other of Anselm's pupils were William of Montfort and Boso of Montivilliers, both high-born, high-bred men who entered Le Bec in early manhood, drawn by the magnetic influence of Anselm's personality, and succeeded in turn to the abbacy. The effect of that influence was prodigious. Towards the close of his priorate the confraternity numbered nearly three hundred monks, including those resident in priories or cells belonging to the abbey on either side of the channel, and the little colony established by Lanfranc at Christ Church, Canterbury.

Among his pupils, Boso, of whom more hereafter, and Maurice, whom Lanfranc carried off to Canterbury, to act apparently as his secretary and amanuensis, were evidently Anselm's especial favourites. To

† Migne, *Patrolog.* clvi. 874.

Maurice, from whom he parted with the utmost reluctance, he writes, after the separation, as a father to a son, alternately deploring his absence and exulting in the favour he has found in Lanfranc's eyes, now exhorting him to repair what was lacking in his own instruction, by attending the lectures of the great grammarian, Arnulf, and reading his Virgil with due diligence, and again showing him how he can still be of service to his old master by procuring for him a copy of the Venerable Bede, *De Temporibus*, or of the Rule of St. Dunstan, or of the Aphorisms of Hippocrates, with glosses explanatory of the Greek or other unusual terms.[1]

In Maurice's absence Anselm found solace in the society of Lanfranc's nephew and namesake, who, with two friends, Guido and Osbern, came to pass his pupilage at Le Bec, and for whose mental, spiritual, and physical well-being he betrays, in his letters to Lanfranc, a solicitude almost maternal.

Both Maurice and Boso had a taste for metaphysics; and with them, and others, probably, whose names we know not, Anselm pursued that method, so easy in appearance, so hard in practice, of familiar and sometimes playful, yet always strenuous and searching, oral discussion which the genius of Socrates, and his greater pupil, established for all time as the most efficient organon of metaphysical investigation.

These discussions led, as such discussions are apt to lead, to that loftiest theme of human discourse, the true relations between Reason and Faith; and so impressed were his pupils by his manner of handling this topic, that they besought Anselm to compose a formal

[1] *Epp.* i. 34, 35, 39, 43, 51, 55, 60, 65, 70.

treatise upon the subject. With some reluctance—for he was diffident of his power to rise to the height of that great argument—he yielded to their importunity, and in due time laid before them a meditation or colloquy of the soul with herself, *de Divinitatis Essentia*, commonly known as the *Monologion*, in which, dispensing with scriptural or other authority, he attempts to establish the congruity of the Catholic faith concerning God and His attributes, with the dictates of Reason.

Not that Anselm is in the common, and, after all, only true sense of the term, a rationalist, though he has been so described. For with the rationalist, Reason takes precedence of Faith, whereas Anselm does not recognize the possibility of any real conflict between the two powers. With him Faith and Reason are "bells of full accord." He is far too good a Catholic to doubt even for an instant that the Church has in her a higher than any human wisdom; but he holds, nevertheless, with all the strength of his deep speculative Gothic intellect, that Reason also has her prerogatives, of which not the least is the right of exploring, in profound reverence indeed, yet not without a certain hardihood, the inmost *penetralia* of the divine mysteries. Though *credere* has of right precedence of *intelligere*, yet the true attitude of the Christian is not that of blind acquiescent *credo*, but of a *credo ut intelligam;* in other words, though the mysteries of the faith transcend Reason, yet there is nevertheless a reason implicit in them, which it is at once the right and the duty of a thinking believer to render explicit.

Accordingly, in the *Monologion*, having assumed the existence of God as a verity of the faith, Anselm essays to prove that it is implicit in ordinary experience. To this end, he begins by analysing the experience of desire. That which we desire, he observes, is always some good, real or apparent, *i.e.* some evident or supposed utility or intrinsic worth, as swiftness or strength in horse or man, or beauty.

But all particular goods, being but varieties of one and the same species, are essentially identical, and must, therefore, have a common original. It follows that there is an archetypal or absolute Good, which is the original of which all particular goods are copies.

The same argument is evidently valid of whatever, by exciting our reverence, falls within the category of the sublime. There must, therefore, be one absolute Good and absolute Sublime.

Having laboured this point with some detail, Anselm proceeds to argue that all particular beings exist in virtue of some universal self-existent being either within or without them, the only alternative being the manifestly absurd supposition of reciprocal dependence.

Moreover, Nature exhibits a scale of being graduated according to worth; and as it is irrational to suppose the scale to be infinite, it follows that there exists a highest Being or a plurality of highest beings. But such a plurality is not thinkable, since it involves the absolute coequality of the supposed highest beings, and such absolute coequality implies essential unity. There must, therefore, be one absolute Summa Natura or Highest Being.

And the unity of this Being must be not only essential, but absolute. In other words, the "Summa Natura" is neither a whole of parts, nor a substance having attributes distinct from itself. For a composite, whether of parts or of attributes, is conditioned by those parts or attributes. But the Summa Natura is unconditioned, therefore it has no parts; and its so-called attributes are merely different ways of denominating its essence or itself. But a being without parts, and of which the attributes are one with itself, is absolutely simple and immutable.

But how are we to conceive the relation of the world of contingent existences to the Absolute?—a question which evidently admits of but one answer. The contingent cannot be a mode of the Absolute, because the Absolute has no modes; neither can it be a part of the Absolute, because the Absolute has no parts. It follows that it was created, *i.e.* absolutely originated, called into being *ex nihilo*, by the Absolute. No other hypothesis is conceivable.

When as yet there was nothing out of which it could be made, the Absolute gave existence to the world of contingent matter; and the existence thus given is dependent for its continuance upon the Power which gave it; otherwise the world would be no longer contingent, but absolute.

Thus, then, it may truly, though figuratively, be said that the Absolute is in and through all things, and that all things are in and through the Absolute.

Moreover: as rational soul is higher in the scale of being than the body, or aught perceivable by the bodily senses, it follows that the Absolute can least inadequately be conceived as rational soul in its highest perfection, as "summa essentia, summa vita, summa ratio, summa salus, summa justitia, summa sapientia, summa veritas, summa bonitas, summa magnitudo, summa pulchritudo, summa immortalitas, summa incorruptibilitas, summa immutabilitas, summa beatitudo, summa æternitas, summa potestas, summa unitas; quod non est aliud quam summe ens, summe vivens."

Such a Being may be said indifferently to be in all places and times, or in no place or time. Omnipresent in the sense of being distributed throughout space and time, He, of course, is not, since He has no parts; but omnipresent He is in the sense that in His undivided essence He is present at once in every part of space and every moment of time.

Thus for God the distinctions of past and future have no existence. He neither was nor will be, He neither foreknows nor remembers; but eternally is and knows. And His knowing, willing, and indeed all His attributes, including His eternity, are one with His essence, with Himself. In strictness of speech, indeed, the terms essence and substance are inapt to denote the perfect simplicity of His nature, which is best defined as absolutely individual spirit.

In the attempt which Anselm subsequently makes, not indeed to explain but to illustrate by human analogies the congruity of the hypostatic triplicity with the individual unity of the Divine nature, Anselm fares no better than most of those before and since his day, who have essayed by the feeble resources of Reason to alleviate the burden of an impenetrable mystery. Our analysis of his argument may therefore rest here.

Neither is this the place for detailed criticism of the argument. To be adequate, such criticism would require more space than is at our command; and anything less than adequate criticism would be manifestly unpardonable. It would, moreover, but involve us in the old mazes which are but too familiar to the theologian. How God can be at once absolutely immutable and yet free, living, exorable, since at least the potentiality of change appears to be involved in freedom and pre-supposed in prayer, while process seems to be of the very essence of life? How His omnipresence, which with Anselm includes His omniscience, is to be reconciled with the reality of change, of contingency; how, if

> Nothing to Him is future, nothing past,
> But an eternal now doth ever last,

He can be the author of change, and therefore cognisant thereof; how if the human will is free, and human action therefore really contingent, He can yet know all the actions of His creatures, and the secret motions of their hearts before they occur? To these dilemmas we can here but advert and pass on. To the last we shall have occasion hereafter to recur; as it is the subject of one of Anselm's later treatises.

These perplexities, however, notwithstanding, the substance of the argument of the *Monologion* is of undeniable force. In the world of experience we are confronted on every hand by the transitory, the contingent, or at least apparently contingent, the imperfect. These features inevitably lead the mind upward towards a Being, conceived as eternal, necessary, perfect; of this Being we stand the best chance of forming a not altogether inadequate idea, if we take as its representative the highest nature which we immediately know, to wit, our own soul, abstracting therefrom all its imperfections. Such anthropomorphism is manifestly—apart from the teaching of the Church—the only possible method by which we can gain anything approaching to a concrete notion of God; and the antinomies which are incident to it, even though they should remain forever unreconciled, will never shake the confidence of the majority of men in its intrinsic validity. The argument of the *Monologion* may therefore be pronounced essentially cogent as against all but the pure positivist. But if we are met at the outset by a refusal to look beyond phenomena; if our sceptical friend hesitates to attempt the logical passage from phenomena to their ground, lest such supposed ground should after all be no more than a bare idea of his own, how are we to deal with him? A question of much pith and moment, which Anselm is so far from ignoring that it causes him no small travail of mind, and brings at last a new argument to the birth.

This passage in Anselm's mental history is described both by Anselm himself and by Eadmer; succinctly, as is the manner of both, but by the latter with such vivacity, that it is evident we are listening to the report of Boso or Henry, or some other of Anselm's pupils who had scanned his demeanour closely during what he felt to be a crisis of supreme importance. We are told that his meditations led him at first, and for long, only farther and farther from his goal, insomuch that his perplexity and anxiety grew so chronic and intense that at last he could neither eat nor sleep, nor duly perform his devotions, so that he began to think the whole train of thought an inspiration of the Evil One, from which it was his duty to divert his mind by all possible means; but that the more he strove so to do the more it haunted him, until one night during vigil the light broke upon his mind, and he felt that he was in possession of the very argument he had so long sought. Snatching his stylus and tablets, he inscribed its substance on their smooth waxen surface, and entrusted them for safekeeping to one of the brothers, by whom they were lost. Another impression narrowly escaped the same fate. The tablets were found in fragments on the dormitory floor; but the wax was gathered up and pieced together, and the argument was thereupon committed to parchment. Copies were multiplied; but with characteristic modesty it was not until 1099, and then only in obedience to the "apostolical authority" of Archbishop Hugh of Lyon, then legate in Gaul, that Anselm consented to attach his name either to it or the *Monologion.*

The argument is in form an "elevation," as it is called in the Church, or aspiration of the soul after God; as is indicated by its title, *Proslogion, seu Alloquium de Dei Existentia.* In substance it is an *Argumentum ad Insipientem,* or confutation of the fool who says in his heart, There is no God; striking, not to say startling, in its boldness, being nothing less than the deduction of the real existence of God from a pure idea.

No man—such in concisest summary is its tenor—not even the fool who in his heart denies God, can, except in words, deny that a *Summum Cogitabile,*[1] or Highest Thinkable exists, at least, in thought; for the term is certainly intelligible, and whatever is intelligible exists in thought. But if it exists in thought, it exists also in fact. For the *Summum*

[1] Anselm does not use this term; but it is the exact equivalent of his somewhat cumbrous circumlocution, "aliquid quo nihil majus cogitari potest," and is as such employed in a treatise, *De Primo Principio,* iv. schol. vii. § 24, which is attributed to Duus Scotus, a master of concise and precise terminology.

Cogitabile manifestly involves the unity of thought and real existence, since any thinkable, however insignificant in the scale of being, which has real existence, is higher than any thinkable, however exalted, which has none. Moreover, necessary existence is higher than contingent existence. It is impossible, therefore, to deny the necessary existence of the *Summum Cogitabile. E vi definitionis*, then, there is a *Summum Ens* existing necessarily both in thought and in fact. And in the idea of the *Summum Cogitabile*, as thus defined, is implicit the idea of God, not indeed in its fulness, for that transcends human thought, but in a measure adequate for the confutation of the fool. For the idea of God is the idea of a Being comprehending within Himself all perfections, self-existent, and the Creator of all finite beings. Now a highest and as such necessary Being must manifestly be self-existent, contain all perfections in indivisible unity, and be related to inferior beings as their Creator. The *Summum Cogitabile*, then, is God. God, then, really and necessarily exists, both in thought and in fact.

In other words, Reason postulates the Absolute as really and necessarily existing, and so in effect postulates God. Reason, therefore, cannot deny God, because she cannot deny herself. He who does so is in very truth a fool; for he has taken leave of Reason. And, in fact, his denial is only apparent. He has not really apprehended what is meant by the *Summum Cogitabile*, for, as soon as he does so, it is impossible for him even to think that it does not really and necessarily exist.

So summary a method of disposing of the atheist was not likely to pass without challenge even in Anselm's day, and it was not long before a monk of Marmoutier, by name Gaunilon, entered the lists with a *Liber pro Insipiente*, or *Apology for the Fool*.[1] His criticism, as might have been anticipated, is just that of common sense. The *Summum Cogitabile*, he says in effect, is a vague idea, and can claim no higher validity than any other idea. Nor does any idea, simply as such, avouch real existence, except, indeed, those which cannot be thought without such avouchment. Of these, the *Summum Cogitabile* is not one.

"Some say that somewhere in the ocean is an island, which, from the difficulty or, rather, impossibility of discovering it (seeing that it does not exist), they call the Lost Island, whereof they fable much more than of the Isles of the Blest concerning the inestimable fecundity in natural resources and all manner of delectable and desirable things, by which, though uninhabited, it excels whatever lands men till. I may hear tell of such an island, and easily understand what I hear, for it presents no difficulty; but if my informant were to add, 'Now you cannot doubt that such an island, excelling all other lands, exists somewhere in fact as well as in your mind, because to exist in fact is more excellent than to exist in imagination, and if it did not really exist,

[1] Near Châteaudun, on the little river Loir, in the fertile plain of La Beauce, lies the hamlet of Montigny-le-Gannelon, in the Middle Ages a fortified town commanded by a strong keep, of which the author of the *Apology for the Fool* was lord. He was also treasurer of the famous Chapter of St. Martin at Tours, and founder of the Priory of St. Hilaire, hard by his castle; but it was at Marmoutier that, *in signo fidei*, we trust, notwithstanding the evidently critical bias of his mind, he ended his days. He was living in 1083. (*Cf. Mem. de la Soc. Arch. de Touraine*, tom. xxiv.; *Hist. de Marmoutier*, i. 363; and RAVAISSON, *Rapp. sur les Bibl. de l'Ouest*, App. p. 410.)

any land which does so would be more excellent than it'—if, I say, by such an argument as this he were to try to convince me of the real, indubitable existence of the island, I should either think he jested, or be at a loss to say whether I or he were the more silly—I, if I should concede the point, or he, for thinking to establish with any certitude the real existence of the island without first proving its existence as a real, indubitable fact in Nature, and not merely as a possibly false or vague somewhat in my mind."

This criticism is trenchant, but Anselm, in his brief rejoinder, or *Liber Apologeticus contra Respondentem pro Insipiente*, easily turns its edge by pointing out the ineffaceable distinction which subsists between the idea of the *Summum Cogitabile* and any empirical idea whatever. Of the existence of the Isles of the Blest of Gaunilon's Lost Island, in short, of any particular object, even though actual, it is possible to doubt, because the existence of such objects is not implied in their idea. Being things of time and sense, they are essentially transitory. If they exist, they had a beginning, and will have an end. No particular idea, therefore, as such, avouches the existence of a corresponding object. But with the *Summum Cogitabile* the case is quite otherwise. "For the *Summum Cogitabile* cannot be thought except as eternal, whereas whatever is thought to be, and is not, may be thought as temporal. The *Summum Cogitabile*, therefore, cannot be thought to be without really being. If, then, it can be thought to be, it of necessity is. Moreover, if it can so much as be thought, it of necessity is. For no one who denies or doubts the real existence of the *Summum Cogitabile* denies or doubts that, if it really existed, it would exist of necessity both in thought and in fact; for otherwise it would not be the *Summum Cogitabile.* Whereas, whatever can be thought, but does not really exist, would, if it did really exist, be capable of not existing either in fact or thought. Wherefore the *Summum Cogitabile*, if it can so much as be thought, necessarily exists.

But let us assume that it need not exist merely because it is thought. Mark the consequence. That which can be thought without really existing would not, if it did exist, be the *Summum Cogitabile;* so that, by the hypothesis, the *Summum Cogitabile* is and is not the *Summum Cogitabile*, which is in the last degree absurd."

In other words, contingent existence, as such, contradicts the idea of the *Summum Cogitabile;* for necessary existence is higher than contingent existence. But it is the mark of necessary existence that it cannot even be thought as contingent. Therefore, the supposition that the *Summum Cogitabile* can be thought without really existing, is self-contradictory.

"It is certain, then, that the *Summum Cogitabile*, if it can so much as be thought, also really exists; *a fortiori* if it can be understood or exist in the understanding.

I will go further. Whatever in some place or time is not, even though in some other place or time it be, can be thought as not being in any place or time, just as well as not being in this or that place or time. For what yesterday was not, and to-day is, as it is known not to have been yesterday, so it can be supposed never to have been; and what here is not, but elsewhere is, since it is not here, so it can be thought as being nowhere.

In like manner, when the parts of a thing do not all co-exist in place and time, they, and by consequence the thing itself, can be thought as not being in any place or time. For though it may be said that time is in all its moments, and space in all places, yet the totality of time is not in each moment, nor the totality of space in every place; and as the several moments of time do not all co-exist, so they can all be thought as never having been; and as the several parts of space do not co-exist, so they can all be thought as being nowhere; for what is composed of parts can be decomposed in thought, and so thought as not being. Wherefore, whatever is not undistributed in some place or time, although it really exist, can be thought as not really existing. But the *Summum Cogitabile* is not something which, though it really exist, can be thought as not so existing; for if it could both so exist, and so be thought, it would both be and not be the *Summum Cogitabile*, which is a contradiction. By no manner of means, then, can there be a place or time in which it is not in its undivided essence present; but in that undivided essence it is present in all times and places."

In short, all that, being real, can be conceived as unreal, can be so conceived because its reality is merely empirical, because being conditioned by space or time, it can be mentally represented as not being when or where it is, and so as not really being at all. But the *Summum Cogitabile* cannot be conceived as not really existing. Whence it follows that it is not conditioned by space or time; and between it and the idea of the Lost Island, or any other empirical idea, there is no parity whatever. And "if anyone will discover for me anything existing either in fact or in pure thought, to which the concatenation of this my argument will apply, I will discover that Lost Island, and make him a present of it, no more to be lost."

The real existence of the *Summum Cogitabile* is proved by the most certain of all principles, that of contradiction; for if it did not exist really, it would not exist at all, *i.e.* not even ideally; but ideally it does exist; therefore it exists also really. "And in fine, if anyone says that he thinks it does not really exist, I answer that what he then thinks is either the *Summum Cogitabile*, or nothing at all. If it is nothing at all, then he certainly does not think the non-existence of that nothing. But if he thinks, he certainly thinks what cannot be thought not really to exist. For if it could be thought not really to exist, it could be thought to have beginning and end; but this is not possible. Whoso then thinks the *Summum Cogitabile*, thinks that which cannot be thought not really to exist. But whoever thinks this, does not think that it does not really exist, otherwise he would think what is not thinkable. It is therefore impossible to think that the *Summum Cogitabile* does not really exist."

Here follows a slight digression into matters which do not concern the substance of the argument; after which Anselm explains his reason for using the term Highest Thinkable in preference to Highest Being (*Majus Omnibus*, or, as we may conveniently say, *Summum Ens*), a distinction of the utmost consequence to the cogency of the argument.

"For if anyone says that the *Summum Cogitabile* either does not, or may not, really exist, or even that it may be thought not really to exist, he may be easily refuted." But not so if *Summun Ens* be substituted for *Summum Cogitabile.* "For it is not so evident that what can be thought not really to exist is not the *Summum Ens,* as that it is not the *Summum Cogitabile.* Nor is it so indubitable that if a *Summum Ens* really exist, it is no other than the *Summum Cogitabile,* or might not be some other like the *Summum Cogitabile,* as it is certain that the *Summum Cogitabile* must be the *Summum Ens.* For were it to be alleged that the *Summum Ens* really exists, and that it yet might be thought not really to exist; and that something higher, though it could not really exist, might nevertheless be thought; would the conclusion, *then it is not the Summum Ens,* follow so evidently as in the parallel case it follows, in the most evident manner possible, that the *Summum Cogitabile* is not the *Summum Cogitabile?* Assuredly not; for in the one case more is needed for the argument than the bare conception of the *Summum Ens;* whereas, in the latter case, nothing more is needed than is already given in the *Summum Cogitabile.*"

In other words, the real existence of the *Summum Ens* can be denied or questioned without contradiction; for it is Reason, and Reason alone, which postulates its real existence; but the real existence of the *Summum Cogitabile* cannot be denied or questioned without contradiction; for the term itself, while it denotes the *Summum Ens,* connotes therewith its real existence as postulated by Reason.

By this time the reader, if he is philosophic, will have so far apprehended the nature of Anselm's reasoning as to perceive that it derives its entire force from the identification of the rational and the real. That which cannot but be thought, that of which the negation is inconceivable, necessarily exists. The ultimate laws of thought are laws of being; logic and ontology are essentially one. Reason postulates an Absolute, in which the apparent opposition between being and thought is overcome; and of the existence of such an Absolute there can be no doubt, because so long as the mind contemplates the Absolute, it necessarily contemplates it as really existing. An unreal Absolute is a contradiction in terms.

Here, then, for the first time in the history of thought, is the formal, explicit, articulate expression of what has since come to be termed the ontological, or *a priori* proof of the being of God—the watershed, as it may fitly be designated, of metaphysical speculation. Rejected, for want of perfect apprehension, by St. Thomas Aquinas[1] and the later scholastics generally, with, however, the notable exceptions of the seraphic and subtle doctors,[2] revived in a modified form by Descartes,[3] and virtually admitted by Leibniz,[4] converted in the Cartesian form to pantheistic uses by Spinoza,[5] subjected to searching criticism after the manner of Gaunilon by Kant,[6] and finally reformulated by Hegel,[7]

[1] *Summ. Contr. Gent.* i. 10. 11.

[2] BONAVENTURA, *Compend. Theol. Verit.* i. 1; I. *Sent.* Dist. viii. pars i. art. i. Quaest. ii.; DUNS SCOTUS, I. *Sent.* Dist. ii. Quaest. ii.; *De Prim. Princip.* iv. schol. vii. § 24.

[3] *Princ.* i. 14.

[4] With curious obtuseness, Leibniz finds one flaw in the reasoning, to wit, that it proceeds upon the assumption of the *possibility* of God. *Opera*, tom. ii. pars i. 221.

[5] *Eth.* i. 5, 6.

[6] *Kritik der rein. Vern.* i., Th. ii., Abth. ii., Buch ii., Hauptst. iii., Abschn. iv.

[7] *Religionsphil.* Th. iii. B. and Anhang. Vorles. 1827 and 1831.

this celebrated theorem will probably continue, in one form or another, to command the assent of the speculative thinker, and provoke the mirth of the man of the world, to the end of time. To make merry at its expense is easy; for that purpose, Kant's imaginary hundred thalers to set against a real debt will serve as well as Gaunilon's Lost Island, though not so pretty a figure in a literary sense; but when the laugh is over, it remains incontestable that the only irrefragable basis of certitude is rational necessity. Assurance of the existence of aught, ourselves included, there is none save the necessity of so thinking. Subject, object, time, space, equality, inequality, likeness, difference, cause and effect, law and phenomenon, the universe in fine, with its fundamental dichotomy of soul and world, all this complicated subtly-woven web of relation and distinction, is what it is for us, is all that it is for us, because we cannot think otherwise. It is not possible, without confusion of thought, to affirm part of it and question the residue, which forms therewith one logical whole. It is possible to argue that it may be all a dream; but it is not possible so actually to think. He who professes so to do merely stultifies himself. And in it is implicit, as its final unity, the idea of a universal, all-comprehensive, eternal, necessary principle, *Summum Cogitabile* and *Summum Ens*, Highest Thinkable and Highest Actuality, Thought and Being in one and in perfection, in a word, God. So much of permanent value for the spiritual interests of mankind was latent in the lonely musings of the recluse of Le Bec; nor, so long as these interests are dear to men, will Anselm lose the place accorded him by

Hegel[1] among the few deep speculative thinkers who have opened new avenues for the human mind.

[1] *Gesch. d. Philos.* Th. ii. Abschn. ii. B. For further exposition and criticism of the *Monologion* and *Proslogion*, the reader whose patience is not already exhausted may be referred to BOUCHITTÉ, *Le Rationalisme Chrétien à la fin du XIe siècle*, Paris, 1842; SAISSET, *De Varia S. Anselmi in Proslogio Argumenti Fortuna*, Paris, 1840, and *Essai de Philosophie Religieuse*, Paris, 1862, ii. 267 *et seq.*; RÉMUSAT, *Saint Anselme de Cantorbéry*, Paris, 1856; ERDMANN, *Grundriss der Geschichte der Philosophie*, Berlin, 1878; RAGEY, *L'Argument de Saint Anselme*, Paris, 1893; WEBB, *Anselm's Ontological Argument for the Existence of God* (a paper read before the Aristotelian Society in 1895).

CHAPTER VI.

ANSELM'S MINOR WORKS: THE *DE VERITATE*, *DE CASU DIABOLI*, AND *DE LIBERO ARBITRIO*—HIS MEDITATIONS, PRAYERS, AND POEMS

THOUGH the most important, the *Monologion* and *Proslogion* were by no means the sole fruit of Anselm's leisure during his residence at Le Bec. To the same period belong four dialogues, entitled respectively, *De Grammatico*, *De Veritate*, *De Casu Diaboli*, and *De Libero Arbitrio*.

The first need not detain us, being of interest only to the curious investigator of scholastic ways of thinking, and as furnishing the student of Dante with the key to the otherwise insoluble enigma, why

> Anselmo e quel Donato
> Ch'alla prim'arte degnò por la mano.

are so closely linked together among the saints of order in Paradise (*Parad.* c. xii. 137–138). The others are worth a passing glance.

The *De Veritate*, as its title implies, is an attempt to solve the ancient, but ever fresh, problem of the nature of truth, and, as might be anticipated, from a point of view, and with a result, as far as possible removed from those of common sense, or empirical philosophy.

Like some earlier and later thinkers, Anselm sees

God in all things, and all things in God. Truth postulates God, for it transcends time, that which is true at all being true always. It is not in the correspondence of our thought with its object that truth consists, for, if so, it would be temporal, coming into and passing out of being with the act of thinking. The truth itself is the object to which, with various degrees of accuracy, our thinking corresponds, or appears to correspond. Truth may therefore be defined as that to which our thinking ought to correspond. And this object is one and indivisible. As there is but one space, and one time, comprehending an indefinite multiplicity of places and moments, so there is but one Truth, to which all so-called particular truths are but approximations. Through the media of sense, judgment, and reasoning, this one eternal Verity is fragmentarily apprehended by us; and so, though our apprehension of it is ever gaining in fulness and depth, yet we habitually think less of the one eternal Truth than of the multiplicity of its appearances. Nevertheless, this parcel truth betrays at every turn its transcendental origin, inasmuch as we always regard it not merely as being, but as being rational, as being necessary (rectitudo sola mente perceptibilis).

Perception, reasoning, are true, in so far as they accurately report this necessary Being, in so far, that is to say, as they reveal to us the mind of God. Thus truth is in the intelligible sphere what justice is in the moral sphere, and, though to us apparently diverse, both have the same archetype, since in God there is no distinction between reason and will, truth and justice. Upon this theory a modern empirical thinker will be apt to remark that, however fine its idealism, it is useless for the practical purpose of discriminating between truth and error in the affairs of daily life, and in the exploration of nature. And this contention, if sustainable, would, of course, be fatal; for an idealism, however fine, which is nothing more than a rhapsodic flight of imagination, is philosophically worthless. But is it really sustainable? What do we when we discriminate between truth and illusion? What is the measure we apply? What but that of coherence with our normal consciousness? That which will not harmonise with the unity of experience we unhesitatingly pronounce false. That which does harmonise therewith we account at least probable, and probable in proportion to the breadth, depth, and subtlety of the resultant harmony. And is not the goal of all our scientific explanation and philosophical theorising a point of view from which, as in Faust's vision, we may discern all modes of being as essentially one—*Harmonisch all' das All durchdringen?* This ideal, however dimly conceived, however thwarted by the multiplicity of phenomena, however clouded by scepticism, has been the hidden source from which, throughout the long travail of the human spirit, not only the meditations of the philosopher and the musings of the mystic, but also the patient, cautious labours of the man of observation and experiment, have drawn their inspiration. This, and this alone, it is which raises scientific endeavour above the level of mere curiosity, gives to the least advance in knowledge an ideal worth, and clothes the masters of the mind with the character of hierophants. And could we but realise this ideal, as perhaps posterity may, should we not verify Anselm's intuition, which is also St. Paul's, of God in all things, and all things in God?

The *De Casu Diaboli*, if not the most satisfactory, is certainly not the least ingenious of Anselm's works. In none of them is the dialectic keener, more subtle; none enables us more vividly to realise how much of abysmal doubt, of intrepid speculation, was harboured in those grey monastic halls. The problem may be stated as follows: Since all finite being owes its origin to and depends for its continued existence upon the will of God, moral evil must evidently be in some sense ordained by Him. More specifically, it is true not only of men, but of angels also, that all that they have, they have received of God. (1 Cor. iv. 7.) Therefore, the will by which the good angels persevered in righteousness, and the will by which the evil angels fell, were alike His gift. How, then, are either the one or the other praiseworthy or blameable? And more specifically still, how is God's omission to endow the Devil with the gift of perseverance to be reconciled with His goodness and wisdom? If we say that the grace was only not given in the sense that, when offered, it was rejected, the difficulty is only removed a stage, since such as in the first instance was the Devil's will, such he received it from God. *Prima facie*, therefore, God would seem to be responsible for his fall. Again, we are told that he fell by inordinate ambition, aspiring to equality with God. And this raises another difficulty. For as God can only be conceived as unique in such sense that nothing like Him is conceivable, how could the Devil desire that which he could not conceive? And if we interpret his desire to be as God as meaning merely the insurgence of his will against the Divine will, nevertheless the old perplexities still return upon us. For whence had he that inordinateness of will? From himself or from God? If we say that he had it from himself, do we not virtually deny his creaturehood? For how can a creature have aught from himself? From God, then? But, if so, then how is he culpable? Moreover, why should a being of so sublime a nature have been so fashioned by God as to be able to change his will from good to bad, but not conversely?

From this apparent *impasse*, Anselm, like Augustine,* finds a way of escape in denying the positive existence of moral evil. If moral evil is nothing positive, if it is a mere defect, then, he argues, the Devil may have had it from himself quite consistently with his having everything from God. The proof that it is nothing positive is as follows:

> "We must believe that justice is the good in virtue of which men and angels are good, *i.e.* just, and the will itself is said to be good or just; and that the evil which makes them and their will bad is injustice, which we define as nothing else than the privation of the good; and therefore we assert that this same injustice is nothing else than the privation of justice. For so long as the will first given to a rational being, and in the giving by the Giver turned—nay, not turned, but made true to its end—persisted in the righteousness, which we call truth or justice, in which it was made, so long it was just. But when it turned itself away from its end, and turned itself towards that which was not its end, then it no longer persisted in its original (so to say) righteousness in which it was made, and in deserting it lost a great thing, and instead thereof got nothing except the privation thereof, which has no essential being, and which we call injustice."

* *De Duab. Animab. contr. Manich.* § 6.

Moral evil, then, being the privation of original righteousness, is irreparable by any act of the creature himself, since he has nothing of his own; but the loss is all his own, since it depended on his free will, and that alone, whether he should adhere to, or deviate from, his original righteousness.

Moreover, the will by which the Devil fell was itself nothing positive, but a mere privation. For every natural propensity, every act or state of will, in so far as positive, is good, being the gift of God. Even the will to be as God is, in itself, good, and the sin of the Devil lay, not in so willing, but in so willing unduly.

The question, Whence came that inordinateness into his will? admits of no answer: it is like asking, Whence came nothing? The act by which he abandoned his original righteousness was one which had no antecedent cause. "It was, at once, its own efficient cause, and, if one may so say, effect." Evil, in short, is a surd in the moral order, existing by the permission, but without the positive ordinance of God, and of which the philosopher can but note the existence, without attempting either to deduce its origin, or explain its final cause.

This theory of moral evil was adopted from Anselm by St. Thomas Aquinas, and so obtained general recognition in the Catholic schools, as the only alternative to Manichaeism. Recast in philosophical form, it holds a conspicuous place in the systems of certain non-Catholic thinkers, as Spinoza[1] and Hegel,[2] and, indeed, is logically involved in every monistic theory of metaphysics. In strict consistency with it, Anselm maintains, in the *De Libero Arbitrio*, that

[1] *Eth.* iv. 64.

[2] *Encycl.* §§ 507 *et seq.*

capacity for sin is no necessary element in moral freedom; but, on the contrary, that an impeccable being, as God, is all the more free by reason of his impeccability. Moral freedom, in his view, is not the power of choosing between alternatives, but the power of persevering in righteousness for its own sake (potestas conservandi rectitudinem propter ipsam rectitudinem); and capacity for sin, so far from enhancing, impairs—though it does not necessarily destroy—this freedom. Sin is, in fact, *pro tanto*, an abdication of freedom—an abdication determined by nothing but the will itself. Even in sinning, then, the freedom of the will is still its power of persevering in righteousness for its own sake, for without that power there could be no sin; and where the power to sin is wanting, it is simply because the will to sin is wanting, and therefore perfect freedom and impeccability are one and the same. In this theory the student of modern philosophy will recognise an adumbration of the essential doctrine of Kant's *Metaphysic of Ethics*; while the theologian will see at a glance how important is its bearing on the subtle questions which concern the relations of sin and grace. Original sin, being in Anselm's view a mere privation, evidently need not involve the total depravity of human nature; and, in fact, he expressly maintains that it does not do so. The Fall, he insists, as it left man reason and will, left him also in possession of "natural" freedom; left him, that is to say, the capacity of recognising the claims of duty, and of fulfilling them. Apart altogether from the influence of Divine grace, the human will is always stronger than temptation, for it is not capable of determination by anything but itself. It is not motives which govern the will, but the will which governs motives. The power of a motive is determined by the will's consent; and, therefore, it is mere idle sophistry to speak of its ever being over-mastered by temptation. But, though original sin does not destroy, it does impair free will, rendering perseverance in righteousness for its own sake a work of difficulty, and fore-closing the way of reformation after a lapse. Hence it renders the sinner dependent for his redemption upon the grace of God. In short, original sin leaves man sufficient freedom to render him culpable, but not enough to justify himself after the commission of actual sin.

Into the question of the relation between human freedom and Divine grace Anselm does not enter here. It is handled, in conjunction with the cognate problem of the reconciliation of freedom with fore-knowledge and predestination, in a separate treatise, projected, doubtless, and pondered during his residence at Le Bec, but only cast into final shape toward the close of his life; and which, being by no means to be regarded as one of his minor works, will receive a separate notice in its proper place.

Amid such heroic wrestlings with the highest problems of speculative thought, Anselm paused from time to time to refresh his soul by the still waters of holy meditation and prayer. His *Meditationes* and *Orationes*, the fruit of these hours of *recueillement*, have been frequently printed, and will probably never lose their charm for people of devout and contemplative mind. The *Orationes* do not lend themselves to quotation, and are inferior in literary quality to the *Meditationes*. The latter cannot but suffer grievously by translation; but of the power which they occasionally display some idea may, perhaps, be gathered from the following excerpt:

"Imagine that you see before you a valley, broad and deep and gloomy, at the bottom whereof are all manner of instruments of torture. Suppose that it is spanned by a single bridge, in width no more than a foot. Suppose that this bridge, so narrow, high, and dangerous, had to be crossed by one whose eyes were bandaged, so that he could not see a pace in front of him; whose hands were bound behind his back, so that it was impossible for him to feel his way by a stick. What terror, what agony of mind, would he not be in? Would he find place for joy, hilarity, pleasure? I think not. Bereft of pride, emptied of vain glory, his whole soul would be enshrouded in the blackness of darkness of the apprehension of death. Suppose, moreover, that monsters and savage birds hovered about the bridge, seeking to draw him down into the abyss, would not his fear be enhanced? Suppose, again, that his retreat is cut off as he advances, the causeway slipping from under his very heels. Would not the anxiety of our wayfarer be thereby greatly increased?

Now learn the meaning of the parable, and brace your mind with divine fear. The deep and gloomy valley is hell, immeasurably deep, shrouded with a horrible veil of murky darkness, and replete with all kinds of instruments of torture, with nothing to alleviate its horror, with everything to terrify, to excruciate, to agonise the soul. The perilous bridge, which whoso treads unwarily is precipitated into the abyss, is the present life, whence they who abuse it fall and go down into the pit. The portions of the causeway which slip from under the heel of the wayfarer are the days of our life, which glide away never to return, and as their number grows less and less urge us ever forward to our goal. The birds hovering about the bridge to lure the travellers to their destruction are evil spirits, whose minds are wholly bent on misleading men and precipitating them into the depths of hell. We ourselves are the wayfarers, blinded with the thick darkness of ignorance, and bound as with a heavy chain by the difficulty of working righteousness, so as not to be able to direct our steps freely to God by the way of a holy life. Consider, then, if in so critical a position you should not with all your might cry unto your Creator that, fortified by His help, you may chant with confidence amid the hosts of the enemy, The Lord is my light and my salvation: of whom shall I be afraid?"—*Meditatio* i. 10.[1]

It must not be supposed that these Meditations of Anselm are pitched throughout in the key of the foregoing passage. On the contrary, there is much in them that is sweet, gracious, tender, and passionate. His Christolatry is of the noblest Catholic type, blended of the reverence due to God, the loyalty of a vassal to his feudal lord, the love that passeth the love of woman, the ecstasy of the mystic:

"O my Saviour and my God," he cries, "let it come; let it come, I pray Thee, the hour when I may at length gladden mine eyes with the vision of what I now believe; may apprehend what now I hope for and greet from afar; may with my spirit embrace and kiss what now with my whole might I yearn after, and be altogether absorbed in the abyss of Thy

[1] The imagery of this sombre passage is probably, as observed by Mr. Martin Rule (*Life of St. Anselm*, i. 48), a reminiscence of the gloomy gorge which connects Cogne with the upper Val d'Aosta. Down this tortuous ravine a torrent, known as the Grand' Eivia (Great Water), writhes its way to the Dora Baltea. At the point where it issues from the neck of the pass, its banks hardly reach an altitude of 180 ft., and are separated by a somewhat less interval. Here it is spanned by a single arch, bearing a gallery and narrow causeway traversable by foot passengers. An inscription on the keystone of the arch informs the traveller that it was built A.U.C. 749 for two Roman magnates—C. Avillius, whose name, more worn by time than his work, reappears in its designation of Le Pondel (Pons Avillii); and C. Aimus Patavinus, who has also left other trace of himself in the name of the neighbouring village of Aymavilles (Aimi Villa). This very striking relic of antiquity must have been frequently seen by Anselm, and may well have left an indelible impression on his mind.

love. But meanwhile, bless, O my soul, my Saviour, and magnify His Name, which is holy and full of the holiest delights."—(*Meditatio* ix. *versus fin.*)

And again:

"Good Jesus, how sweet art Thou in the heart that meditates on Thee and loves Thee. And yet of a truth I know not, for I am not able fully to understand whence it is that Thou art sweeter far in the heart that loves Thee, in that Thou art flesh, than in that Thou art the Word, sweeter in that Thou art lowly than in that Thou art lofty. . . . Jesus, neither can my mind conceive, nor my tongue express, how Thou art worthy to be loved by me, who hast deigned so much to love me. . . . I love Thee above all things, O most sweet Jesus, but far less than Thou meritest, and, therefore, than I ought."—(*Meditatio* xii.)

Once more:

"I have a word in secret with Thee my Lord, King of Ages, Christ Jesus. In the boldness of love the work of Thy hands presumes to address Thee, enamoured of Thy fairness and longing to hear Thy voice. O desired of my heart, how long shall I sustain Thine absence? How long shall I sigh after Thee, and mine eyes drop tears for Thee? . . . .

Thou hast clothed the sun with a splendour pre-eminent among the stars, and brighter than the sun art Thou. Nay, what is the sun, what all created light, but darkness in comparison of Thee? Thou hast furnished forth the heaven with stars, the empyrean with angels, the air with birds, the waters with fishes, the earth with herbs, the thickets with flowers. But there is no form or fairness in any of these that can compare with Thee, O source of all beauty, Lord Jesus!

Thou hast given the honey its sweetness, and sweeter than honey art Thou. Thou hast given its healing to the oil, and more healing than oil art Thou. Thou hast given all the spices their scents, and Thy scent, O Jesus, is above all spices sweet and grateful. Gold among the metals hast Thou fashioned in singular excellence of beauty and preciousness. And yet what is it in comparison of the priceless excellence of the Lord and the glory immeasurable on which the angels desire to gaze? Thy handiwork is every stone that is precious and pleasant to the eyes, sardius, topaz, jasper, chrysolite, onyx, beryl, amethyst, sapphire, carbuncle, emerald. And yet how are they better than straw in comparison of Thee, O King, fair beyond measure and altogether lovely? Thy workmanship is in living jewels and immortal, wherewith, O wise Masterbuilder, from the beginning of the world, Thou hast richly adorned Thy superethereal palace, to the glory of the Father." (*Meditatio* xiii.)

To multiply excerpts would serve no useful purpose. Enough has been done to afford the reader some insight into the bent of Anselm's thoughts in his hours of quiet communing with his own inmost soul. Should he desire to know more, he will, if a tolerable Latinist, find the Meditations by no means hard reading; for Anselm wrote Latin with a purity unusual in his age. In the original they should certainly be read, and with due heed to Anselm's own advice, "in quiet, nor cursorily, but little by little with concentrated and severe reflection" (cum intenta et morosa meditatione).

Besides the *Meditationes* and *Orationes*, not a few *Homiliae* and *Exhortationes*, expositions or applications, more or less formal, more or less familiar, of salient passages of Holy Scripture, such as might well have been delivered in the church or chapterhouse of Le Bec, and which, though the freedom of their mystical exegesis is sometimes enough to make a modern critic's hair stand on end, were not on that account the less likely to be appreciated by the audiences to which they were addressed, find place in Gerberon's collective edition of Anselm's Works, together with a rudely rhythmic Psalter of the Blessed Virgin, a *Carmen de Contemptu Mundi* in hexameters and pentameters, which exhibit a sublime indifference to scansion, and some other metrical trifles. Most of the sermons, however, are of doubtful authenticity, while the only tradition which connects the verse with the saint is both so late and so vague,[1] that it may be confidently set aside; nor is the MS. *Psalterium B. M. Virginis* preserved in the Arundel collection at the British Museum (MS. 157, Plut.), to which attention has recently been drawn by the learned Marist, Père Ragey, notwithstanding that it is indubitably of the twelfth century, and inscribed in the rubric as "editum a sancto Anselmo," much more likely to be his work. This *tour de force* of mystical symbolism consists of a hundred and fifty apostrophes to our Blessed Lady, usually in the form of a trochaic quatrain introduced by the word Ave, and having for motive a verse from one of the Psalms, which are thus traversed in order. There is really nothing better in the whole composition than the beginning: "Et erit tanquam lignum quod plantatum est secus decursus aquarum: quod fructum suum dabit in tempore suo.

Ave Porta Paradisi:
Lignum vitae quod amisi
Per Te mihi jam dulcescit,
Et salutis fructus crescit."

For such work as this it is evident that the most that can be said is that it exhibits a certain smoothness of rhythm, and though it is probable enough that Anselm authorised the use of the Psalter for devo-

[1] The poem *De Contemptu Mundi* is variously ascribed to Anselm's subprior, Roger of Caen, to St. Bernard of Clairvaux, and Bernard of Morlaix.

tional purposes, no one who cares about his literary repute will readily ascribe to him a hand in its production. The same must be said of the two rhythmic prayers to our Blessed Lady, included by Gerberon among Anselm's *Orationes.* That Anselm should have written either of them is simply incredible.

On the other hand, the hymns for the canonical hours, which precede the Psalter in Gerberon's edition, may unhesitatingly be accepted as Anselm's work, and are here printed and paraphrased for the glimpse they afford of the devotional exercises in use at Le Bec.

AD NOCTURNAM.

Lux quae luces in tenebris,
Ex alvo nata Virginis,
Nostram noctem nos exue,
Diemque Tuum indue.

Maria, Dei thalamus,
Posce Te venerantibus,
Virtutibus ut splendeant
Quos reatus obtenebrant.

Gloria Tibi, Domine,
Nato de Sancta Virgine,
Regnanti victo funere,
Cum Patre et Sancto Spiritu! *Amen.*

AT NOCTURNS.

Light that glimmerest in the gloom,
Dayspring from a Virgin's womb,
Haste our night to put away,
And invest us with Thy day.

Mary, Thou who God didst bear,
Pray for us who Thee revere,
That with virtue we may shine
Who in gloom of guilt now pine.

Glory to the Father be,
And the Holy Ghost with Thee,
Who didst conquer death alone,
And now reignest, Mary's Son. *Amen.*

AD LAUDES.

Praefulgens Sol Justitiae,
Ortus de Sacra Virgine,
Splendore tuo noxias
Nostras illustra tenebras.

Orientis castissima
Mater, fac nobis, Domina,
Vita prorsus ut decidat
Vetus, nova proficiat.

Gloria Tibi, Domine, *etc.*

AT LAUDS.

Hail, hail, prefulgent Lord of Morn,
Hail, Sun of Justice, Virgin-born!
With Thy pure splendours penetrate
The noisome shadows of our state.

Mother of Him that rises chaste,
Vouchsafe, we pray, our Lady Blest,
That from the old life we may turn,
And the new life to profit learn.

Glory to the Father be, *etc.*

AD PRIMAM.

O Christe, proles Virginis,
Altissimi compar Patris,
Per Tuae Matris merita
Dele nostra peccamina.

O mundo venerabilis,
Virgo, Mater mirabilis,
Maria, plena gratia,
Ora pro nobis, Domina.

Gloria Tibi, Domine, etc.

At Prime.

Christ, Son of Mary, hear us now,
Peer of the Most High Father, Thou.
Hear us who by her merits pray,
That bore Thee: take our sins away.

Hail Mary, ever-reverend Maid!
Hail mystic Mother, lauds be said
O full of grace, to Thee for aye.
And Thou for us, Blest Lady, pray.

Glory to the Father be, *etc.*

Ad Tertiam.

Quem credimus ex Virgine
Natum, benigne Domine,
Sit nobis haec confessio,
Peccatorum remissio.

Quae genuisti Filium
A Summo Patre genitum
Per haec tua nos merita
A lapsu mortis libera

Gloria Tibi, Domine, etc.

At Tierce
(Before Confession).

O gentle Master, who by birth
Mysterious camest once to earth,
This our confession now receive
And with us Thy forgiveness leave.

Thou that in time didst generate
The Father's Offspring uncreate,
Oh! by Thy merits may we be
Released from mortal pravity.

Glory to the Father be, etc.

ST. ANSELM OF CANTERBURY

Ad Sextam.

Nate, Summe Rex, utero
Mariae de virgineo,
Emunda nos a vitiis,
Et orna sanctis meritis,

Dei Mater, O Domina,
Sublimis tanta gratia,
Tua, fac, exaltatio
Sit nostra relevatio.

Gloria Tibi, Domine, etc.

At Sext.

O King of Kings, who didst assume
Our nature in a Virgin's womb,
That nature cleanse from every stain,
And in Thy likeness mould again.

Mother of God, our Lady Blest,
Of such supernal grace possessed,
Disdain not in Thy Majesty
To lift us upward unto Thee.

Glory to the Father be, etc.

Ad Nonam.

Fili Mariae Virginis,
Da nobis ejus meritis
A peccatis resurgere,
Et ad vitam pertingere.

Cujus est factus Filius
Deus, pro peccatoribus,
Hoc qui fide pronuntiant
Fac ut salutem sentiant.

Gloria Tibi, Domine, etc.

At None.

O Son of Mary, Christ, we pray,
By her sweet merits grant we may
From sin and death deliverance gain,
And sempiternal life attain.

Thou from whom God for sinners' sake
His human substance deigned to take,
To us, Thy faithful servants, grant
The grace to feel what now we chant.

Glory to the Father be, etc.

Ad Vesperas.

Sol casto nascens utero,
Vesperascente saeculo,
Illustra nos perpetue
Nec declines in vespere.

Æterni Solis Genitrix,
Tuis hoc sanctis meritis
Age, quo perpes maneat
Nobis, nec unquam decidat.

Gloria Tibi, Domine, *etc.*

At Vespers.

O Sun that broughtest dawn of light,
The age fast verging unto night,
Shine on us unto endless days,
Nor shades of night obscure Thy rays.

O Mother of the Beam Divine,
By Thy blest merits Him incline
With us forever to abide
In day that knows not eventide.

Glory to the Father be, etc.

AD COMPLETORIUM.

De casta nobis Oriens
Matre Dies indesinens,
Jugi nos fove lumine,
Culpaeque noctem semove.

Mater Diei Perpetis,
Obsiste nostris tenebris,
Ne lucem nobis dissipent
Et nos delictis implicent.

Gloria Tibi, Domine, *etc.*

AT COMPLINE.

O Day that since Thy virgin-dawn
In splendour shinest unwithdrawn,
Dispel, we pray, the shades of sin,
And shine for aye our souls within.

Mother of the Perennial Day,
Against our darkness be our stay,
Lest missing the eternal rays
We wander lost in error's maze.

Glory to the Father be, etc.

Fairest and most fragrant, daintiest and most delicate, perhaps, of all the flowers that blow in the garden of the Mother of God, is the modest yet queenly *Mariale*, a poem of five hundred and thirty-nine stanzas, long attributed to St. Bernard of Clairvaux, but which may now, with somewhat more of probability, be assigned to the saint of Le Bec. Our survey of St. Anselm's minor works would therefore be incomplete without a glance at this poem.

Readers of the *Paradisus Animae Christianae* are familiar with the hardly translatable hymn to our

Blessed Lady therein ascribed to St. Casimir[1] of Poland, for no better apparent reason than that it was used by him in his daily devotions, and was found in his tomb in 1604. St. Casimir's hymn is, in truth, an abridgment of the *Mariale* in six decades, evidently intended for use with the rosary. Those, alas!—in all likelihood but too many—to whom St. Casimir and the *Paradisus* are alike unknown, may gather some idea of the *Mariale* from the few stanzas which here follow:—

Omni die
Dic Mariae
Mea, laudes, anima:
Ejus festa,
Ejus gesta,
Cole splendidissima.
Contemplare,
Et mirare,
Ejus celsitudinem:
Dic felicem
Genitricem
Dic Beatam Virginem.
Ipsam cole
Ut de mole
Criminum te liberet:
Hanc appella,
Ne procella
Vitiorum superet.
Haec persona
Nobis dona
Contulit coelestia:
Haec Regina
Nos divina
Collustravit gratia.

[1] *Cf.* the Bollandists' *Acta Sanctorum Martii* (ed. 1865), tom. i. 355, where the hymn is given *in extenso.*

ST. ANSELM OF CANTERBURY

Lingua mea,
Dic trophaea
Virginis puerperae:
Quae inflictum
Maledictum
Miro transfert germine.

* * * * *

Evae crimen
Nobis limen
Paradisi clauserat:
Haec dum credit
Et obedit
Coeli claustra reserat.
Propter Evam
Homo saevam
Accepit sententiam:
Per Mariam
Habet viam
Quae ducit ad patriam.
Haec amanda
Et laudanda
Cunctis specialiter:
Venerari
Praedicari
Eam decet jugiter.
Ipsa donet
Ut, quod monet
Natus ejus, faciam:
Ut finita
Carnis vita
Laetus Hunc aspiciam.
O cunctarum
Fæminarum
Decus atque gloria:
Quam electam
Et evectam
Scimus super omnia.

Clemens audi
Tuae laudi
Quos instantes conspicis:
Munda reos,
Et fac eos
Donis dignos coelicis.
Virga Jesse,
Spes oppressae
Mentis et refugium:
Decus mundi,
Lux profundi,
Domini Sacrarium.
Ave Maria.

Every day
To Mary pay,
Soul, thy tribute, praises high:
All her glory,
All her story
Celebrate and magnify.
Contemplate
Her lofty state,
Thyself with lowly awe possessed:
Mother hail her,
Neither fail her
To salute as Virgin Blest.
Oh! adore her,
And implore her
Thee from sin to liberate:
Her to aid thee,
When invade thee
Passion's whirlwinds, supplicate.
By this maiden
Bounty-laden
God to earth did once incline:
Queen of Heaven
She hath given
To her children grace divine.

ST. ANSELM OF CANTERBURY

Now thy burden,
Tongue, the guerdon
Of her maiden-motherhood:
Sin's curse shifted
And uplifted
All the human brotherhood!

* * * * *

Eve's offending,
Far descending,
Barred the gate of Paradise:
Mary's credence
And obedience
Ope the portals of the skies.
'T was by reason
Of Eve's treason
Sentence stern on man was passed
By her holy
Hearkening lowly
Mary leads him home at last.
Her to love
It doth behove
And to praise exceedingly:
Her 't is meet,
With reverence sweet,
To extol unceasingly.
Her Son's will
To fulfil
May she not deny the grace:
That the goal
Reached, my soul
May enjoy Him face to face.
Woman fairest,
Virgin rarest,
Robed for aye in peerless sheen:
Whom translated,
And instated,
Earth and heaven acknowledge Queen.

Mother tender,
As we render
Thee our homage, hear our prayer:
Purge our stains,
Heavenly gains
Make us meet with Thee to share
Hope in sorrow
From Thee borrow
Whoso languish, Jesse's Rod;
Ray celestial,
Our terrestrial
Darkness gilding, Shrine of God.
Hail Mary.

The poem, from which are taken the exquisite stanzas thus rudely paraphrased, has a curious history. It was discovered towards the close of the seventeenth century by the Augustinian Jacques Hommey, in a MS. of the middle of the twelfth century[1] preserved in the Royal Library at Paris, and inscribed with the name Bernard. As Saint Casimir died in 1484, the date of the MS. disposed of his claim to the authorship of the hymn which then bore his name, and Hommey, in according the entire poem a place in his *Supplementum Patrum* (Paris, 1684, 8vo.), attributed it to St. Bernard of Clairvaux, but without supporting his opinion by any solid arguments. The news of Hommey's discovery did not penetrate to Poland, where patriotism combined with devotion to enshrine the Hymn of St. Casimir in the hearts of the faithful, until 1866, when Count Alexander Przezdziecki edited the hymn[2] from a MS. in the Vatican Library,[3] with an appendix containing the text

[1] Now MS. Lat. A. 2445 in the Bibliothèque Nationale.
[2] Oraison de Saint Casimir à la très Sainte Vierge, Cracow, 1866, 8vo.
[3] Queen of Sweden's MSS., No. 29, sm. fol.

of the entire poem from the Paris MS. The text, however, was extremely corrupt, and it was at London, and in 1884,[1] that the first critical recension, with the data for determining the authorship of the *Mariale*, was given to the world by the learned and indefatigable research of Père Ragey, who discovered in the Bibliothèque Nationale and British Museum no fewer than eight early transcripts of the poem or some considerable fragment of it. In three of the MSS. in the British Museum the *Mariale* is found intact. Of these, two[2] are of the fourteenth century, and repeat, without confirming, the French tradition that the author's name was Bernard. ("Auctorem sciri si sit revera necesse, Gallia Bernardum Doctorem credidit esse.") In the third,[3] an early thirteenth century codex, this tradition finds no place, while the poem is introduced by the closing paragraph of one of St. Anselm's prayers to the Blessed Virgin (*Oratio* lii [li] in Gerberon's edition), and followed by his prayers to St. John the Evangelist, St. John the Baptist, St. Peter, and St. Paul. This significant collocation affords a strong presumption that the transcriber believed the poem to be Anselm's work; and as he was probably living within a century of Anselm's death, his belief would be entitled to some, though no very great weight. But this is not all. A fragment of the *Mariale*, containing not a few of the stanzas which re-appear in the so-called Hymn of St. Casimir, is found, without any indication of their authorship, in a Psalter[4] compiled by Benedictines of the Province

[1] Sancti Anselmi Cantuariensis Archiepiscopi Mariale studio et cura P. Ragey Societatis Mariæ, olim Theologiæ Professoris. Londini (Burns and Oates) 1884. Editio secunda: Tornaci Nerviorum (Desclée) 1885.

[2] Royal MSS. 7 A. vi., and 8 B i.

[3] Harl. MS. 2882.

[4] Addit. MS. 21927.

of York, at the latest in the twelfth, and very possibly in the latter half of the eleventh century. The later date leaves the question of authorship open as between St. Anselm and St. Bernard. The earlier date would dispose of St. Bernard's claim. Now whoever was the author of this fragment was also the author of the rest of the poem, which is not only written throughout in the same daintily cadenced metre, but has an unmistakable unity of tone. This tone, moreover, is singularly in accord with the passages relating to the Blessed Virgin in Anselm's prose Meditations. What more likely, then, than that a poem which was already in high repute in both France and England during the twelfth century, and contributed more than any other single cause to the popularisation of the devotion to the Blessed Virgin in both countries, should have emanated from the cloister of Le Bec, and had for author no other than its illustrious abbot?

CHAPTER VII.

ANSELM, ARCHBISHOP OF CANTERBURY

WHILE Anselm was Abbot of Le Bec, certain events happened of no small moment to Christendom. The scene at Canossa had raised the spiritual power to a plane transcending, perhaps, the wildest dreams of monastic idealism ; but in its sequel—the desolating civil war in Germany, the king's passage of the Alps, at the head of his victorious chivalry, his unopposed occupation of Ravenna, his investment of Rome (1081), saved from capture for two years only by the strength of her walls, the unwonted loyalty of her citizens, and the pestilence which compelled the intermission of the blockade, the surprise in the third year of Trastevere, all but the Castle of S. Angelo, whence the inflexible Pontiff watched unmoved the triumphant progress of his enemies, the occupation of the Coelian, the consecration of the Anti-pope Guibert, Archbishop of Ravenna (*Clement III.*) in St. John Lateran, the coronation of the king as Emperor of Germany in St. Peter's, the submission of the faithless city, the tardy, but terrible vengeance wreaked upon her by the Norman, Robert Guiscard ; in all this was evidence enough and to spare that the Church was engaged in a struggle, which, whatever might be its ultimate issue, was certain to be prolonged, severe, and exhausting. From the smoking ruins of Rome, Gregory withdrew under his Norman escort to the stronghold of Salerno, and there sank slowly to his eternal rest, murmuring with his latest breath, "I have loved justice, and hated iniquity, and therefore I die in exile." (25 May, 1085.)

For nearly a year, during which the anti-pope gained a partial recognition at Rome, the Holy See was vacant; then Desiderius, Abbot of Monte Casino, reluctantly yielded to the urgency of the Cardinals and suffered himself to be elected. (24 May, 1086.) As if in prophetic irony, he was proclaimed by the style of Victor III.; and at once retreated to Monte Casino, leaving Rome to the mercy of the anti-pope. In the spring of the following year, he was brought back by the Normans; St. Peter's was surprised, and the victorious Pope was consecrated (9 May)—to retire again to his beloved abbey almost as soon as the ceremony was over. Lured thence by the Countess Matilda of Tuscany, he was reinstated in the Vatican after a sanguinary struggle, only to abandon the city once more to the anti-pope, and terminate his ignominious pontificate by a painful death. (16 Sept., 1087.) The same year, the same month, saw the removal from the political arena of the most commanding figure of that iron age. In the first week of September, 1087, William the Norman, the Conqueror of England, lay dying in the little Priory of St. Gervais, near Rouen. He had sent for Anselm to attend him, doubtless to hear his last confession, and administer to him the last sacraments; and Anselm had obeyed, but falling ill, had been removed to the neighbouring Priory of Sotteville, on the other side of the Seine. He thus missed one of the most striking, most memorable scenes in history.

Despite the intense suffering caused by the injuries he had received at Mantes, William retained his composure, the command of his faculties, his sense of public duty, to the last. As the hour of his dissolution drew nigh, he called to his bedside the Bishop of Lisieux, and the Abbot of Jumièges, his two younger sons, William and Henry,[1] and a few of his most trusted councillors; and in the presence of them all and his physicians, made his confession; which was, indeed, not so much a confession as an impartial review of his entire life, in which, while expressing profound contrition for his many misdeeds, he did not fail to urge in extenuation such pleas as were fairly pleadable; the extremely early age at which he became his own master and the master of others, the multifarious and extraordinary temptations inseparable from his position, and as some set-off against the sins of sixty-four years which he despaired of enumerating, his reverential regard, his zeal for Mother Church; he had not sold benefices, simony he had always abhorred, he had preferred persons of merit, as Lanfranc, Anselm, Gerbert of Fontanelle, Durand of Troarn; he had founded abbeys and other religious houses in all parts of his duchy; with more to the like effect. So he craved the prayers of the Church on his behalf, and made her a rich donation from his treasury. He then gave William a letter of nomination to the English throne, kissed and dismissed him; assigned Henry a pecuniary portion; and directed the release of his prisoners of state, in-

[1] The eldest, Robert Courthose, Duke-designate of Normandy, was still a rebel, and in exile.

cluding, after some hesitation, his brother Odo, Bishop of Bayeux. His commerce with the world thus ended, he fell into a deep sleep, which lasted through the night, until it was broken by the sound of the Cathedral bell ringing to prime. "What is that?" he murmured; and was told it was the bell of the Church of St. Mary. Then gathering his whole strength together, he stretched forth his hands, raised his eyes heavenwards, and said audibly, and with deep devoutness, "To my Lady, the Holy Mother Mary, I commend myself, and may she, by her holy prayers, reconcile me to her dearest Son, our Lord Jesus Christ." And so the mighty, heavy-laden, not ignoble spirit, passed to its doom. (9 Sept., 1087.)

None had suspected that the end was so near, and the last sacraments had not been administered. Nobles, clergy, physicians alike succumbed to panic fear, and fled from the corpse, leaving the menials to plunder the room of all that was valuable and portable.

So, unhonoured, the body of the great king lay in the little priory by the Seine, until a certain knight named Herlwin, who here, and here only, emerges into history, placed it on board a ship, which from motives of charity and piety he had hired for the purpose, and carried it down the river, and thence by sea to Caen; where amid a great concourse of nobles and clergy, among them Anselm, it was buried with much pomp and circumstance in the church of the Abbey of St. Stephen.

Not many days later (28 Sept.), Lanfranc consecrated, in Westminster Abbey, the new King of England, William the Red, a prince with whom Anselm, and also a certain monk of Cluny, Otto by name, a native of Châtillon sur Marne, then Bishop of Ostia, soon to be better known as Pope Urban,[1] were destined to come into relations more close than cordial.

On 28 May, 1089, Lanfranc passed quietly away at Canterbury, in the eighty-fourth year of his age, and was buried in the nave of the cathedral. His death set the young king free to indulge his propensities without let or hindrance. And his propensities were fraught with grave peril to both Church and State in England. He was of extravagant habits. To an immoderate passion for the chase he added a taste for coarse, not to say bestial, debaucheries, which he gratified without shame. He had also the ambition to play the part of a great prince, not only in Britain, but, if possible, on the continent. In a supple, adroit, audacious courtier-clerk, by name Ranulf, to whom the treasurer, Robert le Despenser, gave the significant cognomen, Flambard (Firebrand), he had at hand the adviser best fitted to pander to his vices, flatter his hopes, and furnish him with the means of satisfying his desires. Flambard was of low origin, being the base-born son of a priest of no family at Bayeux, but of handsome person, keen and ready wit, insinuating manners, and a cool and calculating unscrupulousness, which permitted nothing to stand between him and his ambition. Thus from a page's place he had risen, by the avenue which the Church then afforded to all men of talent and ambition, to be William's chosen companion, his favourite, and now at last in effect his prime minister, and his evil genius.

[1] Urban II. was consecrated on 12 March, 1088, at Terracina, Rome being in the hands of the anti-pope.

The king required money, and Flambard must find it for him, or forfeit his reputation, his place. Nor was he long at a loss for ways and means. If the existing assessments, based on the Domesday survey, would not yield the needful revenue, there were two very simple expedients by which so monstrous a state of things could easily be set right. The survey itself might be rectified, *i.e.* the taxable area might be fictitiously increased by falsifying the unit of measurement; and the assessment, too, might be rectified, *i.e.* it might be doubled, or even trebled. Moreover, the church lands were a treasure in themselves, and feudal customs could readily be so manipulated as to place and keep the revenues of the more opulent abbeys and sees in the king's absolute control for an indefinite period.

So reasoned Flambard, and having laid his plan wisely, he executed it thoroughly. All England soon groaned under his exactions, and as often as abbey or see fell vacant, vacant it remained; and under colour of the royal prerogative of *advocatio*, its rents passed into the exchequer. Moreover, after Lanfranc's death, appeal to the royal court on any question in which the exchequer was concerned, became an idle formality; for then Ranulf himself was installed as chief justice, while he continued to hold the offices of king's receiver and procurator, or as we should now say, chancellor of the exchequer and attorney-general. Thus, throughout the reign of William Rufus, clergy and laity alike were absolutely at his mercy, and well did he vindicate for himself Robert le Despenser's nickname of Firebrand.

So the oppressed people yearned for a deliverer, and,

instinctively, their thoughts turned towards Lanfranc's pupil, Lanfranc's friend, whom they had learned to know and reverence during his visits to their country. Let but Anselm, they thought, be installed in Lanfranc's place, and the hand of the spoiler would be stayed. The Red King, however, was too well satisfied with the results of Flambard's policy to be eager to fill the vacant see; and Anselm, on his part, was not the man to intrigue, or lay himself open to the faintest suspicion of intriguing, for his own advancement. He remained, therefore, at Le Bec, occupied in writing a treatise against the heresy recently broached by Roscellin, notwithstanding that the acquisition by the abbey of the church of Clare in Suffolk in 1090, and of the church of St. Werburg at Chester, the gift of his old friend, Hugh the Wolf, Count of Avranches, now Earl of Chester, more than justified a visit to England.

In the summer of 1092, however, the Earl of Chester fell ill, and, believing his malady to be mortal, could not rest satisfied to receive the last sacraments from any hand but Anselm's. Yet it was not until Anselm had received three messages from the earl, each more urgent than the last, that he at length made up his mind to obey. He then lost no time, for there was evidently none to spare. Landing at Dover in the first week of September, he hurried through Canterbury, without even waiting to celebrate the feast of the Nativity of the Blessed Virgin, and, after a brief audience of the king, who listened with patience to the expostulations which he did not fail to offer in regard to his treatment of the Church, pushed on to Chester, to find the earl convalescent.

Though the first intention of his visit was thus happily frustrated, Anselm found it much less easy to quit the island than to enter it. The canonry—for such it was—of St. Werburg had to be converted into a regular monastery, in affiliation to the Abbey of Le Bec; the various priories and cells belonging to the abbey to be visited, and counsel to be given to prelates and nobles on all the thorny questions which the disturbed condition of England furnished in abundance. Hence it happened that Anselm kept the Christmas of 1092 with the Red King at Gloucester, waiting a convenient opportunity to crave the royal permit for his return to Normandy. The presence of a man so admirably fitted to fill the chair of St. Augustine, naturally forced upon the attention of the court the still widowed condition of the Church of Canterbury, and led to the adoption of a plan of concerted action. Hence, during the Christmastide festivities, Rufus, to his no small surprise and annoyance, found himself suddenly solicited by the principal magnates of the realm to authorise a form of public prayer for his own guidance in the choice of Lanfranc's successor. So modest a request he could not, in common decency, refuse; but, in granting it, he added scornfully that all the prayers of the Church would not prevent his doing just as he pleased. The task of composing the necessary form of prayer was devolved by the bishops upon Anselm. That duty discharged, he applied to the king for leave to return to Normandy, and met with a refusal. Upon this, he left Gloucester and took up his quarters at a manor-house in the vicinity, there to await the royal pleasure.

Rufus was probably minded that Anselm should become a suitor to him for the archbishopric. At any rate, one day early in March, 1093, hearing one of his courtiers speak of the Abbot of Le Bec's saintliness, how his affections were so set on God that he cared for nothing temporal, the king answered, with a sneer, "No, not even for the See of Canterbury." "That least of all, as I and many more believe," replied the other. "I tell you," rejoined the king with animation, "that if he only thought he had a chance of getting it, he would dance and clap his hands for joy, and throw himself into my arms; but, by the Holy Face of Lucca,[1] for the present neither he nor any but I myself shall be archbishop."

These words had hardly escaped the king's lips when he fell dangerously ill, and a few days later (on Quadragesima Sunday, 6 March) Anselm was summoned to his bedside. Stricken, as he thought, by the just hand of God with a mortal illness, Rufus consented to be shriven by the man whose sanctity he had so lately derided; and, his conscience eased by confession and absolution, made in presence of the assembled prelates and nobles a solemn vow that, if his life should be spared, he would thenceforth order it in clemency and justice.

To lend additional solemnity to the act, he dismissed the bishops to the church to present his vow to the Lord upon the high altar, and at the same time bade a clerk prepare an edict investing it with the form and force of a covenant with the nation.

[1] The "Santo Volto," or "Holy Face," belonging to the ancient crucifix preserved in the Cathedral of Lucca, was held in profound veneration during the Middle Ages, which was doubtless the reason why Rufus was especially addicted to swearing by it.

Anselm, who had withdrawn from the king's bedside, tarried in the room until the edict—which, after proclaiming a general amnesty, discharge of prisoners, and remission of Crown debts, pledged the royal faith to "good and holy laws," and a strict and inviolate administration of justice—was engrossed, read, and ratified. There was then a little buzz of conversation among the councillors who stood nearest to the king, and who urged him to give earnest of his gracious intent by filling at once the vacant See of Canterbury. Rufus assented,[1] and, unprompted, named Anselm primate. Then followed one of the strangest scenes recorded in history.

Dumb, pale, riveted to the floor, stood the archbishop-elect, while the bishops thronged around him, and sought to lead him to the bedside of the king to receive investiture. He remained immovable, deaf to entreaty, expostulation, reproach, pleading his age, his infirmities, his ignorance of secular affairs, his duty to his abbey, his archbishop, his feudal lord in Normandy, to Pope Urban, whom he had already recognised, and from his allegiance to whom he could not swerve for a single hour. All in vain! By main force they partly drew, partly pushed him, towards the king, who added his entreaties to theirs. Still, however, he adhered to his *gran rifiuto*, and

[1] It is plain from the authorities that Anselm had already been virtually elected to the see by the unanimous voice of the clergy and people of England. (*Cf.* Ordericus Vitalis, *Hist. Eccles.* lib. viii. cap. viii.; Milo Crispin. Migne, *Patrolog.* c. 715; Joann. Sarisb. Migne, *Patrolog.* cxcix. 1022; Anon. *de Vita Gundulfi*, Migne, *Patrolog.* clix. 826; and the letters of Osbern and Gundulf in Anselm's *Epp.* Pars. iii. 2, 3.) Yet Freeman, *Norman Conquest*, v. 137, assumes that Anselm received the see "by the gift of the king only."

when excuses failed him, burst into so violent a flood of tears that the blood gushed from his nose. At a word from the king the bishops threw themselves at his feet, but he too prostrated himself, and opposed to their supplications the same stubborn resistance as before. At length, losing patience, they raised and extended his right arm towards the king, who attempted to touch his palm with the crosier; but his fist closed convulsively, nor could they do more than force open a single forefinger, and that only for an instant, though in the struggle they tore the flesh, so that he cried for pain. In the end they were fain to be content with bringing the crosier into contact with his hand, and carrying their captive into the church to the strains of *Vivat Episcopus* and *Te Deum laudamus*, to which he responded with "Nihil est quod facitis," "It is nought ye do."

The religious ceremony appropriate to the occasion was then hurriedly performed, and Anselm returned to the king to enter a formal protest against the entire proceeding as null and void. To the bishops he pleaded once more his inability to sustain the weight of the burden thus thrust upon him. "You are coupling," he said, "beneath the same yoke, an untamed bull and an aged and feeble ewe."

That, in the part he played at this crisis, Anselm was entirely sincere, there is no reason to doubt. Sensitive by nature, and recluse by habit, he was naturally desirous of ending his days in peace in his beloved Le Bec. Nor was his plea of inability to desert his post in any measure overstrained. The news of the election caused the utmost consternation, not only at Le Bec, but throughout Normandy, and it was only with great difficulty, and after prolonged correspondence, that the Archbishop of Rouen, Anselm's old friend, William Bonne Ame, was induced to give it his indispensable sanction. There was further difficulty with Duke Robert, and, most of all, with the monks of Le Bec; nor would the latter consent to renounce their claims upon their abbot, until Anselm himself, convinced at last that duty bade him accept the primacy, had signified his desire to be released from his obligations toward them. His conduct was, of course, misconstrued in Normandy; but as the obstacles to his advancement were one by one removed, the archbishop-elect wept himself half blind for grief.

While, however, there is no reason to seek for any other than the natural explanation of his conduct, it is evident that it may also have been, to some extent, shaped by considerations of policy. To have accepted investiture of the spiritualities from the king would have been an uncanonical act. To reject the crosier when offered by him, and yield only to the force put upon him by the bishops, was undoubtedly, as the event proved, the best available method of safeguarding the prerogatives of the Church. Moreover, Rufus sick unto death was one man; Rufus risen from his sick bed was likely to be quite another. Nor was it, as he well knew, merely, or mainly, with the king that Anselm had to deal, but with the much more astute, more resolute, more formidable Ranulf Flambard, who looked to enrich himself no less than his master by the plunder of the Church, and was not likely to be diverted from his purpose by any regard for law—human or divine.

With such a monitor at his side there was little likelihood that, in the event of his recovery, Rufus would long adhere to pledges wrung from him by fear of instant death. Common prudence, therefore, would dictate that the archbishop-elect should defer his acceptance of the see until it was certain whether the king was to die or recover, and how, in the latter event, he was disposed to behave.

The king's illness was not of long duration, and, on his recovery, his good resolutions vanished like smoke. "By the Holy Face of Lucca," he swore to the Bishop of Rochester, "God shall have no good thing from me after all the evil He has done me." He lost no time in revoking the edict which testified to the contrition of which he was now ashamed; and though he made Anselm a formal grant in writing of the temporalities of the See of Canterbury, the document was too vaguely worded to be of much more value than the parchment on which it was engrossed.[1] Even Lanfranc, great though his ascendancy over the Conqueror had been, had not been able to restore the See of Canterbury to all its ancient opulence; and to pluck from the grasp of Rufus lands of which he had already enjoyed the revenues for nearly four years, bade fair to be a task of no ordinary difficulty and danger. Moreover, Pope Urban II. had not, as yet, been recognised in England, and, without such recognition, it was unlawful even for an Archbishop of Canterbury to hold correspondence with him. In all this there was matter enough to daunt a bolder, or teach caution to a less wary, man than Anselm.

Accordingly, Anselm, who awaited at Rochester, as

[1] RYMER, ed. Clarke, i. 5.

the guest of his friend, Bishop Gundulf, the arrival of the letters from Normandy which were to release him from his duties at Le Bec, seized the occasion of the king's passage through the city on his return from an interview with Robert, Count of Flanders, at Dover, to advise him that his acceptance of the see must be conditional upon the restitution to it of all the lands which had belonged to it in Lanfranc's time, and an equitable adjustment of the claims of the see to the other possessions of which it had been despoiled before Lanfranc's time. He added that he hoped the king would accept him as his spiritual director, and in regard to Urban he frankly informed him that he had already acknowledged him as Pope. Rufus made answer that he would restore the lands which had been held by the see under Lanfranc: as to the other points, he would say nothing. He afterwards—doubtless at the suggestion of Ranulf Flambard—sent for Anselm to Windsor, and sought to withdraw from the scope of his promise certain estates which he had granted to vassals on hereditary tenures; but Anselm held him to his original bargain, hoping that thus, even at the eleventh hour, he might be honourably relieved from the dreaded burden of the archbishopric, and suffered to end his days in the seclusion of the cloister.

It was not to be, however. Yielding to the indignant remonstrances of his court, Rufus summoned him to Winchester, and made him such ample promises that he had no choice but to accept the see. Investiture he, of course, did not receive from the king; that Rufus, doubtless, though erroneously, supposed he had already given when he applied the crosier to his hand during the memorable scene of the preceding 6 March; but, following Lanfranc's example, Anselm did not scruple to do the king homage for the use of the archiepiscopal temporalities—an act which the Church had not, as yet, pronounced uncanonical. The homage done, the king gave him seisin of the temporalities. He took formal possession of the see on the fourteenth Sunday after Pentecost (11 September), the gospel for which day, then, as now, opened with the words from the sixth chapter of St. Matthew, "In illo tempore: Dixit Jesus discipulis suis 'Nemo potest duobus dominis servire'"—words amply significant to the least superstitious mind in the circumstances in which Anselm stood. His enthronisation at Canterbury took place on 25 September, the august ceremony being marred by the noisy intrusion into the cathedral of Ranulf Flambard, who chose that occasion to serve the archbishop with a citation to appear before the royal court, and that, too, as Eadmer informs us, in a matter of which, in fact, the royal court had no cognisance.

The consecration followed on 4 December, the rite being performed by the Archbishop of York, assisted by the entire episcopate of England, with the exception of the Bishops of Worcester and Exeter, who were sick.[1] Nothing occurred to disturb the harmony of the proceedings, except that, during the reading of the formal record of the election, the Archbishop of York took exception to the words, "totius Britanniae Metropolitana," by which the church of Canterbury was therein designated, as derogatory to the dignity of his own metropolitan church of York. The objection was held well founded, and the word "Metropolitana" was

[1] The See of Lincoln was at this time vacant.

accordingly struck out, and replaced by the term "Primas."[1] This technical flaw amended, Anselm was consecrated in the usual form, except that, in taking his vow of obedience to the Roman Pontiff, he did so in general terms, thus leaving open the momentous question who the true Pope might really be.

[1] In point of fact, the Archbishop of Canterbury, as inheritor of the authority delegated to St. Augustine by Gregory the Great, was Primate not merely of Britain, but also of Ireland and the adjacent Isles. As such, Anselm consecrated the Bishops-elect of Dublin and Waterford soon after his assumption of the pallium.

CHAPTER VIII.

THE BEGINNING OF THE STRUGGLE

IF any doubts lingered in Anselm's mind as to the royal disposition towards him, they were soon and rudely dispelled. The consecration over, he hurried to Gloucester, where Rufus, revolving warlike schemes, kept the festival of peace. Normandy was to be wrested from Duke Robert, and money for the expedition was in great demand, and, alas! in short, very short supply.

Anselm, accordingly, thinking to propitiate the king, offered him a modest aid of £500. Considering how long the king had enjoyed, and how recently surrendered the revenues of the See of Canterbury, the gift was perhaps as much as he could fairly expect, and he at first accepted it; then, suddenly changing his mind, he returned it, doubtless expecting that it would be increased. Anselm, however, merely renewed his offer, explaining, with much frankness, that though the first, it would not be the last of his gifts, and that small and frequent aids made in good will would be more profitable to the king, and more consonant with his dignity, than occasional inordinate contributions extorted by force as from a slave; adding with emphasis, "I and all that is mine shall be at your service, so only it be a friendly and a free service;

but on terms of servitude you shall have neither me nor mine."

"Keep your gifts to yourself," replied the king in a passion. "All that I need I have. Begone!"

So the interview terminated, and Anselm, after some fruitless overtures towards reconciliation, at last took his leave of the court, and congratulating himself that he had escaped a possible imputation of simony, returned to Canterbury by way of Harrow on the Hill, where he consecrated to the service of God the noble parish church which Lanfranc had built, but had not lived to dedicate. (January, 1094.)

Meanwhile, Rufus mustered his forces and marched to Hastings, there to wait for a favourable breeze to carry him across the Channel. Notwithstanding his irritation, he was not too proud to send for Anselm to bless his enterprise. As in duty bound, Anselm obeyed, and towards the end of January was at Hastings.

There, on 9 February, he consecrated Robert Bloet to the See of Lincoln. The wind continued adverse for some weeks; so that the beginning of Lent (23 February) found the royal army still on shore. Anselm profited by the occasion to read certain of the young courtiers, whose long elaborately-dressed hair, flowing robes and mincing gait betrayed, even at the penitential season, their nameless shame, an Ash Wednesday homily on the duty of reforming their lives, and to urge upon the king the advisability of convening a council to devise measures to stem, if possible, the flood of moral corruption which, emanating from the court, bade fair to contaminate the whole of English society; and also to fill the various vacant abbacies, and otherwise set the house of the Church in order.

Rufus listened with manifest impatience. He would not allow that Anselm had any responsibility either for the morals of the nobles, or the state of the abbeys. The last were absolutely his own, to do with them, or leave undone, what he pleased. Anselm reminded him that he held them in trust for God and His service; whereupon the king peremptorily commanded him to be silent. His language was displeasing; nor had Lanfranc ever dared to use the like to his father. So Anselm took his leave.

On sounding his suffragans on the probable cause of the king's obduracy, he was given plainly to understand that the affair of the £500 still rankled in the royal mind. Rufus would give nothing for nothing, and if the primate wished to have his "peace" he must even be prepared to pay for it. A *douceur* of £1000 would work wonders with him.

Anselm replied that he was not prepared to purchase the king's good will at the expense of the Church, or, indeed, at all; that the voluntary aid which he had offered had been rejected, that most part of it had now been applied in charity, that he had nothing more to offer.

When these words of just and grave rebuke reached the king, they elicited a characteristic outburst. "Tell him," he said to the bishops, "that much as I hated him yesterday, to-day I hate him more, that to-morrow and each succeeding day I shall hate him with an intenser and more bitter hatred; that I shall never more account him father or archbishop, that I utterly execrate and reject his benedictions and prayers. Let him betake himself whithersoever he will, and wait no longer here to bless my passage."

On receipt of this message, Anselm at once returned to Canterbury. Not long afterwards, the wind shifting, Rufus effected a landing in Normandy, which, in the excellent, succinct words of Eadmer, "at the cost of an immense sum of money, he entirely failed to subjugate." Trouble in the Welsh marches recalled him in high dudgeon to England at the end of the year. While making preparations for the invasion of the Principality, he fixed his quarters at Gillingham, near Shaftesbury, in Dorset, and thither, in January, 1095, came Anselm, to crave the king's permission to make the usual journey to Rome, to receive his pallium from the hands of the Pope. The rule which prescribed that, upon his consecration, an Archbishop of Canterbury must with all due speed resort to Rome to receive this stole of white wool, woven from the fleeces of the lambs of S. Agnese fuori le Mura, and ornamented with purple crosses, the symbol at once of the plenitude of his authority and its dependence upon the Holy See, dated from a period long anterior to the Norman Conquest. Anselm was therefore only proposing to do what Lanfranc and other of his predecessors had done, and what was strictly in accordance with canon law. Moreover, his year of grace had already expired, and it was only by special favour of the Pope that he could hope to receive the pallium at all. If it were to be refused, the see would at once become vacant. The delay had been caused by the king's refusal to recognise Pope Urban, a refusal in which he still persisted. "The Pope?" he said, as soon as Anselm had broached the matter—"from which

Pope would you receive the pallium?"[1] And when Anselm named Urban, he answered that he had not yet acknowledged Urban as Pope, nor so far deviated from his own and his father's settled usage (*consuetudo*) as to suffer anyone to name a Pope within the realm of England without his leave, and that whoso should endeavour to invade this, his prerogative, should be dealt with exactly as if he had sought to rob him of his crown. Anselm reminded him of what had passed at Rochester; how, before accepting the see, he had informed him that he was already pledged to Urban, and that under no circumstances could he violate his pledge. Rufus angrily replied that Anselm could not retain his allegiance to the Holy See, if it came in conflict with that which he owed to his sovereign. Thereupon Anselm craved that the question might be referred to a council composed of bishops, abbots, and magnates of the realm, adding that if they should decide that the two allegiances were incompatible, he should desire leave of absence from the kingdom until such time as Rufus should recognise Urban, rather than deviate for an hour from the duty which he owed to the Holy See.

The king assented, issued the necessary writs, and on Sunday, 25 February,[2] 1095, all that was noblest

[1] At this date the castle of S. Angelo, with the Vatican and Lateran, was still held by the Antipope Guibert of Ravenna, who, it will be remembered, shortly before the death of Gregory VII., had got himself consecrated, and assumed the style of Clement III., and given the Imperial crown to Henry IV.

[2] "Tertia septimana Quadragesimae," the third week in Lent, according to Eadmer, *De Vita Anselmi*, lib. ii.; the Sunday within which, as Easter Day, 1095, fell on 25 March, must have been 25 February. Yet in the *Hist. Nov.* lib. i., Eadmer gives another date, viz. "quinto Idus Martii," *i.e.* 11 March, the fifth Sunday in Lent, or Passion Sunday.

in the Church and State of England met in solemn conclave in the church of the royal castle of Rockingham, to determine whether the country should still remain part of Catholic Christendom, or plunge into schism at the behest of a despotic prince. President there appears to have been none. Rufus himself was not present, nor was he officially represented. He remained, however, in the castle, so that from time to time one or other of the prelates could report progress to him, or carry messages from him. He had probably little fear of the result, for he knew the stuff of which the Norman bishops were made. From the outset Anselm found the minds of the spirituality, with the sole exception of his old friend Gundulf, Bishop of Rochester, hopelessly prejudiced against him. He opened the proceedings himself.

"My Brothers," he began, "children of God's Church, all ye who are met together here in the name of the Lord, hearken, I pray, and lend, as far as in you lies, the aid of your good counsel to the matter for the discussion of which you are here assembled. And as many of you as have not as yet fully understood the nature of the matter in hand, listen, if it so please, and you shall shortly hear it. Between our lord the king and me certain words have passed, which seem to engender discord between us. For when of late, according to the custom of my predecessors, I craved of him permission to resort to Urban, Bishop of the Apostolic See, to receive from him my pallium, he replied that he had not as yet acknowledged Urban as Pope, and, therefore, would not suffer me to have recourse to him for that purpose. Furthermore,

The discrepancy was first pointed out by Mr. Martin Rule, in his scholarly edition of Eadmer in the Rolls Series (1884), *Preface*, p. 62, and is doubtless to be explained, as he suggests, by supposing that Eadmer, in writing the passage in the *Hist. Nov.*, inadvertently postdated Easter-day by exactly a fortnight. The same error will reappear later on.

he said, 'If, in my realm, you acknowledge as Pope, or treat as so acknowledged, either this same Urban or anyone else, without my recognition and authorisation, you act in breach of the allegiance which you owe to me, and wrong me no less than if you were to attempt to take away my crown. Know, then, that you shall have neither part nor lot in my realm unless you give me the most unequivocal assurances that you will renounce, as I require you, all submission to the authority of this Urban.' Which hearing, I was lost in wonder. I was, as you know, an abbot in another realm, leading, by the grace of God, a life without reproach in the sight of all men. It was neither hope nor desire of episcopal office that brought me hither, but certain just obligations which I could by no means ignore. When the king fell ill, all ye, who were then about him, urged him before his death to provide, by the institution of an archbishop, for the well-being of his mother, and yours, the Church of Canterbury; and, in brief, the king approved your counsel, and concurred with you in electing me to the office. I made several excuses, desiring to escape the responsibility of the primacy, but ye would not have it so. Among other pleas I urged this, that I had already acknowledged Urban as the successor of the Apostle, and that, so long as I lived, I would not depart for a single hour from my allegiance to him. To all this you had none of you a word to object. Your reply was to seize me by force and thrust upon me the common burden, upon me, I say, whose burden of physical weakness was already so great that I was scarce able to hold myself upright. Therein, perchance, you thought to answer my secret desire. How I desired your gift, how sweet I have found it, what pleasure I have had of it, I think it needless at present, since in truth it is nothing to the purpose, to explain. But lest any, through ignorance of my inner mind, should find occasion to misconstrue my conduct in this matter, I profess, in all sincerity, that, saving the submission due to the will of God, I had preferred at that time, had the option been given me, to be cast on to a stack of blazing faggots to be burned, than to be raised to the archiepiscopal dignity. But, seeing your importunity, I yielded to you, and accepted the burden which you laid upon me, confiding in the hope of the aid which you promised me. Now, then, is the time, now the occasion for you to lighten my burden by your counsel. For to the end that I might have your counsel, when these words of which I have spoken passed between our lord the king and me, I craved an adjournment to the present day, that, meeting together, you might, by your collective wisdom, examine this matter—whether I am able, without trenching upon my allegiance to the king, to maintain intact my submission to the Holy See. I craved, I say, an adjournment, and I had it; and lo! by the grace of God, you are here present. All, therefore, but you especially, my Brethren and colleagues in the episcopate, I pray and exhort that you examine diligently of these matters, and, with a well-considered judgment, such as is worthy of you, and on which I may securely rely, advise me how to reconcile the submission which I owe to the Pope with my fealty to our lord the king. Ill can I brook the idea of setting at nought the authority of the Vicar of Blessed Peter, or of breaking the faith which, under God, I have sworn to the king, or that it is impossible for me to adhere to the one without violating the other."[1]

When Anselm had done, the bishops drily answered that on so weighty a matter they could not presume to advise a man of his recognised wisdom and sanctity. They hinted, however, that he had better make unconditional surrender to the king, to whom, with his permission, they would report the substance of his speech. Anselm bowed assent, and the session was adjourned. On the morrow the council reassembled, and the bishops reiterated their sentence of the preceding day. Then Anselm, in an impassioned speech,

[1] This speech is from Eadmer (*Hist. Nov.*, lib. i.) who was present on the occasion, and whose scrupulous veracity is universally admitted. It is, probably, as nearly as possible in the actual words used by Anselm.

appealed from them and their king to the supreme Pastor and King of kings, who had given His apostles and their successors the power of binding and loosing on earth and in heaven, and bidden them render unto Caesar the things that are Caesar's, and unto God the things that are God's. "Know then," he concluded, "all of you, that in those matters that are God's I will yield obedience to the Vicar of Blessed Peter, and in those things that rightly appertain to the state of my earthly king I will render him, to the best of my capacity, faithful counsel and service."

Upon this the bishops, with one accord, rose in tumult, and refused to carry such high words to the king. Anselm accordingly saw Rufus himself, and represented to him the substance of his speech. The audience over, he returned to the church, and went quietly to sleep in his chair.

Meanwhile the bishops were closeted with the king in long and anxious consultation. Few of them probably bore Anselm any positive ill-will, or were specially zealous for the royal prerogative, or cared or knew much about the merits of the controversy. They were, for the most part, ignorant, apathetic, subservient courtiers who looked on the Church as a means to their worldly advancement. John of Touraine, Bishop of Bath, was more skilled in the use of simples than in the Scriptures, or canon law; Losinga, Bishop of Thetford, was an accomplished sycophant; Robert Bloet, the recently-consecrated Bishop of Lincoln, an indifferent-honest man of the world. These, and such as these, were likely to take an extremely practical view of the situation. Anselm's high ideas might be all very well for him, but Urban's position was not yet secure, and it was a far cry from Rockingham to Rome. The Red King did not brook contradiction, and had a heavy hand. They were his men, and his will must be law to them. At the same time there was no good reason why they should whet the edge of his anger against the primate; for who could say what, after all, the ultimate issue of the contest might be? So, like Dante's

> Caitiff brood
> Of angels, who nor faithful to God were
> Nor yet rebellious, but for themselves stood
> (*Inferno*, c. iii. 37–39),

they temporised, counselled submission to the primate in the church, and propounded no definite policy to the king in the privy-chamber.

Among them, however, was one of another stamp—William of St. Calais, Bishop of Durham, an able and ambitious prelate—who hoped, by compassing Anselm's downfall, to succeed to his place. This man had been Rufus' prompter and evil genius throughout the affair, and he now came forward as the king's accredited agent.

Towards evening Anselm was awakened to hear the royal ultimatum—unconditional and instant surrender—to which the bishops added their doubtless well-meant and, by this time, very explicit counsel, that, in his own interest, he "should renounce his obedience to that Urban, who, in a quarrel with the king, could be of no manner of help to him, and, if he made his peace with the king, could do him no manner of hurt; should shake off the yoke of subjection, and freely, as became an Archbishop of Canterbury, submit his will in all matters to that of his lord the king," with more in a similar strain; to which he answered, as before, that "renounce his obedience to the Pope he would certainly not," adding that "the day was far spent, let the session be adjourned to the morrow, and he would then give his final decision, as God might direct him." The king, however, at the suggestion, and through the mouth, of William of St. Calais, insisted on having Anselm's final answer there and then. If he delayed further, added the bishop in a tone of menace, he would assuredly be called to account for his presumption. Brought thus to bay, Anselm replied with quiet dignity that "if any sought to call him to account for maintaining inviolate his allegiance to the Pope, he would answer the charge as and where he ought."

These words completely changed the aspect of affairs; for they brought to mind the forgotten fact that an Archbishop of Canterbury was amenable to no jurisdiction but the Pope's. Moreover, signs were not wanting that the feeling of the laity was on Anselm's side. A murmur of indignation ran through their ranks, and at length a knight, more courageous than the rest, approached Anselm, knelt before him, and said, "My Lord and Father, your children, by my mouth, pray you not to let your heart be troubled by what you have heard, but to bethink you of blessed Job who, on his dunghill, conquered the Devil, and avenged Adam, whom the Devil had conquered in Paradise."

This timely manifestation of sympathy was of invaluable service to Anselm. The voice of the people, he said to himself, is it not the voice of God? And so with fresh courage and beaming face he resumed the debate, and with triumphant logic maintained it until the approach of night rendered a further adjournment necessary.

On the morrow, the difficulties of the situation became only more apparent. The primate could not be legally tried; the temper of the laity plainly forbade the forcible removal from the archbishopric and expulsion from the kingdom which William of St. Calais now proceeded to urge as the only practical expedient. In vain Rufus, through the bishops, formally withdrew from Anselm his confidence, countenance, and the protection of the law; in vain the latter, at the king's bidding, renounced their fealty to him, and declared their intention of holding no more intercourse with him. Anselm replied with suave dignity:

"I understand you. In withdrawing from me all the obedience, fealty, and friendship which you owe me as your primate and spiritual father, because I am determined to maintain inviolate the obedience and fealty which I owe to Blessed Peter, the Prince of the Apostles, you do ill. But God forbid that I should return you evil for evil. On the contrary, I shall manifest towards you the charity of a father and brother; I shall hold you ever as my brothers and the children of our holy mother, the Church of Canterbury; I shall do my utmost, so far as you will permit me, to reclaim you from the error into which fear has led you, and by the power which the Lord has given me to recall you to the path of rectitude. As for the king, who deprives me of the protection of the law within his realm, and refuses any longer to recognise me as his archbishop and spiritual father, I promise to give his laws all possible support, and to render to himself every service that is in my power; and if he will permit, I will have the care of a loving father for the interest of his soul, while remaining faithful to the service of God and maintaining undiminished the power, reputation, and office of

Archbishop of Canterbury, whatever may be the persecutions to which, in my worldly estate, I may be subjected."

This answer served, of course, only to exasperate the king still further. "What he says is altogether an offence to me," he broke out, "and I renounce whosoever may take his side." He then appealed to the barons to follow the good example set them by the bishops, by making a formal renunciation of "faith and friendship" to the disgraced primate.

This move was miscalculated. The haughty barons of England were by no means inclined to proceed to extremities against the man whom they had raised to the rank of first grandee of the realm, at the bidding of a monarch of whose power they had too good reason to be jealous. Moreover, they had their answer ready. "We were never his vassals," they said. "We cannot abjure a fealty which we have never sworn. He is our archbishop; his it is to govern the Church in this country, and by consequence we, as Christians, cannot withdraw ourselves from his authority, more particularly as there is not a single blot upon his life which could incline us to act otherwise."

These words, so grave, so well-weighed, so unanswerable, were received by the king with mute, ill-disguised chagrin, and by the laity at large with transports of joy. The prelates hung their heads in shame, as "Judas the traitor," or "Pilate," or "Herod," or some other laconic and expressive comment on their and their master's part in the day's transactions, came hissing through the stern lips of baron or knight.

The cup of their humiliation was filled up when the suspicious king called them to his presence one by one, and required them to answer, categorically, the embarrassing question, whether, in renouncing fealty to Anselm, they had done so unconditionally, or only with respect to what he might enjoin upon them in the name of the Pope. Taken thus off their guard, the majority took refuge in prevarications and evasive circumlocutions; only a few had the consistency to make their repudiation of the primate's authority complete and unequivocal. These received every mark of the royal favour, while the former were banished to a distant part of the castle, there to await their sentence. They acquired their liberty by the one unfailing method of conciliating the Red King—the payment of a round sum of money.

It was now evident to Anselm that the time had come for bringing matters to a decisive issue. The king had done his utmost to array both clergy and laity against him, and had in effect declared him an outlaw: it ill became the dignity of an Archbishop of Canterbury to acquiesce in a position so humiliating. He would leave the kingdom, or be reinstated in the position of trust and honour which belonged to his office. He accordingly applied to the king for a safe conduct to the coast. This demand, as Anselm doubtless foresaw, had the effect of still further aggravating the embarrassment of the king. To suffer the newly-elected primate to leave the realm, to receive, doubtless, the pallium from the hands of the Pope, to enlist the sympathy of the faithful throughout the length and breadth of Christendom in his behalf, while the Church of Canterbury remained widowed and desolate, could not fail to reinforce to a dangerous degree the already strong and growing discontent of the English laity.

It was a prospect which Rufus dared not face. He accordingly laid Anselm's proposition before the barons, and by them it was decisively rejected. With the good sense of practical statesmen, they advised that the whole question should remain in abeyance until the octave of Pentecost, the king, in the meantime, guaranteeing the archbishop the protection of the law, and maintaining with him as friendly relations as possible. During this period of time they doubtless anticipated that some compromise would be effected. Their proposal was communicated to Anselm in the church, on the fourth day of the council, and was at once accepted by him. The king also assented, and the council thereupon broke up, Anselm returning at once to Canterbury. So ended the first phase in the struggle for the rights of the Church, in which Anselm was destined to be involved during the best part of the remainder of his life.

CHAPTER IX.

THE COMPROMISE

ANSELM had not long to wait before he discovered that the "truce" arranged at Rockingham was, on the part of the king, but a veiled war. One by one the monks on whom he most relied for help in the administration of the practical affairs of the diocese were banished the realm—among them his especial friend Baldwin—while the chicanery of the law was strained to the uttermost to harass the vassals of the Church of Canterbury. Meanwhile, two of the royal chaplains, Gerard (afterwards Bishop of Hereford and Archbishop of York) and William of Warelwast[1] (the future Bishop of Exeter) were busy at Rome, commissioned to ascertain who the true Pope really was, and to induce him, if possible, as the price of his recognition by the king, to transmit to him the pallium of the Archbishop of Canterbury, leaving undecided the all-important question who the Archbishop of Canterbury might be.

Evidently, if the Pope should fall into this trap, William, the precious pallium once in his hands, would be able to confer it on whomsoever he might contrive to get elected in Anselm's place, and so, by the Pope's own act, render himself independent of the Holy See

[1] Now Veraval, near Yvetot, in Normandy.

during the lifetime of the new primate. The plot, however, was far too transparent to succeed, and Urban, whom the envoys found themselves compelled to recognise, while he made no difficulty about sending the pallium to England, took care to commit the sacred stole, enclosed in a silver casket, to the custody of his own legate, Walter, Cardinal-bishop of Albano, who landed in England with the chaplains shortly before Pentecost. On his arrival he went straight to court, avoiding all intercourse with Anselm, who remained as ignorant as the rest of the world of the object of his mission. In his interviews with the king the legate observed strict silence in regard to the question of the pallium, but in all other matters assumed an air of entire subservience to the royal will. He thus induced Rufus to accord Urban a formal recognition, and then listened with polite surprise while the king made proffer of certain liberal annual subsidies to the Holy See as the price of Anselm's deprivation. With profound chagrin Rufus heard his overtures summarily rejected by the cardinal. He perceived that he had been caught in his own snare, that by his clumsy stratagems he had but succeeded in covering himself with shame. He had appealed to Rome, he had recognised Urban as Pope in the hope of obtaining the disposal of the pallium. The pallium was actually in England, but as far from his reach as when it lay on the tomb of St. Peter. He had attempted to corrupt the Holy See, and the Holy See, in the person of its legate, had disdained his bribes. As all this flashed upon his mind his heart failed him. Anselm, it was plain, must have the pallium, but perhaps he might be induced, even at the eleventh hour, to take it from him, and pay him well for it.

Accordingly, when Pentecost arrived, Anselm, who kept the feast at the archiepiscopal manor of Mortlake, received a summons from the king to attend him at Hayes, in the neighbourhood of Windsor Castle, and there, through certain of the bishops, was given to understand that the royal amity and, indeed, the pallium, now actually in the country, were to be had for a due pecuniary consideration. The least he could offer, they urged, would be the cost of the journey to Rome, which he was now spared. Anselm, however, cut them short. "Neither that," he said curtly, "nor aught else will I give him, or do for him on this account. You waste your words. Have done."

Foiled again, Rufus now condescended to summon Anselm to court, and to treat him with an ostentatious appearance of cordiality, which elicited from the legate the ironical comment, "Lo! how good and sweet it is for brothers to dwell together in unity!" Meanwhile certain of the courtier-bishops buzzed about him, insinuating that at least he might now so far conciliate the king as to consent to receive the pallium from his hands. This resource, however, also broke down before the primate's suave inflexibility. He "could not, if he would," he quietly observed, "receive from the king that which did not lie in the king's gift, but in that of the successor of Blessed Peter." This logic admitted of no reply, but Rufus was obstinately determined that the pallium should not be given by the legate. Matters thus seemed at a deadlock until, at length, a marvellous expedient was discovered whereby, without abatement of the papal claims, the royal dignity was salved.

The legate carried the pallium to Canterbury, and there, on the second Sunday after Pentecost, in presence of a vast concourse of clergy and laity assembled in the cathedral, laid it upon the high altar. Then Anselm, robed in full canonicals, but walking barefoot, and attended on either hand by most of his suffragans, two of whom, Robert of Lorraine, Bishop of Hereford, and Osmund, Bishop of Salisbury, had already craved and received his absolution for their defection from him at Rockingham, advanced to the altar, took down the pallium, and after it had been devoutly kissed by the assembled multitude, in token of reverence to St. Peter, vested himself with it, after which he celebrated high mass. The gospel for the day was the same which had furnished his prognostic, on his consecration; viz. the parable of the great supper, from which the bidden guests with one accord made excuse for absenting themselves. This ominous coincidence is duly noted by Eadmer, who thereby affords the means of rectifying the error by which, repeating a previous miscalculation, he fixes the date of this curious scene as 10 June, *i.e.* the fourth Sunday after Pentecost. A glance at the contemporary Canterbury lectionary, preserved in Harl. MS. 562, shews that then as now, the parable in question was appropriated not to the fourth, but to the second Sunday after Pentecost, which in 1095 fell on 27 May.

In this curious compromise, the Church, it is evident, had the best of the bargain; inasmuch as besides recognising the Pope, the king tacitly waived his claim to confer the pallium. To this result grave political anxieties probably contributed, no less than the subtlety of the legate and the constancy of Anselm. Conspicuous by his absence from the court, notwithstanding the peremptory summons of the king, was the stern warden of the Scottish marches, Robert of Mowbray, Earl of Northumberland, nephew and heir of Geoffrey de Mowbray, Bishop of Coutances, and nephew-in-law of Hugh the Wolf, Earl of Chester. This haughty and powerful noble was suspected of being the head of a widespread conspiracy, having in view nothing less than the deposition of the king in favour of his cousin, Stephen of Aumale, son of Odo, Count of Champagne, and Lord of Holderness, by Adelaide, sister of William the Conqueror. His absence was therefore tantamount to a declaration of war, and was so understood by the king. At such a crisis, William had neither time nor patience to spare for the protraction of an ecclesiastical dispute, however important might be its ulterior issues. Mowbray was understood to have active and powerful friends in Normandy, and, by the custom of the realm, the Archbishop of Canterbury was, *virtute officii*, warden of the south coast. As soon, therefore, as the reconciliation with Anselm was effected, he received the king's orders to attend him at Nottingham, to pronounce his benediction upon the army which William had hastily gathered there for a forced march upon Earl Robert's stronghold of Bamborough Castle. He obeyed, and, after blessing the troops, returned at William's command to Canterbury, there to muster the array, and hold himself in readiness to resist any descent which might be made upon the coast.

Meanwhile, Rufus pushed rapidly northward, surrounded by traitors. In a certain wood, on the confines of Northumbria, an ambush had been placed, and next the king rode the very men who were to give the signal for his assassination. At the pinch, however, their resolution failed, or their conscience smote them; and their ringleader, Gilbert of Tunbridge, falling on his face before the king, confessed the plot, and implored his forgiveness. Thus forewarned, William passed the wood in safety, reduced Newcastle-upon-Tyne and Tynemouth, and invested Bamborough. As the reduction of this strong fortress bade fair to be a slow process, William varied the monotony of the siege operations by making, with part of his forces, a raid into Wales; but before Christmas Bamborough had fallen, Earl Robert, taken in a monastery in which he had sought sanctuary, was a prisoner, and the king had returned to Windsor.

Meanwhile the legate, after making certain inopportune proposals to Anselm for a conference on ecclesiastical abuses, a thing impossible in the absence of the king, had left England, carrying with him to the Council of Clermont, which opened its memorable ten days' session on 18 November, not only the formal announcement of Urban's recognition by the King of England and Anselm's investiture with the pallium, but, *mirabile dictu*, some arrears of Peter-pence. So far, thanks to firmness, patience, and the political chapter of accidents, has the spirit of concession to Rome been at length carried in England. But if the Church has on the whole been a substantial gainer by the compromise of Windsor, there is, it must be observed, another and less satisfactory side to the transaction. Hugh of Flavigny speaks of a convention made between the king and the legate "ne legatus Romanus ad Angliam mitteretur nisi quem rex praeciperet";[1] whence it would appear that Cardinal Walter had

[1] MIGNE, *Patrolog.* cliv. 353.

carried his complaisance towards the king to the point of ostensibly investing him with a new prerogative, that of choosing whom the Pope should send him as legate. The convention, of course, was *ultra vires.* No legate could by his own act annul the freedom of the Pope in so vital a matter as the choice of his own agent, and it is hardly conceivable that the cardinal acted in good faith. He probably gave the pledge, foreseeing that it would be repudiated at Rome, because to do so would smooth his relations with the king; perhaps—for there is no reason to suppose that his virtue was of a very austere type—because it was profitable to himself. An act of such signal bad faith on the part of so high a dignitary of the Church could not fail to seriously damage her prestige and justly exasperate the king when its true character came to be discovered. But this was not all, or the worst. Hugh of Flavigny continues: "And to such a degree had the authority of Rome been degraded among the English by the avarice and greed of legates, that in the presence of the same Bishop of Albano [the cardinal-legate] without protest on his part, nay, with his consent, and even by his direction, the Archbishop of Canterbury had sworn fealty to Blessed Peter and the Pope so far as consistent with his fealty to his lord the king (salva fidelitate domini sui regis)."

This oath, of which Eadmer says nothing, must have been taken by Anselm on the reception of the pallium. It is evident that it was susceptible of two interpretations: on the one hand, the king could urge that in case of conflict it postponed Anselm's fealty to the Pope, to his fealty to his sovereign; on the other hand, Anselm could plead that "salva fidelitate domini regis" was no more than a courtly form of words; that it was impossible for an Archbishop of Canterbury to swear conditional fealty to the successor of St. Peter; that, if he attempted so to do, his oath would be invalid in the sight of God, and therefore in no way binding on his conscience; and that, by waiving his claim to confer the pallium, the king had virtually decided the question raised at Rockingham in the Pope's favour.

The compromise, therefore, was no final settlement, but only a temporary makeshift; and it was inevitable that the entire question of the relation of Church and State in England should be reopened at no distant date. In the meantime, the condition of the Church remained what it had been before the advent of the legate. The royal prohibition against holding intercourse with the Pope remained still in force; the royal grasp was still tight on church lands and revenues; the See of Worcester, then vacant, and that of Hereford, which had since fallen vacant, were vacant still; the See of Durham [1] was also in the king's hands, and likely there to remain; little or nothing was done to restore ecclesiastical discipline, and a simoniacal and profligate clergy daily betrayed the cause they should have defended throughout the length and breadth of the land.

The report, therefore, which Cardinal Walter carried from England to the Council of Clermont was such as to afford Pope Urban food for anxious meditation; and though he was occupied with no less weighty a matter

[1] William of St. Calais, the Bishop of Durham, was one of Mowbray's adherents; and on the suppression of the rebellion was arrested and confined in Windsor Castle, where he died on 1 Jan., 1096. The see was afterwards leased by the king to Ranulf Flambard.

than the marshalling of the hosts of united Christendom against the Saracen, he did not allow himself to be so engrossed with it as to neglect the English question.

Conspicuous among the potentates of Europe by the ostentatious indifference which he exhibited towards the sufferings of the Eastern Christians, and the desecration of the Holy Sepulchre, was the King of England. Rufus was evidently what in these days would be called an enlightened monarch. He was for non-intervention, except where English interests were concerned, and English interests were in his mind in no way concerned in the Crusade. If certain dark stories told by the chroniclers can be credited, he was capable at times of repeating the sin of Judas; and it is likely enough that his intellectual hold on the Christian faith had become seriously impaired.

In any case, the Crusade was to him but a fool's errand, to further which he was not prepared to sacrifice a single English man-at-arms. But, however indifferent he might be to the Crusade itself, it incidentally opened to him a prospect to which he was by no means indifferent. His gallant but improvident brother, Duke Robert, had taken the cross, but lacked the means to equip a contingent of troops befitting his rank. He must therefore borrow money upon the security of his duchy; and to whom should he so naturally apply for the needful loan as to his dear brother of England? William had always coveted Normandy; and were he once in possession of the fair province, it would go hard, even supposing Robert to return from the Holy Land safe and sound, if he ever relaxed his grasp of it. Meanwhile, the opportunity which the situation afforded for renewed intervention in English affairs, did not escape the watchful eye of the Pope, and he lost no time in despatching another legate to England, for the purpose, in the first place, of negotiating the loan between William and his brother, and then doing what might be done to repair the mischief wrought by Cardinal Walter, and seriously grapple with the grave questions which he had ignored.

The new legate, who landed in England in the spring of 1096, was Abbot Jarenton, of Dijon, a man of tried sagacity, probity, and firmness, in every way a contrast to the supple Cardinal-bishop of Albano. William saw at a glance that he was not a man to be cajoled, bribed, or intimidated. He therefore assumed an air of cordiality, and lent his best attention to the legate's outspoken remonstrances and reproofs; so that "all the faithful," says Hugh of Flavigny, "were overjoyed at the advent of one in whose presence the Church breathed more freely, and regained with the free exercise of the authority of Rome, her ancient glory and vigour."

Their delight was soon exchanged for consternation, when, shortly before Whitsuntide, the legate suddenly left England in obedience to what he took to be a papal mandate. He is said by Hugh of Flavigny, who appears to be the only authority for this obscure passage of history, to have been imposed upon by some nephew of the Pope or petty official of the Curia, whom Rufus, with the royal sum of ten marks, had bribed to personate a special envoy sent by Urban with authority to postpone until Christmas the further discussion of the various matters at issue between the king and the Holy See, in consideration of the prompt payment of what was due in the way of Peter-pence. However this may be, it is certain that, for some reason or other, Jarenton abruptly left the country without accomplishing the main purpose of his mission. Rufus had, indeed, so far yielded to his representations as to suffer the vacant Sees of Worcester and Hereford, and the vacant Abbey of Battle, to be filled. Otherwise the state of the Church remained what it had been—or even grew worse.

The most probable account of the legate's mysterious return to the continent would seem to be that the negotiations between William and Duke Robert required his presence with the latter. Certain it is, in any case, that he had an interview with Duke Robert, and arranged with him the terms of a treaty by which the duchy was pawned to William for three years or five years—the chroniclers differ about the length of the term—for the sum of ten thousand marks; that thereupon the duke set out for the Holy Land, attended by the legate as far as Pontarlier, and that in the following September William crossed to Normandy, and took possession of his pawn.

The ten thousand marks were raised by contributions levied upon the religious houses, a fifth part of the amount being furnished by the monastery of Christ Church, Canterbury; to secure which Anselm assigned for seven years his archiepiscopal manor of Peckham. Thus the king got his lease of Normandy for nothing, and the Church paid for setting Duke Robert free to fight her battles.

CHAPTER X.

FURTHER TROUBLE—THE APPEAL TO ROME

THE Crusade was not the only topic of European interest discussed at Clermont. The misconduct of Philip I. of France, who had put away his wife Bertha, to marry the fair Bertrade, Countess of Anjou, could not escape the censure of a Synod of the Church, even though it sat in his dominions; and Urban's first act, after opening the proceedings, was to excommunicate him. He then passed to the perennial question of the relations of Church and State. The mantle of Gregory VII. had fallen upon him, and he had proved himself worthy to wear it. He had strengthened the hands of the Church's faithful daughter, the Countess Matilda of Tuscany, by uniting her with the son of Guelf the Great, Duke of Bavaria. He had vindicated, in the most exemplary manner, the sanctity of Christian marriage, by parting the Emperor from his injured but guilty spouse, and laying him once more under the ban of the Church. He had enlisted his son, Conrad, in the Church's cause, had recompensed his devotion and confirmed his loyalty by the gift of the crown of Italy, and made assurance doubly sure by wedding him to a daughter of Roger Guiscard, Count of Sicily. He had reduced the antipope to impotence. The time was now come to resume the struggle for the emancipation of the Church. So, before giving rein to that impassioned eloquence, which, kindling at once the military spirit and the religious fervour of the Frank, hurled the flower of Western chivalry against the armies of the alien, Urban not only renewed the decree of the Council of Rome against lay investiture, but took the further and extremely bold step of forbidding the clergy any longer to do liege fealty to the laity. It is evident, from the wording of his decree, "*Ne episcopus vel sacerdos regi vel alicui laico in manibus ligium fidelitatem faciat,*" that the liege fealty which he prohibited was no mere oath of fealty, such as at a later date came to be recognised by jurists as the proper homage of a "man of religion," but "manual homage"—homage, that is to say, in the strictest, most onerous sense of the term, "liege fealty by intromission of hands;" by which, whoever paid it became thenceforth the "liegeman" of his lord, bound to aid him on all occasions, in all quarrels, just or unjust, to the utmost of his ability, on pain of forfeiture of his goods, his lands, and even his life. It is evident that homage of this sort must at this time have been commonly, if not generally, exacted from churchmen by their feudal superiors, otherwise it would not have been worth the Pope's while to prohibit it; evident, also, that it was radically incompatible with the character, the duties of a "man of religion," whose undivided liege fealty was due to Christ and His Vicar. If the Church was ever to regain the independence needful for the fulfilment of her spiritual mission, liege homage by the clergy must clearly go the way of lay investiture; and, in so decreeing, Urban did not act an hour too soon.

It is probable, though not certain, that it was liege homage which had been exacted from Anselm by Rufus upon his consecration; and though Anselm was not present at Clermont, he was represented there by his friend Boso.[1] We may therefore assume that the decree was made, if not at Anselm's suggestion, at any rate with special reference to his case; with the view, that is to say, of strengthening his hands in the event, which could not be far distant, of an open rupture with the king, or the possible early demise of the latter. If so, events amply justified the action of the Pope.

Early in 1097, William was recalled to England by an insurrection, which the united forces of the Earls of Chester and Shrewsbury had failed to quell. Before marching westward, he demanded from Anselm a contingent of troops for the war; which Anselm, as in feudal duty bound, provided from the tenantry of the archiepiscopal estates. Apparently these warriors gave but a sorry account of themselves in the brief campaign from which the king returned triumphant towards Whitsuntide; for Anselm then received from him a curt missive, informing him that he would be held to account in the royal court for the ill-found condition and unsoldierly bearing of the men. Rufus was evidently determined that the Primate of England should learn the duties belonging to a vassal. He also doubtless hoped that Anselm would compound the suit by a liberal aid. Anselm, on his part, chafed at the anomalous position in which he found himself. Secular business of all kinds he detested; military affairs he held in especial horror; and that he, who had spent the best part of his life in a cloister, should now in his old

[1] *Vit. Bos.* (Patr. Eccl. Angl. *Lanfranc* i.) § 2.

age be called upon to act as commissioner of array, and be held personally responsible for the equipment and behaviour of the men-at-arms, whom, at a hasty summons, he put into the field, was more than even a saint's patience could well be expected to endure. Moreover, he had no faith in the sort of treatment he was like to meet with in the royal court, believing, with too good reason, that there the tyrant's will would be the only law recognised. Meanwhile, for aught that he could do to succour the forlorn state of the English Church, he might as well be at Le Bec. He could not remain indefinitely an idle spectator of wrongs he could not right, a passive recipient of affronts which lowered his order in the eyes of all men. At all costs he would repair to Rome, and seek the counsel of the Pope. He therefore ignored the royal letter, went to court as usual, and at the close of the Whitsuntide festivities, craved, through certain of the barons, the king's leave of absence for his projected journey to Rome, alleging no particular reason, but only "absolute necessity."

William either was, or feigned to be, amazed at the audacity of the proposal. "He shall by no means go," he answered abruptly, "for we do not credit him with having committed any sin so heinous as to oblige him to seek the absolution of the Pope himself; and so far are we from supposing that he stands in need of advice in any matter, that we know that the Pope stands in greater need of his advice than he of the Pope's." After delivering himself of this curiously frank testimony to Anselm's abilities, Rufus, who evidently feared to push him to extremities, directed that the suit against him should be suspended; nor were the proceedings ever resumed.

It was not long before Anselm renewed his request; which was again refused. Nothing daunted, he made at Winchester, in October, a third application; upon which the king fairly lost patience. "Such excessive importunity about a matter which he had made up his mind not to concede, was vexatious. He would hear no more of it; and Anselm must make such satisfaction as should be adjudged for the annoyance he had already caused."

Therefore Anselm raised his tone, no longer praying the leave of absence as a favour, but claiming it as a right, which he was prepared to vindicate by argument. Rufus would hear no argument, and gave him to understand that if he left the country the entire see would be confiscated, and he would never be reinstated as archbishop.

This ultimatum caused no little excitement at court, where Anselm still had his sympathisers. In the hope that even at the eleventh hour the king might be induced to relent, they prevailed upon him to defer his answer to the royal message until the following morning.

The king, however, remained inexorable, and Anselm persisted in his determination to quit the realm, if possible with his leave; if not, without it. Then followed a scene closely resembling that at Rockingham.

Anselm called a council of such of his suffragans as chanced to be at court, Vauquelin, Bishop of Winchester; Robert, Bishop of Lincoln; Osmund, Bishop of Salisbury; John, Bishop of Bath; and making them sit down on his right and on his left addressed them thus:—"Brethren, I have called you to me, because your office it is, postponing all other matters, to discuss, order, and maintain the things which belong to God. For you are bishops, prelates in the Church of God, sons of God. If then you are prepared in my cause to devote to the maintenance of the rights of God and His justice the same faithful and exact consideration which in the case of the king you devote to the maintenance of the laws and customary rights of a mortal man, and will so promise; I will unfold to you, as to the faithful servants and sons of God, the scope of my present design, and will hear and follow such counsel as your faithful zeal to Godward may suggest." Whereto the bishops replied:—"We will speak, if it please you, together, and will then give you our joint answer." They then rose, exchanged a few words apart, and sent the Bishops of Winchester and Lincoln to the king to seek his instructions. On their return Anselm received the joint answer of the four Fathers in God, as follows: —"Lord and Father, we know that you are a religious man and holy, and that your conversation is in heaven. We, however, attached to earth by our kinsfolk whom we support, and the multiplicity of secular affairs which we love, confess that we cannot rise to the height of your life, and disdain the world with you. But if you are willing to descend to our level, and walk in the same way with us, we will make your interest ours, and in your affairs, whatever they may be, when occasion shall arise, will give you our aid as if they were our own. But if you have made up your mind to go on as you have begun, having your regard fixed on God alone, you will be in the future as in the past entirely isolated from us. We shall not deviate from the fealty which we owe to the king." "You have well said," rejoined Anselm, "Go, then, to your lord; I will remain faithful to God." Thereupon the bishops withdrew, and left Anselm alone with a few faithful adherents occupied in silent prayer for Divine guidance in this emergency. Their orisons were soon interrupted by the return of the bishops, accompanied by some of the barons, who brought a message from the king. The message briefly recapitulated the course of events since the Council of Rockingham, Anselm's reconciliation with the king, the oath he had taken on the assumption of the pallium, which bound him thenceforth in all respects to observe, and faithfully maintain against all men, the laws and customs of the realm; characterised his "threat" of going to Rome without the royal licence as a manifest breach of good faith; and required him, without more ado, to forswear appeals to Rome in all cases whatsoever, or forthwith to leave the realm. In the event of his taking the prescribed oath he was to be tried by the royal court for having repeatedly harassed the king, by advancing a claim in which he was not prepared to persevere.

This message delivered, Anselm craved, and obtained, an audience of the king; and, seating himself, as was usual, on his right hand, repeated it to him word for word, and asked him if it were really his. Satisfied on this head he proceeded: "You say that I have promised to observe your customary rights, and faithfully to maintain them against all men; that, I profess, I would acknowledge to be true, if, in so saying, you recognised the distinction which, at the time when the promise was made, I distinctly remember to have been admitted in respect of them. I mean that I know that my promise was to the effect that, in accordance with the will of God (*secundum Deum*), I would observe and maintain, by all just means, to the full extent of my power, the customary rights which you have in your realm, in accordance with the just law of God (*per rectitudinem et secundum Deum*)." Here he was interrupted by the king and his nobles, who asseverated, not without oath, that the promise had contained no mention of either God or justice. "How then," cried Anselm, promptly demurring to their objection, "if the oath had, as you say, no mention in it of God or justice, whose is its sanction? Far be it from any Christian to observe or maintain laws or customary rights which are known to be contrary to God and justice."

To this the king and council returned no answer but inarticulate noises, and gestures of dissent, which ceased as Anselm, with unruffled mien and irrefragable logic, proceeded with his argument. No custom of the realm, he urged, could foreclose the right, or annul the duty, of an Archbishop of Canterbury to seek counsel of the Vicar of Christ, in matters pertaining to the well-being of Church and State. Nor could he justly be charged with breach of faith in persisting in his intention so to do, since the whole force and validity of an oath depended on its supernatural sanction, and therefore could not be pleaded in justification of that which was contrary to the law of God, as the alleged custom unquestionably was. The demand that he should renounce the right of appeal to Rome was tantamount to a demand that he should renounce Christ. When he did so, and not till then, he would submit to whatever sentence the royal court might impose upon him for the wrong he had done in applying for the leave of absence.

Unable to deny the force of this argument, Rufus, as Anselm was leaving the presence-chamber, sent messengers after him with the required leave. "You shall go," ran the curt formula, "but understand that our lord forbids you to take with you anything that is his."

"I have horses, clothes, and personal chattels," replied the Primate; "perhaps it will be said that these belong to the king. If he forbids me to take them, let him know that I will rather go naked and afoot than desist from my purpose."

This shamed the king. "Oh," he said, "I did not mean that he should go naked or afoot. But he must be at the port of departure on the eleventh day from now, and there he will meet my messenger, who will tell him what he and his suite are at liberty to take with them."

Nor did he refuse Anselm's parting blessing, when, in the fulness of his great heart, the saint returned to thank him for the concession thus tardily and hardly wrung from him. This, which proved to be Anselm's last interview with the king, took place on 15 October, 1097.

Returning with all speed to Canterbury, he took the staff and scrip of a pilgrim, bade an affectionate farewell to the monks and good people of the city, and, accompanied by Baldwin and Eadmer, rode post-haste to Dover. There he was detained for a fortnight by an adverse wind; and, when at last he was about to embark, the messenger of whom Rufus had spoken, who proved to be William of Warelwast, arrested his baggage on the beach, and subjected it to rigorous scrutiny, as if he had been suspected of carrying away what did not belong to him. This last indignity endured, he received permission to depart, and set sail for Wissant, a port to the south of Boulogne, then much frequented, which he gained after an unusually speedy and tranquil passage.

From Wissant, Anselm and his two companions journeyed to the celebrated Abbey of Saint Bertin, near Saint Omer, where they were hospitably entertained, and rested some days. But the news of Anselm's arrival being carried to Saint Omer, a deputation of canons from that church waited on him, and prayed him, without delay, to go thither to dedicate their new altar to St. Lawrence the Martyr. He complied, and, after performing the ceremony, and dining with the canons, courteously declined their eager proffer of further hospitality, by quoting our Lord's injunction against going from house to house, and announced his intention of returning at once to Saint Bertin. Some years, however, had elapsed since the good folks of Saint Omer had seen a confirmation, and Anselm was not suffered to leave the town without administering that sacrament to a multitude of young people of both sexes. It was thus late at night before he reached Saint Bertin. Nevertheless, the next morning saw him again in the saddle, his face set towards Burgundy; and though his progress was somewhat retarded by the immense and enthusiastic crowds which assembled at every principal halting-place to do him honour, he succeeded in reaching Cluny before Christmas. After a brief halt there he pushed on to Lyon, where, fairly worn out with fatigue, he was fain to make a prolonged stay under the hospitable roof of Archbishop Hugh. Meantime he wrote to Urban, advising him of the cause of his journey, and received in reply an urgent summons to Rome. The letter gave him new vigour; and, quitting Lyon on 16 March, the Tuesday before Palm Sunday, 1098, and maintaining the strictest incognito, for the partisans of the anti-pope were known to be in force on both sides of the Alps, he pushed rapidly across the Mont Cenis, and was in Rome soon after Easter.

CHAPTER XI.

A BREATHING-SPACE—SCHIAVI—LEARNED LEISURE

ON his arrival at Rome, Anselm found that by the forethought of the Pope, rooms had already been assigned him in the Lateran Palace, where Urban was then residing. A day was allowed him for repose; and on the morrow the Pope, surrounded by the Roman nobility, received him with marked distinction. Waiving the customary homage, Urban had a chair placed for him that he might be seated in his presence, and when Anselm, passing the chair, knelt at his feet, the Pope at once raised him, gave him the kiss of peace, and amid the acclaims of the Curia, bade him welcome to Rome; concluding with an eloquent tribute to his intellectual and spiritual eminence, his devotion to the Holy See, and his profound humility.

"Yes," so ran the peroration of his speech, "even so it is. And yet this man, trained from his youth up in all the learning of the liberal arts, whom we hold as our master, whom we deem justly to be reverenced as in some sense our peer, the Pope and patriarch of another region, is yet so humble, and in his humility so consistent, that neither the perils of the sea, nor the fatigues of a long journey through foreign countries, have deterred him from presenting himself here to do homage to Blessed Peter in our humble person, and crave, touching his affairs, advice from us, who, with far more reason, might seek advice from him. Bethink you, then, with what love, with what honour, he is to be received and embraced."

Passing then to business, the Pope listened while Anselm laid before him a detailed account of the forlorn condition of the Church in England, and of his own relations with the Red King. The gravity of the situation was thus, for the first time, revealed to him in its full extent and degree. He pledged himself to support Anselm to the uttermost, and at once wrote an admonitory letter to the king, which, with another from Anselm himself, went to England by the same messenger.

From this by no means excessive exertion of apostolic authority Anselm probably expected nothing; it was dictated, however, by the extreme caution which in Urban tempered a resolution hardly less heroic than that of Hildebrand; there was nothing for it but to await in patience the answer of the king. Meanwhile, by the Pope's desire, Anselm remained at the Lateran until the summer heats rendered change of air necessary. Then he was claimed by an old *alumnus* of Le Bec, John, now Abbot of S. Salvatore, a monastery situate between Telese and the confluence of the Calore and Volturno, who carried him off to his villa on the neighbouring plateau of Schiavi,[1] on the skirts of the Samnian Apennines. As he drank in the pure and delicate air of this ideal summer retreat, and scanned its vast ethereal prospect, "Here," said the

[1] Schiavi will be sought in vain on the modern map of Italy, progress, as understood in that country, having changed the name to Liberi. It is situate in the district of Formicola, towards Caserta.

weary saint, with a sigh of relief, "here is my rest—here will I make my habitation"; and with the delight of one who, after much wandering in foreign lands, finds himself at length at home, he resumed once more the old life of devout exercises and profound theological meditation, for which he had never ceased to sigh since he had left Le Bec. Nor did he forget what was due to the simple folk among whom he sojourned, but gained their confidence at once by his ready sympathy and gentle, gracious ways; so that they came to look upon him as a being belonging to a sphere little removed from the celestial, yet by no means disdainful of ordinary mortals and their common earthly needs. One so learned, wise, and holy must surely, they thought, know where to sink a well; and where was such a gift more opportune than at Schiavi, where there was but one well, and that by no means always adequate to the wants of the inhabitants? The brother from S. Salvatore, who acted as major domo at the villa, made their necessity known to Anselm, and had great hopes that God would work a miracle by his agency, if with prayer and benediction he would choose a spot for the men to dig, and himself begin the operations. Unwilling to offend his host, Anselm consented, led the way to one of the rocks which overhung the villa, and, having prayed that God would thence grant an abundant and unfailing supply of sweet water, struck it thrice, and bored a small cavity in its surface. The villagers then proceeded to deepen the cavity, and after a few days thus spent were equally delighted and amazed by the sight of a limpid fountain welling up out of the hard rock; which, though lapse of time has changed much in the neighbourhood, still perpetuates the memory of St. Anselm among their descendants by the abundant supply of sweet water which, in the popular belief, it has never failed to yield.[1]

Pentecost had come and gone when Anselm, still at Schiavi, was recalled to a sense of the outer world by the arrival of messengers from Roger Guiscard, who had succeeded to the Dukedom of Apulia on the death of his father, Robert, in 1085.

He was now, with Count Roger of Sicily and a well-found army, before the walls of Capua, intent to bring the city back to the allegiance, which it had renounced, to its Norman prince, Richard of Aversa. With him also was his wife Adela, daughter of Robert, Count of Flanders, and Queen-dowager of Denmark—a devout woman, whom Anselm had known in earlier days; and it was, we may suppose, rather at her suggestion than of his own motion that the duke had sent to Schiavi to invite Anselm to visit his camp and witness some of the operations. However reluctant the saint might be to exchange the peace of his mountain hermitage for the clash of arms, he was too gracious to decline a proposal dictated by courtesy; and the duke consulted the tastes of his guest by providing him with a tent in the quietest part of the camp. Thither too, in due time, came Urban, to offer his mediation between the belligerents.[2] His overtures were rejected by the infatuated city, which was reduced after no long resistance; but, pending the negotiations, he occupied a pavilion immediately adjoining Anselm's tent, so that the two men lived for a time in the closest intimacy, and were able to discuss at their leisure the news from England; which proved,

[1] RULE, *Life and Times of Anselm*, ii. 192.
[2] MURATORI, *Rer. Ital. Script.* v. 47, 600.

as might have been anticipated, far from reassuring. Hardly had Anselm left the country when the king resumed possession of all the estates belonging to the See of Cantérbury, annulled all that Anselm had done since his consecration, and instituted a persecution of the Church so ruthless and systematic that the tribulations which had followed Lanfranc's death seemed trifling in comparison. His animosity had pursued Anselm to Italy. Duke Roger had received a letter from him defamatory of his guest; and, by secret emissaries well provided with money, he had attempted to create a party hostile to Anselm in the camp. There were also dark rumours afloat that he was on the very verge of open apostasy.

William's machinations failed entirely with Duke Roger, who, on the fall of Capua, made Anselm an earnest proffer of further hospitality, nay, even gave him the choice of his fairest domains, to be his, if he so willed, for life.

This noble offer Anselm declined, and, having taken leave of the duke and duchess, quitted Capua with the Pope for Aversa. The bad news from England preyed on his mind, and for the time completely broke his resolution; so that at Aversa Urban listened with surprise and undisguised indignation to his importunate entreaties to be released from the burden of the archbishopric, administered a sharp reproof, and dismissed him to Schiavi, with a monition to attend a council which would meet in the autumn at Bari, where his cause would be fully discussed.

At Schiavi, Anselm found such leisure for literary work as he had not known since he had left Le Bec. In England, indeed, the storm and stress of his conflict with the king, and the heavy burden of his official duties, had rendered much sustained intellectual effort impossible; and, except the treatise against the heresy of Roscellin, begun at Le Bec, none of his works can be assigned to that period. This work had for him a special and personal interest, for Roscellin, upon the first censure of his thesis, had sought to make both Anselm and Lanfranc sponsors for it. Anselm had lost no time in vindicating both his own and his master's orthodoxy in a letter to his old pupil, Fulk, Bishop of Beauvais, which Fulk was authorised to communicate to the Council of Soissons (1092), before which the heretic was cited to appear.[1] Meanwhile he had quietly proceeded with the formal refutation of the obnoxious thesis, intending to give it the shape of a letter to the Pope, but laid it aside on hearing of Roscellin's recantation. When, however, Roscellin retracted his recantation, Anselm took up again his unfinished work, reçast and completed it, retaining of the original epistolary form no more than a prefatory dedication. The work thus slowly elucubrated, which bears the title *De Fide Trinitatis, seu de Incarnatione Verbi*, was probably complete, and in the hands of the Pope, before Anselm's final rupture with the king. The present, however, is the most convenient place to give account of its contents.

John Roscellin, a native of Compiègne, studied at Soissons and Reims, and taught logic at Tours and Locminé, near Vannes, in Brittany, where he had for pupil the illustrious Abelard. He afterwards held a canonry at Besançon. He was a bold thinker, and has

[1] *Epp.* ii. 35, 41; *De Fid. Trin.* Praefat. Baluz., ed. Mansi, 1761, ii. 174. Prantl, *Gesch. d. Logik*, ii. 77.

been classed among nominalists; nor, though we have not his logical doctrine in his own words, is there reason to doubt that it was substantially identical with that afterwards developed by Abelard, and which, whether strictly nominalistic or not, certainly involved the denial of the reality of universals. Such a doctrine, it is evident, if applied to theology, would be utterly subversive of Catholic orthodoxy; for the Catholic doctrine of the Holy Trinity imports that, while God is simple—numerically one—in respect of His essence, He is, nevertheless, universal in respect of the comprehension therein of a threefold personality. The nominalist must therefore make his option between Sabellianism and tritheism. Which alternative Roscellin ultimately adopted is not clear; but the trend of his thought was apparently tritheistic. "If," he argued, "the three Persons are but one Being (*res*), and not merely three Beings, each separate from the other, like three angels or three souls (but so that they have one and the same will and power), it follows that, in the incarnation of the Son, the Father and the Holy Spirit were also incarnate." In other words, the assumption of human nature by the Son alone is incompatible with the unity of the Godhead. Such was the thesis censured at Soissons, and to the confutation of which Anselm addressed himself in the *De Fide Trinitatis*.

Before asking how far he is successful in this undertaking, something must be premised concerning the philosophical question thus early raised by Roscellin's imperious logic, and which, in one shape or another, has occupied the subtlest minds of every succeeding age. His postulate, it is evident, is that the individual is that which exists in and by itself; in a word, the atomic. Grant this, and his logic is irrefragable, *actum est de Fide Catholica.* But is the assumption justifiable? Is not the individual *per se,* the mere individual—as mere an abstraction as the universal *per se?* Is not the actual a blend, so to speak, in which the universal and the individual exist as mutually determining elements? Consider any given object, as this rose or ring, abstract all that it has in common with other roses or rings, all that they and it have in common with other objects of sense-perception, and how much of its actuality is left behind? Evidently nothing at all; for its individual characteristics are not self-supporting, they exist only in the synthesis which, by your analysis, you have destroyed. Every object, then, so far as given in perception, is at once individual and universal; nor is there any reason to suppose that in. itself, if in itself it really exist, it exists as a mere individual. The unknown cause or combination of causes, whatever it may be, which affects me with the sensuous impression of an object having both individual and universal characteristics, must surely have corresponding characteristics. In itself, then, as well as for us, it would seem that actuality is essentially universal and individual. At the present day, this is easily seen and said; but it was otherwise in the eleventh century, and therefore we must not expect from Anselm any formal refutation of Roscellin's logical doctrine.

It is enough for him that Roscellin is one of "those dialecticians, nay rather dialectical heretics of our time, who reckon universals nothing more than empty words." So crazy a theory he will not deign even to examine, but passes at once to a criticism of his theological position.

It is remarkable, however, that his criticism presupposes throughout the true realism. Roscellin's fallacy, he says, in effect, consists in treating the universal and the individual as essentially repugnant *inter se*, whereas, in fact, they are not so. Each of the Persons of the Godhead is what is common to all, and is also what is peculiar to Himself. They are therefore in very truth three Beings, but not three separate Beings, like three angels, or three souls; and the incarnation took place by the assumption of human nature into the unity of the Godhead, not as immanent in all three Persons, but only as immanent in the Person of the Son. The union, indeed, in one and the same spiritual subject, of three Beings individually distinct, is a matter for which human experience furnishes no perfectly apt analogue; yet we are not wholly left without type and symbol to illustrate this transcendent mystery.

"Let us suppose a fountain, whence issues a stream, which flows until it is gathered into a lake, and let us call it the Nile. Speaking then precisely, we use these three terms—fountain, stream, lake, distinguishing the fountain from the stream, and both from the lake. Yet the fountain is called the Nile, and the stream is called the Nile, and the lake is called the Nile; and the two together, the fountain and the stream, are the Nile; and the fountain and the lake are the Nile; and the stream and the lake are the Nile; and the three together, the fountain, the stream, and the lake, are the Nile. But as there is not one Nile, and another Nile, but only one and the same Nile, whether each of the three severally, or two together, or the three together are called the Nile; so there are three—fountain, stream, and lake, and yet one Nile, one river, one nature, one water; and it is impossible to define exactly what the three are. For the three are neither three Niles, nor three rivers, nor three natures, nor three waters, nor three fountains, nor three lakes. Here, then, one is predicated of three, and three are predicated of one; and yet the three are not predicated equivalently. But if Roscellin objects that no one of the three, neither the fountain, nor the stream, nor the lake, nor any two of them, are the perfect Nile, but only parts of it; let him consider that this whole Nile, from the moment when it begins to be, to the moment when it ceases to be, throughout its entire life, so to speak, does not exist in its entirety, but only in part in any given place or time, and, in fact, is not complete until it ceases to be. For the Nile has some similarity to human speech, which, while it flows from the fountain of the mouth, is incomplete, and by the time it is complete, no longer is. For whoso attentively considers until he understands this matter, will see that the fountain, the stream, and the lake are equally the whole Nile; and yet that the fountain is neither the stream nor the lake; that the lake is neither the fountain nor the stream. For the fountain is not the same as the stream or the lake, although the stream or the lake is the very same as the fountain, *i.e.* the same Nile, the same river, the same water, the same nature. So then three are here predicated of one perfect whole, and one perfect whole is predicated of three; and yet the three are not predicated equivalently. And although it is only in another much more perfect manner that this can hold good of that Nature which is perfectly simple, and free from all conditions of space, and time, and composition of parts; yet if it is seen to hold good to some extent of that which is composed of parts, and subject to conditions of space and time, it renders it not incredible that it may hold good perfectly in that highest and unconditioned Nature. This also is to be considered, that the fountain is not from the stream, nor from the lake; but the stream is from the fountain alone, not from the lake; while the lake is from the fountain and the stream; and so the entire stream is from the entire fountain, and the entire lake both from the entire fountain and the entire stream; just as we affirm of the Father, Son, and Holy Spirit. And just as it is in one way that the river is from the fountain, and in another way that the lake is from the fountain and the stream, so that the lake is not called the stream; so it is in one way peculiar to Himself that the Word is from the Father, and in another way that the Holy Spirit is from the Father and the Word, so that the same Holy Spirit is not Word or Son, but proceeding. I have yet another thing to add, which amid much dissimilarity, nevertheless offers a certain similitude to the Incarnation of the Word; and though the reader may perhaps scorn it, I will nevertheless mention it, because I myself should not scorn it, if it had been said by someone before me. If, then, the stream were to run in a conduit from the fountain to the lake, should we not say that it was the stream alone (though in fact it is as much the Nile as the fountain or the lake) that was enclosed in the conduit? Even so it is the Son alone that was incarnate, though no other God than the Father and the Holy Spirit."

The similitude is ingenious, and subtly wrought out; but like all other attempts to illustrate by physical analogies mysteries which transcend the scope of human reason, it is only likely to be of service to those whose faith hardly needs corroboration; and it is with a certain sense of relief that on turning the page we find ourselves once more in the company of Blessed Augustine and the Holy Apostle Paul, and are reminded that to them no more than to us was it given in this life to see God as He is; but only as through a glass darkly, and by way of figurative adumbration to catch some distant, albeit not delusive, glimpses of His shrouded majesty.

CHAPTER XII.

THE CUR DEUS HOMO?

THE masterly little treatise analysed in the last chapter has its appropriate sequel in a much more elaborate work, which has attained a wide and enduring celebrity, rather, perhaps, by reason of its theme, style, and popular method of treatment, than the intrinsic merits of its thought. Begun in England "in great tribulation of heart," finished in the serene atmosphere and restful solitude of Schiavi, it is unquestionably, from a literary point of view, Anselm's masterpiece, and even at the present day can be read with pleasure by those least versed in the mysteries of Catholic theology.

Cur Deus Homo? such is its title; but its scope is not, as might be inferred, the determination of the final cause of the Incarnation. We should look in vain in its pages for an anticipation of the subtle question afterwards discussed by Duns Scotus, whether the Incarnation was contingent upon the Fall, or did not rather lie in the Divine idea as the complement, so to speak, of the creation, so that it would equally have taken place though man had persevered in his original righteousness; but, assuming that its final cause was the restoration of the fallen race to its pristine dignity,

Anselm seeks in this treatise to vindicate its propriety if such an expression be allowable, as the economy of redemption.

Was the Incarnation derogatory to the majesty of God? What was the nature of the obstacle which the Fall opposed to the Divine forgiveness? Could not that obstacle have been removed in some other way than by the Incarnation? How, as a matter of fact, was it removed by the life, suffering, death, and resurrection of the Incarnate God?

Such are the questions with which Anselm deals, working the subject out dialectically in the shape of a dialogue between himself and his friend Boso, the latter playing the part of *Advocatus Diaboli* against the entire providential scheme.

The first question discussed relates to the necessity of the Incarnation. Was it necessary? If so, how is such necessity compatible with the Divine omnipotence? Could not God have redeemed man in some other way than by Himself assuming his nature, and suffering and dying on his account? If He could have so done, why did He choose so painful and costly a method instead of one exempt from cost and suffering? Are we not compelled either to bind God fast in fate, or to save His freedom at the expense of His wisdom?

Having thus propounded his antinomies, Boso proceeds to notice—only to reject, not without a touch of scorn—the solution propounded by Origen, the theory, that is to say, of a ransom paid to the Devil, whose vested interest in man, acquired through the Fall, God could not in justice disturb without providing an adequate compensation. Boso sees clearly enough that it was not in the power of His Satanic Majesty to acquire any such vested interest; and Anselm smiles assent while he triumphantly dismisses that theory to the limbo of grotesque fictions. He then presses Boso for a more exact definition of his objections. Why should that which the Church confesses in the article of the Incarnation be deemed a thing unreasonable? To which Boso replies that it seems unworthy of the Highest that He should stoop so low, of the Omnipotent that He should take such pains. This Anselm meets by a simple enunciation of what he takes to be the Catholic faith concerning the hypostatic union. The Incarnation, he suggests, involved no humiliation or labour on the part of God, but simply the exaltation of humanity. After, as before, the assumption of humanity into Himself, God remained in His Divine nature impassible; the seat of His suffering and humiliation was His human nature.

This, it is evident, is not wholly satisfactory; and Boso might fairly have urged in reply that, though it was only as man that Christ suffered and was heavy laden, yet, inasmuch as His human nature was anhypostatic, His suffering was, in very truth, the suffering of God; and, indeed, that it was essential to the redemption that it should be so. To deny that God, in very truth, suffered on the cross, would be a form of Nestorianism; and therefore, though the initial act of the Incarnation did not, its sequel certainly did involve humiliation; so that the objection is not met.[1]

[1] Dante, whose theory of the Atonement need not be ignored by theologians, merely because it is enshrined in noble verse, had evidently

Boso, however, does not take this point; but proceeds to argue the case in another way. Assuming the validity of Anselm's distinction, he takes exception to the entire idea of vicarious satisfaction, as involving nothing less than the condemnation of the just in lieu of the unjust, the punishment of the guiltless, in order that the guilty may go free.

This Anselm repudiates as a gross misconception. The Passion was not, he insists, in any sense a punishment, but merely the natural result, in the circumstances in which Christ was placed, of His adherence to His righteousness; and was in no other sense willed by the Father than as He was consenting to it, in order that thereby man might be saved. But on this head Anselm has so much to say that is interesting and suggestive, that he must be allowed to speak for himself.

deeply pondered this problem. His solution, perhaps the best that can be offered, is given in the *Paradiso*, c. vii. 109–120.

> La Divina Bontà, che il mondo imprenta,
> Di proceder per tutte le sue vie
> A rilevarvi suso fu contenta.
> Nè tra l'ultima notte e il primo die
> Sì alto e sì magnifico processo,
> O per l'una o per l'altra fu o fie.
> Chè più largo fu Dio a dar sè stesso,
> A far l'uom sufficiente a rilevarsi,
> Che s'egli avesse sol da sè dimesso.
> E tutti gli altri modi erano scarsi
> Alla giustizia, se il Figlinol di Dio
> Non fosse umiliato ad incarnarsi.

> The Love Divine, who all creation's frame
> Seals with Himself, in His great bountyhead,
> To raise you up by every means did aim.
> Nor aught so noble, so sublime was sped,
> Or ever shall be, from the primal morn,
> Till night shroud all things, as that twofold deed.
> For more of grace He showed who showed the way,
> Himself that way, for man himself to raise,
> Than had He him dismissed, no debt to pay.
> And justice, too, had failed by other ways:
> Nought could suffice, but that the Son of God
> To take our nature should Himself abase.

"*Ans.* You do not deny that the rational creature was created in righteousness, and to the end that he might be blessed in the enjoyment of God?

Bos. No.

Ans. You would think it incongruous if God, having created man in righteousness for a beatific end, should compel him to be miserable though he had done no wrong? Now to die against one's will is to be miserable.

Bos. It is plain that, had man not sinned, God ought not to have exacted death from him.

Ans. Therefore God did not compel Christ to die, in whom was no sin; but He Himself, of His own accord, endured death in obedience to a law, which required not of Him the surrender of His life, but the maintenance of His righteousness; in which He so bravely persevered that thereby He brought death upon Himself. . . . . . . And as for that saying of His, 'I came not to do my own will, but His who sent me' (John vi. 38), it is much the same as that other, 'My doctrine is not mine' (John vii. 16); for that which one has not from oneself, but from God, one must call not so much one's own as God's. But no man has from himself the truth which he teaches, or a righteous will, but from God. Christ, therefore, came to do not His own will but the Father's, because the righteous will which He had was not from His human nature, but from His Divine Nature. And the words 'God spared not His own Son, but delivered Him up for us all' (Rom. viii. 32), mean no more than that He did not liberate Him. For many similar phrases are found in the Holy Scriptures. But where He says, 'Father, if it be possible, let this cup pass from me: nevertheless not as I will, but as Thou wilt' (Matt. xxvi. 39); and 'If this cup may not pass away from me, except I drink it, Thy will be done' (*Ibid.* 42); He signifies by His own will that natural instinct of self-preservation, by which His human flesh shrank from the pain of death. And He speaks of the will of His Father, not because the Father preferred the death of His Son to His life, but because the Father was unwilling that the human race should be restored unless man should do some great act such as was that death. . . . . .

It may also fairly be understood that, by that pious will by which the Son willed to die for the salvation of the world, the Father gave Him (yet not as by compulsion) the command and the cup of suffering, and spared not Him, but delivered Him up for our sake, and willed His death; and that the Son was obedient unto death, and learned obedience by the things which He suffered. For as it was not from Himself as man, but from the Father, that He had the will to live righteously; so it was only from the Father of Lights, from whom is 'every good gift and every perfect gift' (James i. 17), that He could have that will by which He willed to die, that He might accomplish so great a good. As the Father is said to draw those to whom He gives a will; so He may not incongruously be said to impel them. For as the Son says of the Father, 'No man cometh to me, unless the Father draw him' (John vi. 44); so He might have said, *Unless the Father impel him.* Similarly He might have said, 'No man goeth cheerfully to death for my name's sake, unless the Father impel or draw him.' For since every man is drawn or impelled by his will to that which he steadfastly wills, God is not incongruously said to draw or impel him when He gives him such a will; in which drawing or impulsion is understood no coercion of necessity, but only the man's spontaneous and loving adhesion to the good will which he has received. If then, in this manner, it cannot be deemed that the Father in giving His Son the needful will, drew or impelled Him to death, who may not see that it was in the same way that He gave Him the command to suffer death voluntarily, and the cup, to drink it not unwillingly? And if the Son is rightly said not to have spared Himself, but for our sake, by a spontaneous act of will, to have delivered Himself up to death, who would deny that the Father, from whom He had that will, did not spare Him, but for our sake delivered Him up to death, and willed His death? In this way then, also, by steadfastly and of His own accord holding fast the will which He had received from His Father, the Son was made obedient unto death, and learned, by the things which He suffered, obedience; *i.e.* how great a work may be achieved by obedience. For therein is true and pure obedience, when a rational being, not of necessity, but of his own accord, holds fast the will which he has received from God. There are other ways, also, in which it may fairly be understood that the Father willed the death of the Son. For as we say that he wills who makes another to will, so we say that he wills who does not make another to will, but approves his willing; and when we see one willing bravely to endure hardship that he may accomplish a righteous will, although we confess that we will him to bear that suffering, yet we do not will or delight in his suffering, but in his will. We are also accustomed to say that he who, being able to prevent, does not prevent, wills that which he does not prevent. Since, then, the will of the Son was pleasing to the Father, and He did not prevent Him from willing or fulfilling what He willed, He is rightly said to have willed that the Son should so piously, and to such good purpose, endure death, though He did not take delight in His suffering. And as for what He said, that the cup could not pass away unless He drank it, He said that, not because He could not have avoided death had He so willed; but because, as has been said, it was impossible that the world should be otherwise saved, and He Himself steadfastly willed rather to suffer death than that the world should not be saved. And His purpose in saying these words was to teach us that the human race could not otherwise be saved than by His death, not to signify that he could in no wise avoid death. For this, and all similar utterances concerning Him, must be interpreted consistently with the belief that He died not by necessity, but of His own free will. For He was omnipotent, and of Him we read that 'He was offered, because He Himself so willed' (Isaiah liii. 7); and He Himself says, 'I lay down my life, that I may take it again. No man taketh it from me, but I lay it down of myself. I have power to lay down my life, and to take it again.' (John x. 17.) What, then, He Himself did by His own power and will, He can by no means rightly be said to have been compelled to do."

To these arguments Boso replies that the real question, after all, lies much deeper; for "why was God unable to save man otherwise? or, if He was able, why did He choose this method? For it seems incongruous that God should have saved man in this way; nor does it appear how the death availed to the salvation of man. For it is marvellous, if God has such delight in, or need of, the blood of an innocent person, that, except by His death, He is unwilling or unable to pardon the guilty."

This objection is evidently crucial, and Anselm feels that he must, as lawyers say, change the venue. "Let us assume, then," he says, "that the Incarnation, and what we have said of the Incarnate God, had never been; and let it be agreed between us that man was created for a blessedness which is not to be had in this life, and to which none can attain unless his sins be forgiven, and that no man can pass through this life without sin, and other things which must be believed in order to eternal salvation." Boso assents, and Anselm proceeds to deduce from these postulates a rationale of the atonement, which may be summarised as follows:—

Man, as a creature, owes to God absolute obedience, and that debt he cannot, by reason of his original sin, pay. By the commission of actual sin he incurs a debt which cannot be satisfied by penitence, since that is merely its due sequel. Neither can God exercise His prerogative of mercy by merely ignoring sin, since it necessarily defeats the end for which man was created, to wit, union with God. In order, therefore, to the reconciliation of the race with God a man must arise, who shall not only perfectly fulfil the Divine law, but also offer to God satisfaction for the sin of his fellow-creatures, not merely adequate, but so superabundant as may entitle him to claim the race as his own possession for ever, that by his example, and the infusion of his grace and merits, it may be conformed unto his likeness, and so restored to its pristine dignity. But a work so great as this was beyond the power of any mere man to accomplish. The Incarnation was, therefore, so far as human reason can judge, the only possible means of effecting the redemption and regeneration of man. By His sinless life and His voluntary submission to death, from which, by reason of His sinlessness, He was merely as man exempt, Christ did as man discharge the debt due from the creature to the Creator, and also provided a superabundant satisfaction for the sins of the whole world; in virtue whereof, upon His resurrection and ascension, He received from the Father all power over men, and became to them not merely an ensample for their imitation, but a perpetual fountain of grace and of merit.

Such, in brief, is the view of the economy of redemption developed by Anselm in this lively dialogue, the course of which is interrupted from time to time by digressions into matter more curious than relevant. Despite its lucidity and ingenuity, its hard juridical character, the limitations to which it seems to subject at once the love, the freedom, and the omnipotence of God, prevented its gaining acceptance either among the schoolmen or the later doctors of the Church. It did much, however, to stimulate thought on the profound and, perhaps, impenetrable mystery of which it treats, and, in fact, marks a new epoch in theological speculation.

CHAPTER XIII.

THE COUNCIL OF BARI—THE PROCESSION OF THE HOLY SPIRIT

ON the morning of 1 Oct., 1098, Duke Roger of Apulia's new Church of St. Nicholas, at Bari, built, as became a Norman Duke, in all the austere grandeur of vaulted roof and granite column, wore an unwonted festal appearance. The floor of the sanctuary, from the shrine of St. Nicholas to the gradual, was carpeted with rich fabrics woven in the looms of the East. In the nave sat Pope Urban, in chasuble and pallium, near him the aged Archbishop of Benevento, magnificent in a golden broidered cope, the gift of Ægelnoth, Archbishop of Canterbury, whom as a young man he had visited, on an errand of charity, in the days of pious Canute and good Queen Emma: on either hand a hundred and eighty-three prelates, some of them Easterns, in their copes, besides abbots and other high dignitaries not a few; among whom Anselm, attended by Eadmer, glided unheeded to a lowly place.

The acts of this noble council, as Baronius calls it, have perished; but from Eadmer, and William of Malmesbury, we learn that the first matter discussed thereat was the long-standing controversy with the

Eastern Church, concerning the dogma of the Procession of the Holy Ghost; and that it afforded Anselm an unexpected and unique opportunity for the display of his theological learning and dialectical skill.

The preliminary mass over, the Pope ascended the gradual, and taking his stand on the predella with his back to the high altar, opened the discussion with the Greeks.

How he handled the subtle question in dispute we know not, except that in the course of his argument he drew upon Anselm's treatise against Roscellin, quoting, doubtless, the similitude of the fountain, stream, and lake—in which the lake may be said with justice to proceed from both fountain and stream, not as two separate sources but as one undivided source—by way of illustrating the Latin doctrine of the Procession "*ab utroque*"; but that finding himself hard pressed by the objections of the Greeks, he at length interrupted his discourse, and eagerly scanning the assembled Fathers cried out, with a loud voice:

"Father and Master Anselm, Archbishop of the English, where art thou?"

Whereupon Anselm, rising from his seat, responded, "Lord and Father, what are thy commands? Here am I."

Upon which the Pope bade him come up into the sanctuary, and succour Mother Church in her struggle with those who were seeking to rob her of the integrity of her faith.

Amid some confusion and many murmurs of "Who is he?"—for to most of the bishops the Archbishop of the English was as yet quite unknown—Anselm obeyed; and when order was restored, the Pope introduced him to the council as a man of holy and laborious life, who had suffered many persecutions for righteousness' sake, and had at length been unjustly expelled from his see: after which it seemed good to adjourn the session until the morrow, that the Archbishop of the English might have freer scope for the exposition of his views.

The morrow came; and Anselm standing where the Pope had stood on the preceding day, "so handled, discussed, concluded the matter, the Holy Spirit guiding his mind and tongue, that in the assembly there was none but was convinced by his argument."

At its close, when the hum of applause with which it was received had died away, the Pope rose, and, turning towards him, pronounced his solemn benediction: "Blessed be thy heart and thy mind, blessed be thy mouth and the words which it hath uttered."

To the argument thus struck out, as it were, on the spur of the moment, Anselm afterwards gave articulate and permanent form in a systematic treatise, *De Processione Spiritus Sancti*, which, though completed only shortly before his death, displays in perfection his rare aptitude for keen dialectic and luminous exposition; and as the principal monument of mediæval thought on the subtle question with which it deals, still merits the attention of all serious students of Christian theology. Before, however, proceeding to analyse its contents, a word or two must be said on the previous history of the controversy, which, abstruse and barren though it may at first sight appear, is yet not without its own peculiar interest.

That the Holy Spirit is in some very real sense the Spirit of the Son, as well as of the Father, lay in the mind of the Church from the beginning, being, in fact, implicit in what is revealed in the New Testament concerning His mission by the Son. But the Church defines nothing until it is absolutely necessary; and so long as she was preoccupied with the question of paramount importance at issue in the first phase of the Arian controversy, she had no occasion to formulate her Pneumatology with nice exactitude; nor was it until the second General Council (381) confessed the Holy Spirit's personality and procession from the Father, that the question of His relation to the Son acquired substantive importance. Then, as the Church pondered on all that is implicit in the unity of the Godhead, it gradually became apparent to her that, in proceeding from the Father, the Holy Spirit must also proceed, either immediately or derivatively, from the Son. The Eastern Church, in which the tendency towards Arianism was never wholly overcome, adopted the theory of a derivative procession from the Son, the theory, as it came to be formulated, of a procession from the Father through the Son. The Western Church, with her deeper sense of the co-equality of the three Divine Persons, felt that such as is the relation of the Holy Spirit to the Father, such also must be His relation to the Son, and spake accordingly of the procession as from Father and Son; and her instinctive wisdom was amply justified by events.

Towards the close of the fourth century the Spanish Church became deeply infected with Gnosticism, in the form given to that farrago of heresies by the gloomy and fantastic genius of Priscillian, and in the succeeding age the militant Arianism of the Visigothic invaders threatened to sweep the Catholic faith from the peninsula.

The history of the struggle with these heresies is written in the acts of the Councils of Toledo; in which nothing is more remarkable than the prominence given to the Latin doctrine of the Procession of the Holy Spirit. To enter here into the vexed question of the precise date at which the doctrine made its appearance in the Spanish Church would be waste of labour. Its early reception there is sufficiently attested by the sanction obtained for it from Pope Leo the Great by Bishop Turibius of Astorga in 447;[1] upon which it was formulated in a confession of faith.[2] Evidently Leo felt with the Spanish theologians that so long as it remained open to regard the Holy Spirit as holding to the Son a relation essentially diverse from that which He holds to the Father, neither the coequality and consubstantiality of the Persons of the Holy Trinity could be made good against the Arians, nor the reality of the hypostatic "proprieties" be vindicated against the Priscillianists. Evidently also the latter, at any rate, regarded the Latin doctrine as implicit in the Nicene Creed, at least as amplified by the Second General Council; for, in imposing that creed under anathema upon King Reccared and his subjects on their abjuration of Arianism in 589,[3] they did not scruple (notwithstanding the prohibition of every "other faith" by the Council of Chalcedon) to render it explicit by the insertion of the words "et Filio."

[1] See Leo's Letter (*Ep.* xv.) in MIGNE, *Patrolog.* liv. 678.

[2] MANSI, iii. 1002 vi. 494.

[3] MANSI, ix. 990.

Thenceforward the doctrine maintained its position as an integral part of the faith of the Spanish Church; from which, passing the Pyrenees, it made its way into the Frankish Church, and into the Athanasian Creed, if, as is most probable, that symbol is of Frankish and seventh century origin. In England it was acknowledged as a fundamental verity of the faith as early as 680, at the synod held in that year by Theodore of Tarsus, Archbishop of Canterbury, and his suffragans at Hatfield.[1] As such, a century later, it was reaffirmed in the *Caroline Books* (iii. 3) in opposition to the Greek formula, ἐκ τοῦ Πατρὸς διὰ τοῦ Ὑιοῦ, approved by the Patriarch Tarasius at the Seventh Œcumenical Council (Second of Nicaea) in 787.

Tarasius had communicated his profession of faith to Pope Hadrian I., who had suffered it to pass uncensured. The Carlovingian theologians, however, detected the Arian tendency latent therein, and, so far as in them lay, made good what they doubtless deemed the Pope's lack of zeal for the Catholic faith. They argued,[2] not without force, that the Greek formula was open to misconstruction, as if the Holy Spirit were in temporal and creaturely dependence upon the Son—doubtless with reference to the text, "For of Him, and through Him, and to Him, are all things" (Rom. xi. 36);

[1] BEDA, *Hist. Eccl.* ed. Stevenson, 1841, § 304.

[2] "Ex Patre enim et Filio . . . procedere recte creditur et usitate confitetur: quia non per Filium ut pote creatura quae per ipsum facta sit, neque quasi posterior tempore, aut minor potestate, aut alterius substantiæ procedit, sed ex Patre et Filio ut coaeternus, ut consubstantialis, ut coaequalis, ut unius gloriae, potestatis, atque divinitatis, cum eis existens procedere creditur. Alteram namque vim habet, praepositio *ex*, et alteram *per*. Unde et Dei Filius natus ex homine, non per hominem creditur, idest non per coitum, non per humanam operationem sed ex Virgine carnem assumendo natus." *Lib. Carol.* iii. 3 (MIGNE, *Patrolog.* xcvii. 1118).

by which, in fact, it was commonly supported—whereas the Latin doctrine was entirely consonant with the coeternity, consubstantiality and coequality of the three Persons.

The answer to this criticism is not apparent; nor did Hadrian, in adverting to the question in his letter to Charlemagne upon the recent council, which had discussed without deciding the question,[1] attempt any; but contented himself with citing a number of patristic authorities in favour of the Greek doctrine. He was getting old, was indisposed authoritatively to determine the question, and was principally concerned to preserve the peace of the Church. His irenicon, however, failed, as irenicons are apt to fail, of its intended effect. It was an age of active theological speculation. The Frankish Church was distracted by the Adoptianist controversy; and lax views of the doctrine of the Holy Trinity were widely prevalent.[2] Charlemagne felt that it was not a time to bate a jot or tittle of the Catholic verity, and gave practical effect to his views by introducing the word "Filioque" between "Patre" and "procedit" in that version of the Nicene Creed which it was already the custom to chant in his chapel at Aix.[3] There some monks belonging to the Frankish monastery of Mount Olivet heard it so chanted, and on their return to the East introduced the same practice in their house. Taxed with heresy in consequence, they appealed to Hadrian's successor, Leo III., citing the imperial precedent. Leo forwarded their

[1] MANSI, xii. 1120, xiii. 759.

[2] See the Acts of the Councils of Frankfort (794), Friuli (796), and Rome (799), in Mansi.

[3] It was not as yet the practice to chant the Nicene Creed at Rome.

letter to Charlemagne, who in November, 809, convened, at Aix la Chapelle, a council at which nothing was determined; but the entire question, both of the comparative orthodoxy of the Latin and Greek doctrines and the lawfulness of the addition made to the creed, was remitted by legates to the Pope. A curious report of the conference between Leo and the legates may be read in Baronius, *Ann.* 809, liv. In the result the Pope decided nothing except that the Latin doctrine was orthodox, and therefore binding on all who could attain to an explicit belief in it, and by all means to be taught. By reason, however, of its extreme subtlety and mysteriousness, he deemed it unfit for incorporation with the creed. At the same time he did not peremptorily enjoin the erasure of the Filioque; but advised that the practice of chanting the creed in the imperial palace should be discontinued. It is plain that he did not regard the Chalcedonian canon as in itself precluding any and every addition to the creed; but merely held that the particular doctrine in question was not one in favour of which an exception should be made. Later popes were less cautious; and by giving countenance, if not express sanction, to the general use of the amplified symbol, furnished Photius with the most specious of the pretexts by which he sought to justify his rupture with the Holy See.

This supple and accomplished courtier and scholar, who in 857 supplanted the austere Ignatius in the favour of the Byzantine Emperor, Michael III., and in the Patriarchate of Constantinople, sought by an affected zeal against Iconoclasm to obtain recognition by Pope Nicolas I.

Before according it, Nicolas through his legates

demanded evidence of the voluntary resignation of Ignatius, and learned instead that after a fruitless attempt to wring a resignation from him by torture, a forged abdication had, with the connivance of his bribed or terrified legates, been accepted as authentic by a synod subservient to Photius. He therefore (863) passed sentence of excommunication against Photius and all his adherents, and decreed the restoration of Ignatius to his office. Both decrees, however, remained *bruta fulmina*. Secure in the protection of the Emperor and the adhesion of his servile suffragans, Photius met anathema with anathema, excommunication with excommunication, arraigned the Roman Church of heresy and schism in eight articles, among which the corruption of the sacred symbol of Constantinople, by the insertion of the Filioque, held a place of capital importance, and asserted the primacy of the See of Constantinople (867). He had hardly done so, however, before he was deposed and banished by Basil the Macedonian, the murderer and successor of Michael III., who restored Ignatius to the Patriarchate. He was reinstated in the Patriarchate on the death of Ignatius (877); and in return for his recognition by Pope John VIII., convened (879) a synod at Constantinople, by which an anathema was launched against all who should make spurious additions to the Nicene Creed.[1] Thus, in personal ambition, political intrigue, corruption, and violence, was initiated that revolt of the Eastern Church, which culminated under the Patriarch Michael Caerularius in the definitive schism of 1054. Thereafter the controversy slumbered, until in 1098 the Crusade suddenly drew East and West together, and

[1] MANSI, xv. 159-179, 803-812, xvii. 515,

brought the Greek bishops to Bari, to try if by any means short of submission the breach might be healed —with what result we have seen.

In the *De Processione Spiritus Sancti*, Anselm's argument moves in the main within the lines traced by St. Augustine in his classical treatise, *De Trinitate*.[1] The unity of God is absolute, save so far as limited by His threefold personality. The Son and the Holy Spirit differ from the Father only in respect of their relations to Him, and *inter se* only in respect of the diversity of those relations. In this diversity there is nothing to preclude the Holy Spirit from bearing to the Son the same relation as to the Father; and as it is more consonant with the Divine unity that so it should be, even so it must be. Such is Augustine's, and such also is Anselm's essential idea, though the later thinker has of course given to it that articulate and elaborate expression, which only stress of controversy elicits.

He begins by setting forth what both sides hold in common: one God in three Persons, Father, Son, and Holy Spirit, of whom the third is in a certain sense relative to the other two. "For although the Father is spirit and holy, and the Son is spirit and holy; yet the Father is not predicated of a subject as the spirit of that subject; neither is the Son so predicated; as, on the other hand, the Holy Spirit is; for He is the Spirit of God, and the Spirit of the Father and the Son. For notwithstanding the Greeks deny that He proceeds from the Son, yet they do not deny that He is the Spirit of the Son.

They believe also, and confess, that God is from God by generation, and that God is from God by procession;

[1] v. 14.

for the Son is God from God the Father by generation, and the Holy Spirit is God from God the Father by procession. Nor do they think that there is one God who is generated, and another by whom He is generated; one God who proceeds, and another from whom He proceeds; although the terms, importing that there is a being from whom a being is generated, and a being who is generated from a being, and a being who proceeds from a being, acknowledge a plurality; so as that the Father, the Son, and the Holy Spirit are several and distinct from one another.

Moreover, the Greeks concur with the Latins in holding that the relations between the Father and the Son, and the Father and the Holy Spirit, are diverse. "For the Son is from His Father, *i.e.* from God, who is His Father. But the Holy Spirit is not from God His Father, but only from God who is Father. Therefore the Son, in respect of His being from God, is said to be His Son, and He from whom He is said to be, His Father; but the Holy Spirit, in respect of His being from God, is not His Son, nor is He from whom He is, His Father. It is also agreed that God is not Father or Son or Spirit save of God, and that God is no other than this same Father, Son, and Holy Spirit. And as God is one, so there is but one Father, one Son, one Holy Spirit. Wherefore, in the Trinity, the Father is the Father of the Son, and of the Son alone; the Son is the Son of the Father, and of the Father alone; the Holy Spirit is the Spirit of the Father and the Son, and of the Father and Son alone. Herein, then, alone and essentially consists the plurality which is in God, that Father, Son, and Holy Spirit cannot be predicated equivalently, but are distinct one from another, because God is from God in the two ways aforesaid; which may all be summed up in the term relation; for since the Son is from God by generation, and the Holy Spirit is from God by procession, they are so related to each other by the distinction between generation and procession as to be diverse and distinct from one another."

From these premises Anselm deduces the Latin doctrine of the Procession of the Holy Spirit by the following cogent argument. The unity of the Godhead prescribes that whatever is predicable of God, as such, is predicable of His three Persons save so far as their individual characteristics may stand in the way. Either, then, (1) in being begotten of the Father, the Son is also begotten of the Holy Spirit; or (2), in proceeding from the Father, the Holy Spirit also proceeds from the Son. But we know by necessary implication that the Son is not begotten of the Holy Spirit; otherwise it would not have been expressly revealed that He is begotten of the Father. The first alternative may, therefore, be unhesitatingly dismissed. With the second alternative it is otherwise. We know by express revelation that the Holy Spirit is the Spirit, not of the Father alone, but also of the Son, and therefore His proceeding from the Father by no means necessarily implies that He does not also proceed from the Son; nor can due effect be given to the unity of the Godhead except by assuming such procession. The assumption is, therefore, not only legitimate, but necessary.

Against this logic the only resource of the objector is to deny that the Holy Spirit is God from God, a position which, it appears, was actually taken by one of the bishops at Bari. Evidently, if the Holy Spirit is not God from God, then, as He is not essentially one with the Father and the Son, His procession from the Father, however it is to be understood, will not necessarily imply His procession from the Son. This desperate expedient, however, involves the denial either (1) of the Godhead of the Father, or (2) of the Godhead of the Holy Spirit, or (3) of the procession of the Holy Spirit from the Father; and is thus equivalent to an apostasy. But if it be admitted that the Holy Spirit is God from God, the argument from the silence of the Nicene Creed can no longer be urged against His procession from the Son; for that symbol is equally silent as to His being God from God.

In short, the Holy Spirit is God from God proceeding, and when He is said, whether in the Gospel or the Creed, to proceed from the Father, no less is intended than that He proceeds from the unity of the Godhead, and thus equally from the Father and the Son; and this view is corroborated by the fact that His temporal mission is expressly revealed to be from both Father and Son.

To the objection that the Latin doctrine, by making the procession of the Holy Spirit conditional upon the generation of the Son, introduces an element of gradation into the Trinity, Anselm answers that its entire force is derived from a confusion between temporal and metaphysical conditionality; as if the generation of the Son were the *temporal prius* of the procession of the Holy Spirit, whereas in fact both are coeternal. As the Son is none the less very God of very God because He is begotten of the Father, so the Holy Spirit is none the less very God of very God because

He proceeds from the Son; and His procession, though from the Son, is yet coeternal with the generation of the Son.

This misconception disposed of, Anselm adverts to the rival Greek doctrine of the Procession from the Father through the Son; which he finds to be neither supported by authority—for the single text urged in its behalf, the "Quia ex Ipso et per Ipsum et in Ipso sunt omnia" (Rom. xi. 36) evidently has reference to creation—nor intelligible in itself; inasmuch as there is no sense in saying that the procession is through the Son, when it is one and the same Deity that begets, and is begotten, and proceeds.

And if it be objected that the same logic which proves that in proceeding from the one Godhead the Holy Spirit proceeds equally from the Son as from the Father, proves also by a parity of reasoning that He proceeds from Himself, the simple answer is that such a conclusion is negatived by the character of the hypostatic relations. As well might it be argued that in being begotten of the Father the Son is begotten of Himself. This, we know, is not the case; and the unity of the Godhead being consistent with the generation of the Son by the Father and the Father alone, is equally consistent with the procession of the Holy Spirit from the Father and the Son alone.

In short, the Latin doctrine is consistent both with the unity of the Godhead and the fixed character of the hypostatic relations; while the Greek doctrine either makes a distinction without a difference, or rends the unity of the Godhead, by annulling the coinhesion of the three Persons. In being begotten of the Father, in proceeding from the Father, the Son and Holy Spirit do not depart from the Father, but remain within Him. Unless this be denied, there is no force in the distinction between proceeding "through" and proceeding "from" the Son.

The Greek doctrine can only be made significant by being made heretical.

From this same principle of the coinhesion of the three Persons it follows that the procession of the Holy Spirit is from the Father and the Son, not as from two principles, if, where all are coequal, such an expression may be allowed, but as from one. In other words, it is not from the Father and Son as distinct Persons, but from the one God who is both Father and Son, that the Holy Spirit proceeds.

Nor can any objection be raised against the Latin doctrine from the silence of our Lord when, in promising the Paraclete, He calls Him the Spirit of Truth who proceeds from the Father. (John xv. 26.) For this is only a compendious mode of speech not unusual with Him; as when He says to Peter "Blessed art thou, Simon Bar-Jonah: for flesh and blood hath not revealed it unto thee, but my Father which is in heaven" (Matt. xvi. 17), He cannot be taken to mean that either the Son or the Holy Spirit had no part in giving the revelation. "For, since it is not as Father that the Father reveals, but as God, and the same God is also Son and Holy Spirit; it follows that what the Father reveals, that is also revealed by the Son and the Holy Spirit. And when He says 'No man knoweth the Son, but the Father; neither knoweth any man the Father, save the Son, and he to whomsoever the Son will reveal Him' (Matt. xi. 27); as if the Son alone knows and reveals the Father and Himself, and the Father alone knows the Son—then it is to be understood that this revealing and knowing is common to the three Persons; for it is not by virtue of their distinctness, but by virtue of their unity, that the Father, and Son, and Holy Spirit know and reveal. For when He says that the Father knows the Son and the Son knows the Father, and reveals Himself and the Father, He plainly means it to be understood that the Father knows the Holy Spirit, and that the Son knows and reveals the Holy Spirit; since what the Father is and what the Son is, that also is the Holy Spirit. Similarly, when He says 'Who seeth me, seeth also the Father' (John xiv. 9), the Holy Spirit is not to be excluded; since he who sees the one God who is Father, Son, and Holy Spirit, cannot see one of these three Persons without the other two. Of the Holy Spirit, also, He says to the apostles:

"'But when that Spirit of Truth is come, He shall teach you all truth' (John xvi. 13), as if the Holy Spirit alone were to teach all truth; whereas He cannot teach the truth without the Father and the Son. For it is not in that He is the Spirit of the Father and the Son, but in that He is one with the Father and the Son, *i.e.* in that He is God, that He teaches all truth."

From all which Anselm draws the very evident inference that, throughout the Holy Scriptures, what is affirmed of any one of the Persons of the Holy Trinity is to be understood of the others, except so far as their hypostatic "proprieties" preclude such an interpretation; and so returns to the point from which he set out, viz. that in proceeding from the Father the Holy Spirit must likewise proceed from the Son, unless (*per impossibile*) the Son should be begotten of the Holy Spirit.

He then clinches the argument by the following very neat dilemma. The Greeks confess that the Holy Spirit is the Spirit of God, the Spirit of the Father, and the Spirit of the Son. Now this must be understood either univocally or equivocally; *i.e.* either the Holy Spirit is the Spirit of God, the Spirit of the Father, in the same sense in which He is the Spirit of the Son, or in some other sense. But He is the Spirit of God, the Spirit of the Father, in the sense that He proceeds from God, from the Father. Either, then, He is the Spirit of the Son in the sense that He proceeds from the Son, or in the sense that He is given by, without proceeding from, the Son; for which neither reason nor authority can be alleged. The Greeks must therefore either accept the Latin doctrine, or adopt one which is entirely arbitrary; in which case they ought in fairness to give up censuring the Roman Church for drawing a plain deduction from premises acknowledged by themselves, in a matter not expressly determined by revelation.

Passing to the subordinate question of the addition made to the Nicene Creed, Anselm defends it as necessary for the quieting of doubts among the less intelligent members of the Church, and in no way contrary to the true spirit of the Chalcedonian canon; and urges, in justification of the independent action taken by the Roman Church in the matter, her own inherent prerogative and the confusion of the times, which rendered the assembling of a general council a matter of extreme difficulty.

He then concludes with a lengthy recapitulation of the whole argument, in which we need not follow him. Equally needless is it to trace the subsequent course of the controversy, if indeed that can be called a controversy in which all the sound reasoning is on one side.

That the Greek Church, after twice acknowledging the truth of the Latin doctrine—once, on its definition by Clement IV., at the second Council of Lyon in 1274,[1] and again at Florence in 1439—remains still in schism, is a fact known to all the world, as also that there is no apparent likelihood of the schism ever being ended.

[1] The Council was held under Gregory X.; but the definition had been framed by his predecessor. (BARONIUS, *Ann.* 1274, xiv.; MANSI, xxiv. 81.)

CHAPTER XIV.

CLOSE OF THE COUNCIL OF BARI—THE COUNCIL OF ROME—RETURN TO LYON

FROM the dizzy altitudes of theological speculation, the council of Bari descended to discuss the posture of affairs in England, and the misdeeds of her king. Urban dilated on his oppression of the Church, his gross and shameless profligacy, his contumacy towards the Holy See, his iniquitous treatment of Anselm, and appealed to the Fathers for their advice. They were unanimous that the time had come to "strike with the sword of St. Peter," and the fatal "Ita est" fell from the Papal lips. The blow, however, was not struck; and it was by Anselm that it was averted. Throwing himself on his knees before the Pope, he prayed that the sentence of excommunication might not pass, and Urban reluctantly yielded to his intercession. Shortly afterwards the council was dissolved, and Anselm returned with the Pope to Rome.

Anselm's conduct on this occasion is inexplicable. To appeal to the Holy See against the delinquent, and then stand between him and the just reward of his evil deeds, was certainly as illogical as it seems impolitic. We can only conjecture that he yielded to one of those sudden impulses which sometimes completely overpower sensitive natures. The sequel, however, will show that, as a matter of fact, nothing was lost by the suspension of the decree.

Meanwhile the nuncio bearing Urban's letter, and that which accompanied it from Anselm, had reached the English court. Anselm's letter Rufus had refused so much as to receive, and the papal missive he had treated with hardly less conspicuous contempt. Though he made himself acquainted with its contents, he disdained a written reply, and recognising the nuncio as one of Anselm's men, bade him make his best speed out of England, or, by the Face of God, he would put his eyes out. At the same time he commissioned his trusty henchman, William of Warelwast, the same who had overhauled Anselm's baggage on Dover beach, to proceed to Rome with a verbal answer, and such an answer!

"My lord the king," said Warelwast as soon as he was admitted to the Papal presence, "lets you know that it is a matter of no small amazement to him that it should so much as enter your mind to address him on the subject of the restitution of the temporalities to Anselm. If you want to know the reason, it is this. When he proposed to leave the country the king openly threatened him that, on his departure, he would confiscate the entire see. Now, as Anselm paid no heed to this threat, but left the country, he deems that, in acting as he has done, he has acted justly, and is unjustly censured by you."

"Does he accuse him of aught else?" enquired the Pope.

"No," replied Warelwast.

"Oh!" exclaimed the Pope, forgetting his dignity in his excitement, "whoever heard the like! To despoil a primate of all his temporalities simply because he would not forego a visit to the Holy Roman Church, the mother of all churches! Truly and unreservedly we may say that nothing of the kind was ever heard since the world was. And was it to deliver such a message as this, strange man, that you gave yourself the trouble of coming hither? Return—return with all speed—and lay upon your master the injunction of Blessed Peter, that, without further parley, he reinstate Anselm in all his temporalities on pain of excommunication. And see that he lets me know what his intentions are before the council, which I am about to hold in this city, in the third week after Easter. Otherwise, let him be assured that in that same council he will incur the punishment of the just sentence which he has provoked."

The speech was worthy of the successor of Hildebrand; but it fell on sceptical ears, and only elicited from the Norman clerk the cynical rejoinder, "Before I go I must deal more secretly with you."

Warelwast tarried accordingly in Rome; where, though apparently he had no further interview with the Pope, he succeeded, by a liberal bestowal of money and promises among the prelates who formed the papal court, in averting the threatened excommunication, and eventually, at Christmas, secured its formal postponement until the following Michaelmas.[1]

On learning of this arrangement, Anselm applied to

[1] According to William of Malmesbury, *De Gest Pontif.* (Rolls Ser.), p. 34, it was the Pope himself whom Warelwast bribed. This, however, is by no means borne out by Eadmer, whose account has been followed in the text.

Urban for leave to return to Lyon and his good friend Archbishop Hugh. But of this Urban would not hear, and kept him in Rome, giving him legal title to his rooms in the Lateran, and precedence before all other dignitaries in public receptions, processions, and other solemn functions. He also frequently visited him, and, in short, endeavoured, by every means in his power, to mitigate the inevitable bitterness of his exile. Thus the weeks slid by; winter passed into spring, and with the spring came bishops to the number of one hundred and fifty, besides a multitude of abbots and other clergy, from all parts of Italy and beyond the Alps, to discuss once more in council the perennial questions of discipline and the relations of Church and State.

At this council, which assembled at St. Peter's on 25 April, 1099, there was much ado to determine Anselm's proper precedence. The presence, says Eadmer, of an Archbishop of Canterbury at a Roman council was a thing as yet unwitnessed, unheard of, and none knew where he ought to sit. The Pope, however, ordered his chair to be placed in the corona, or hemicycle—a position of no small dignity. There he sat, wrapt in melancholy meditation, while Bishop Reinger, of Lucca, who was chosen for the purpose because he was tall and strong of lung, read out the decrees to the somewhat tumultuous assembly. Worded with peculiar care, so as to avoid, as far as possible, misconstruction or evasion, they reaffirmed the Hildebrandine canons against lay investiture, and that of the Council of Clermont against liege fealty, placing under excommunication not only all laymen who should give investiture of spiritualities, and all clerks who should receive such investiture, or should consecrate such recipients, but also all clerks who should do homage to laymen for their temporalities, affirming it to be "a thing execrable beyond measure that hands which were exalted to such super-angelic dignity as by their ministry to create God the Creator of all, and offer Him before the eyes of God the Father Almighty for the redemption and salvation of all the world, should be degraded to such an abyss of ignominy as to become subservient to hands which day and night were polluted by contact with obscenities, and stained by habitual commerce with rapine and the unjust effusion of blood."

This tremendous assertion of sacerdotal prerogative was preceded by other decrees of minor importance, the reading of which proved a somewhat tedious business; and Reinger had not proceeded far with it when, either by a happy inspiration or of premeditated purpose, he diverted the attention of the Fathers from the dry questions of law to the concrete facts represented by the presence among them of the Archbishop of Canterbury. Fixing his audience with an eager, penetrating glance, he exclaimed with sudden animation of tone and gesture, "But alas! what shall we do? We burden subjects with our ordinances, and withstand not the ruthless atrocities of tyrants. For of the oppressions wherewith, in their unbridled license, they afflict the churches, despoiling those who are set to watch over them, come daily tidings to this see, from which counsel and aid are sought, as from the head of all; but with what effect, alas! is known to, and deplored by, the entire world. From the farthest part whereof one, even now, sits among us, distinguished by his gentle mien and modest reserve, whose silence is an eloquent appeal, whose humility and patience, the more lowly they are and long-suffering, are the more exalted in the sight of God, and the apter to move our sympathies. He has come hither—he of whom I speak—most cruelly oppressed, most unjustly despoiled of all that he has, to implore, in his behalf, the justice and equity of the Apostolic See. It is now more than a year since he came among us; but alas! what succour has he so far found? If by chance any of you are ignorant of whom I speak, know that it is Anselm, Archbishop of England."

So spoke the stout Bishop of Lucca, and, as he concluded, struck the pavement thrice with his crosier, while a low hiss of rage escaped his tightly-compressed lips.

Then Urban's bland voice was heard: "Enough, enough said, Father Reinger; good counsel shall be had in this matter."

"Ay, it had need," retorted Reinger, with real or simulated impatience, "else the Judge of all will not pass it over." He then concluded the reading of the decrees, after which he again briefly adverted to Anselm's wrongs, and the session terminated.

The council over (1 May), Anselm at once set out on his return journey to Lyon. The ordinary routes, however, were unsafe, by reason that the Anti-pope Guibert, who had not yet ceased to trouble the peace of the Church, being minded to play the brigand, had snatched a sketch of the saint's features, and distributed copies among his partisans with instructions to waylay and arrest him. He therefore turned aside, and made a long détour by way of Piedmont and the Black Forest, resting some days under the quiet roof of Kloster Hirsau, the scene of the devoted labours and holy death of his old correspondent, Abbot William; and leaving memories behind him which still smell sweet in the pages of a later abbot, good, gossipy John Tritheim, or Trithemius, of Spanheim, in whom, in the fifteenth century, the archives of Hirsau found an editor.[1] He also spent some time with his sister, Richera, and her husband, Burgundius, though whether at Aosta, or elsewhere, is not clear. Richera, it will be remembered, was Anselm's junior by many years, and her husband had still so much vigour in him that he was thinking of breaking a lance in the holy war. They had had several children, but only the eldest, a lad who bore his uncle's name and was resolved to tread in his uncle's footsteps, had survived.[2] So when Anselm left, Richera bade a tearful adieu to her son; and when Anselm reached Lyon, he wrote her a tenderly affectionate letter to assure her of young Anselm's safety and well-being, and, as far as might be, to console her for her loss. This letter, as it shews the saint in a new light, may fitly close this chapter.

"Anselm, Archbishop of Canterbury, to his dearest sister, Richera, health, and the consolation of God in all her tribulations. I know, sister best beloved, that there is no man on the earth, except your husband, of whose health and well-being you would so gladly hear tidings as of my own and that of your son, Anselm, who is with me; for I am your only brother, and he your only son. Of what concerns us, our messengers will be better able to inform you by word of mouth than I by letter. Know, however, that your son, my dearest nephew, after he left you, had a long and severe

[1] The incident is recorded under date 1077, but the context shows that it belongs to 1099.

[2] He was afterwards successively Abbot of S. Saba in Rome and St. Edmunds in Suffolk. He died in 1148.

illness, from which, by the mercy of God, he is now completely recovered. Of myself, I may say, with truth, that I am well in body, but my mind is distraught with great tribulation. For so it is, that abandon England, for the fear of God, I dare not, nor yet live there in any peace, tranquillity, or quietude. I live in daily suspense, as if about to go hence; but, however I may be situated, I rejoice, on your account, because your messengers have brought me tidings of your health and good fortune. But, as the good and evil fortune of this life are brief and transitory, let us despise them, study to avoid that evil fortune which is eternal, and strive, by living well, to earn that good fortune which is perpetual. So then, dearest sister, as you have not, in this life, that wherein your heart may take delight, turn it all to God that, in the life to come, it may be able to have joy in Him. Farewell! If your husband, on his return, desire to come to me, I bid him on no account so to do."

CHAPTER XV.

REST AT LYON—THE *DE CONCEPTU VIRGINALI*—ENGLISH AFFAIRS ONCE MORE

SOON after Anselm's arrival at Lyon, Pope Urban closed, in curious contrast to Gregory VII., a pontificate of exile, by a peaceful death at Rome. He had been consecrated at Terracina; and, after holding a single council at Rome (1089), had been compelled to abandon the city to the anti-pope; nor did he recover possession of it until, in 1097, the expulsion of his rival from the Castle of St. Angelo sealed the discomfiture of the imperial faction. Thus the council at which Anselm was present was only the second, as it was also the last, which Urban held in Rome. He died on 29 July the same year, just a fortnight after the storm of Jerusalem by Godfrey of Bouillon, in the palace of the Frangipani, which then adjoined S. Nicola in Carcere, between the Tiber and the Capitoline Hill; and was laid to rest in St. Peter's, near the oratory of his great predecessor, Hadrian I. His successor, like himself a Cluniac monk, was Cardinal Rainer, Abbot of S. Lorenzo fuori le Mura, who took the style of Paschal II.

Paschal was elected by the unanimous vote of the Sacred College; and the death of the Anti-pope Guibert, followed not long after. He had to contend, however, with three successive pretenders, whom the disaffected had still strength enough in Rome to array against him; and the affairs of Germany, where the emperor was mustering his forces for a final trial of strength, demanded his vigilant attention. England and Anselm were, therefore, for a time neglected.

During this period of suspense, Anselm was entertained by Archbishop Hugh less as a guest than as his superior lord and honoured master. By a gentle compulsion, he found himself forced against his will to play the leading part, in the less laborious and more honorific ecclesiastical functions of the archdiocese; which served to wean his mind from melancholy reflections, while leaving him abundant leisure for pursuing his favourite theological studies. Two opuscula were the fruit of these tranquil hours. The one, which bears the title *Meditatio de Redemptione Humana* (xi. in Migne's collection), is an informal summary of the main argument of the *Cur Deus Homo?* and calls for no special notice. The other, a systematic tractate, *De Conceptu Virginali et Originali Peccato,* is devoted to the discussion of the perplexing problem implicit in the then prevalent opinion of the Blessed Virgin's subjection to original sin. From St. Augustine Anselm inherited not indeed the traducian theory of the origin of the soul, but the belief in the transmission of original sin by natural procreation. Applying this principle to the mystery of the Incarnation, he found himself face to face with the question which it was not in his nature to shirk, "Quomodo Deus accepit hominem de massa peccatrice humani generis sine peccato?" In what way did God assume human nature from the sinful substance of the human race, yet without sin?

In other words, as Christ took His human nature

from the substance of His mother, and she was conceived in the natural way of procreation, and therefore subject to original sin, how is the blasphemous conclusion to be avoided, that He took from her a nature tainted with original sin?

The solution of this formidable problem Anselm seeks in the virginal birth of our Lord; arguing, somewhat inconclusively, it must be owned, that parthenogenesis is in itself a bar to the assumption of original sin, so that even had Christ been mere man He would equally have been the second, unfallen, Adam. In the curious reasoning by which he reaches this result we need not follow him; for, until the adoption by the Church of the Augustinian theory, it has little relevance. That which is of capital interest to us is the relation of his argument to the doctrine of our Lady's sinlessness. Was that sinlessness a necessary part of the economy of redemption, or merely congruous therewith? That is the real question which is in Anselm's mind; and his treatise is designed to answer it in the latter sense.

Into the question of the Immaculate Conception of our Lady he does not enter, being doubtless swayed by the example of his master, St. Augustine, who, throughout his polemic against the Pelagians, practises a studious economy in regard to that topic. But that when our Lord took flesh of her substance, that substance was sinless, he assumes; and his whole contention is that it was so not of necessity, but only of congruity. Such a position is manifestly quite compatible with the doctrine of the Immaculate Conception.

But Anselm had best be allowed to state his doctrine in his own words; which he does as follows:

"Although, then, the Son of God was most truly conceived of a most pure Virgin, yet was not this of necessity: it was not that, in the nature of things, it was not possible for a righteous offspring to be generated by this mode of procreation from a sinful parent, but only that it was congruous that the conception of that Man should be by a mother most pure. Congruous, indeed, was it that with a purity, than which none greater is conceivable below the Divine, that Virgin should be adorned to whom God the Father decreed to give His only Son; whom, begotten from His own heart, equal with Himself, He loved as Himself; that, entering the natural order, He might become her Son as well as His; and whom the Son Himself chose to make His mother, substance of His substance; and of whom the Holy Spirit willed and decreed to effect that of her should be conceived and born He from whom He Himself proceeds. Of the manner in which, before the conception, she was purified, I have spoken in that place where I have given another account of this matter." (*De Concept. Virg.* cap. xviii.)

The other account here referred to is the *Cur Deus Homo?* cap. xvi., in which the material passage is the following:

"*Ans.* That Virgin, from whose substance that Man was assumed, was of those who, before His birth, were purified from sin, and in her purity He was assumed from her substance.

Bos. What you say would please me much were it not that, whereas He ought to have His purity from sin from Himself, He seems to have it from His mother, and not by Himself to be pure, but by her.

Ans. Not so. But since His mother's purity, by which He was pure, was only derived from Him, He was Himself pure by Himself and from Himself."

Briefly stated, then, Anselm's position is as follows: It was not necessary that the Blessed Virgin should be immaculate in order that her Son should receive from her an immaculate human nature; but it was fitting that so it should be, and therefore she was entirely sanctified before she conceived of the Holy Spirit. Whether she was herself conceived immaculate he leaves an open question, but it is manifest that the argument from congruity, if valid at all, is valid *a fortiori* for the doctrine of the immaculate conception. What more congruous with the Divine majesty can be imagined than that the Mother of God should, in virtue of her foreknown faith and obedience, be full of grace from the first moment of her conscious life? Assuredly if the argument from congruity is valid at all, coherent thinking demands that it be pressed to its logical result.

And perhaps, after all, this is not Anselm's last word on the topic. We know that the Feast of the Immaculate Conception was already observed in England in the first half of the twelfth century, and ancient and credible tradition attributes its inauguration to St. Anselm;[1] while a short tractate containing a lucid exposition of the doctrine, included by Migne among the spurious works ascribed to him, is unquestionably assignable to his nephew and namesake, and may therefore represent his final opinion.[2] The observance of the feast at Lyon, in 1140, is attested by one of the letters of St. Bernard of Clairvaux, and, taken in connection with the known nature of Anselm's studies during his sojourn there, raises a fair presumption that it was due, directly or indirectly, to his influence.[3]

[1] Mansi, xxv. 829.

[2] Migne, *Patrolog.* clix. 302, *et seq.*; Osbert of Clare, *Ep.* viii. (Caxton Ser.).

[3] Migne, *Patrolog.* clxxxii. *Ep.* clxxiv.; Raynaud, *Hagiolog. Lugdun.* (1662) p. 328; Ragey, *Hist. de Saint Anselme*, ii. 243-247.

From these abstruse scholastic studies Anselm found relief, from time to time, in visits to the neighbouring towns and religious houses—to Vienne, to Mâcon, to Chaise Dien (in Auvergne), to Cluny—celebrating mass, preaching, healing the sick in mind and body wherever he went, and everywhere receiving the same tribute of devout homage.

Nor was he unobservant of the course of affairs in England, though the prospect of return to that distracted island seemed only to grow more remote. On hearing of Urban's death Rufus had remarked, with his usual good taste, "God's enmity attend him who regrets it." Then he had asked what manner of man was his successor, and being answered, "Such a one in some respects as Anselm," had responded, "By the Face of God, then, if such he is, he is no good; but let him keep himself to himself. For this time I vow his Popeship shall not get the better of me. Meanwhile I will use my freedom to do as I like." What that meant we know.

The See of Durham, vacant since the death in 1096 of William of St. Calais, he had just bestowed, doubtless not without due consideration, on Ranulf Flambard, to whom he had also leased the now vacant See of Winchester, besides eleven abbeys scattered throughout the country. The profits arising from these nefarious transactions, added to the revenues of the See of Canterbury, would be augmented as often as another abbey or see lapsed, as before the end of the year the See of Salisbury actually did lapse, by the death of Bishop Osmund, into the voracious maw of the royal fisc. Such was the freedom which Rufus meant to use as he chose. "God," he had once said to the Bishop of

Rochester, "shall never have any good thing from me in return for the evil He has done me." And he meant to keep his word.

All this, and probably much more, was only too well known to Anselm, who received regular advices from England, and was once perhaps tempted to hope for better things by the appearance of a royal envoy at Lyon, who bore a commission to discuss his case with Archbishop Hugh. What terms Rufus offered we do not know; but, whatever they were, they were rejected, and on the departure of the envoy, Anselm, as a last resource, appealed once more to Rome. His letter,[1] which has fortunately been preserved, is as follows:

"To his Lord and reverend Father, Paschal, Supreme Pontiff, Anselm, slave of the Church of Canterbury, his heart's due submission and the good offices, if aught they avail, of his prayers.

That, after I rejoiced and gave thanks to God, to hear certain tidings of your elevation, I delayed for so long a time to send a messenger to Your Highness, was by reason that a certain envoy of the King of the English came to our venerable Archbishop of Lyon to discuss my affairs, bringing, however, no proposition that could be accepted; and having heard the archbishop's answer, returned to the king, promising shortly to come back to Lyon. His return I awaited, that I might know what I might be able to impart to you concerning the king's disposition, but he came not. And so I now lay before you my cause, succinctly, because during my stay at Rome I often detailed it to Pope Urban and many others, as, I think, Your Holiness knows. I observed in England many evils, the correction of which belonged to my office, which I could neither correct, nor, without sin, tolerate. For the king required of me, as of right, that I should accede to his wishes; which were neither in accordance with the law of

[1] *Epp.* iii. 40.

the land nor the will of God. For he forbade recognition of the Pope to be had, or appeal to him made, in England, without his authorisation; forbade me to communicate with him by letter, or receive a letter from him, or obey his decrees. He suffered no council to be held in his realm from his accession for the space of—as it now is—thirteen years. The lands of the Church he gave to his own men. In regard to all these and similar matters, if I sought advice, all in power in his realm, even my own suffragan bishops, refused to give any but such as chimed in with his will. Observing these and many other things, which are contrary to the will and law of God, I sought leave of the king to pay a visit to the Apostolic See, that I might there receive ghostly counsel and instruction in regard to my duty.

The king replied that the mere making such a request was an offence against him, and gave me the option either to make satisfaction to him as for a fault, and pledge myself to him never again to repeat it, and on no occasion to appeal to the Pope, or to quit his dominions forthwith. I chose rather to leave the country than to concur in iniquity. I came to Rome, as you know, and laid the whole matter before the Pope. The king, as soon as I had left the country, laid tax upon the very victuals and clothes of our monks, invaded the entire see, and converted it to his own use. Admonished and enjoined by Pope Urban to set this right, he treated his words with contempt, and therein still persists.

It is now the third year since I left England. The little money which I brought with me, and the large sums which I borrowed, and for which I am still a debtor, I have spent. So, more owing than having, I am detained in the house of our venerable father, the Archbishop of Lyon, being supported by his benign generosity and generous benignity. I say not this as being desirous of returning to England, but because I fear lest your Highness should resent my not notifying it to you. I pray, therefore, and beseech, as earnestly as I may, that you by no means bid me return to England, unless on such conditions as may enable me to set the law and will of God and the apostolic decrees above the will of man; and unless the king shall have restored to me the lands of the Church, and whatever he has taken from the archbishopric on account of my recourse to the Apostolic See, or at least have made the Church a sufficient compensation therefor. For, otherwise, I should give countenance to the idea that I ought to prefer man to God, and that I was justly deprived of my temporalities for determining to have recourse to the Apostolic See. And it is evident how injurious, how execrable a precedent this would be for posterity. Some not very sagacious people ask why I do not excommunicate the king; but the wiser and better advised counsel me not to do so, because it does not belong to me to both lay the plaint and execute judgment. And, in fine, some of my friends who are subjects of the same king have sent me word that my excommunication, if it took place, would be despised and turned into ridicule by him. In regard to all these matters, your authority and wisdom need no advice from me. I pray that God Almighty may so direct all your acts as that they may subserve His good pleasure, and that His Church may long rejoice under your prosperous governance. Amen."

From this letter it appears that Anselm had all but given up hope of restoration to his see on honourable terms during the life of the king; and as he was now aged and infirm, while Rufus was in the prime of life, that meant a virtual postponement of his return until the Greek Calends. He was only solicitous lest, in a moment of weakness, Paschal should accept an unworthy compromise. The residue of his days could at most be but brief; and he would rather spend it in honourable exile at Lyon, than in splendid ignominy at Canterbury.

Meanwhile, Rufus flourished like the proverbial green bay-tree. His sway was absolute, his will was law, in England as in Normandy. Only in Maine, the suzerainty of which he claimed as appendant to Normandy, had he cause for anxiety. The sturdy Manceaux disputed his title to their allegiance, and under Hélie de la Flèche, Count of Le Mans, had asserted their independence, and only been subdued after an obstinate struggle, which Hélie suddenly renewed in the summer of 1099. William heard the news as he was on his way from Clarendon to the New Forest upon a hunting expedition. With characteristic precipitancy, he at once turned his horse's head, rode almost unattended to the coast, and threw himself into the first available ship. The sky was overcast, the wind contrary, the sea boisterous, the ship unfit to face rough weather; the crew shrank from attempting the passage. But William would not hear of delay. "I have never heard," he said, "of a king perishing by shipwreck. Cast loose the cables, and you will see that the elements will conspire to obey me." And a prosperous passage, and safe landing at Touques, seemed to justify his boast.

Hastily gathering an army, he marched straight on Maine, relieved the garrison of Le Mans, failed to take another town or two, and satisfied with this partial success, hurried back to England to mature much larger plans of conquest.

William, Count of Poitou and Duke of Aquitaine, was bound for the Crusade; but, like Duke Robert, was sorely in need of ready cash. The freedom which Rufus had used with the lands of the Church placed him in a position to advance the money, of course upon a proper mortgage of the Duchy of Aquitaine. Aquitaine in his power would serve as a base for the extension of his dominion far into the south of Gaul. As he revolved his schemes of aggrandisement in the spring of 1100, he promised himself that he would be at Poitiers by Christmas. Some, however, of those who watched the culmination of his star, cast his horoscope very differently. During the summer a presentiment that his end was at hand, taking shape in dreams and visions, ran like an epidemic through England and Normandy, and even reached Anselm's ears, though he closed them against it.[1]

The sequel is matter of general history. On Thursday, 2 August, 1100, William was hunting with Anselm's old friend, Walter Tirrel, near Brockenhurst, in the New Forest, when, whether by accident or design will never now be known, he was stricken through the heart by an arrow, and fell lifeless on the ground. The corpse was carried to Winchester, and buried hastily and unceremoniously in the Old Minster. On the following Sunday, Henry I. was crowned at Westminster by Maurice, Bishop of London.

[1] This presentiment seems to be too well and widely attested to be dismissed as a mere *vaticinium post eventum*. The evidence is collected by Freeman, *Reign of William Rufus*, vol. ii. 318 *et seq.*, 657 *et seq.*

CHAPTER XVI.

RETURN TO ENGLAND—FIRST RELATIONS WITH HENRY I.

IT was towards the end of August when Anselm, then at Chaise Dieu, heard of the death of Rufus. Unmanned for a moment by the horrible news, he burst into tears; then, mastering himself by a convulsive effort, he protested, amidst his sobs, that to save the king such a fate he would willingly have died himself. Then came the inevitable reflection that the removal of the king materially altered his own position, and he lost no time in taking horse for Lyon. Arrived there, he found a letter awaiting him from the Christ Church monks, urging his immediate return to Canterbury. So, early in September, he bade an affectionate farewell to Archbishop Hugh, and, amid the liveliest demonstrations of grief on the part of the good townsfolk, took his departure from Lyon, making, in the first instance, for Cluny. On the way he was stopped by a messenger from the new King of England, who bore a missive for the Archbishop of Canterbury. Anselm broke the seal and read as follows:

"Henry, by the grace of God, King of the English, to his most pious, spiritual Father Anselm, Bishop of Canterbury, health and all friendly greetings.

Know, dearest Father, that my brother, King William, is

dead; and I, by the will of God, being chosen by the clergy and people of England, and, though against my will by reason of your absence, already consecrated king, call upon you, as my father—joining my voice to that of the entire people of England—to come hither with your best speed to afford me, and the same people of England, the care of whose souls has been committed to you, the help of your counsel. Myself and the people of the entire realm of England I commit to your guidance and theirs who ought to unite with you in council; and I pray you not to be displeased because I have received consecration from other hands than yours; for from you would I more gladly have received it than from any other man. But needs must in such a case; for my enemies designed to rise against me and the people whom I have to govern; and, therefore, my barons and the same people would not consent to a postponement; in such an emergency, therefore, I received it from your suffragans. I would have made you a remittance of money by some of my courtiers, but the death of my brother has caused such a commotion throughout the dominion of England that they could by no means have reached you in safety. I therefore advise you not to travel by way of Normandy but by Wissant, and I will have my barons at Dover to meet you with money; so that you will find, by God's help, wherewithal to repay what you have borrowed. Make haste, then, Father, to come hither, that our mother, the Church of Canterbury, long agitated and distressed on your account, may sustain no further loss of souls.

Witness, Gerard, bishop, and William, Bishop-elect of Winchester, William of Warelwast, and Count Henry, and Robert, son of Haymon, and Haymon, lord chamberlain, and others both bishops and barons."

Fair words, and not quite as false as fair. Henry was a scholar, and, though licentious, was not without a certain dim sense of religion. He had viewed with disgust the bestial orgies and shameless ecclesiastical policy of his brother. He was really anxious for an accommodation with the Church. He dismissed Ranulf Flambard, purged the palace of the effeminates who had ministered to his brother's pleasures, and formed his council from his father's companions in arms, among whom was Anselm's old friend Hugh the Wolf, Earl of Chester. In short, he was bent upon treading in his father's footsteps. He would not bate a jot of what he deemed his prerogative, but neither would he assume an attitude of wanton hostility to the Church. Anselm he respected, perhaps revered, as a scholar and a saint; and, moreover, Anselm could be of real service to him.

Duke Robert was hourly expected in Normandy, and might even show his face in England. Anselm's presence would give moral support to Henry's as yet by no means secure tenure of the throne. Anselm must therefore return without delay, and then perhaps means might be found of arranging matters with the Pope. Anselm could read between the lines, and the significance of the royal letter could hardly be missed by him, as he turned its contents over in his mind, while he rode towards Cluny. No time was evidently to be lost; so he pushed on at a rate which must have been extremely trying to a man of his years, landed at Dover on 23 September, and at once hurried to Salisbury, where Henry had his court. There, or on his way, he was apprised of two facts which gave him cause for rejoicing: (1) Ranulf Flambard was already in the Tower on a charge of malversation; (2) Henry had signed, upon his coronation, a charter, by which he "made the Church of God free"; free, that is to say, as a subsequent clause explained, from simoniacal traffic and confiscation of her revenues by him.[1]

About investiture and homage the document was silent; and in his first audience of the king, Anselm found that he was as little disposed as his predecessor to concede the papal claim in regard to them. Henry plainly intimated that he expected Anselm to do him homage, and to receive investiture from him; and Anselm as plainly answered that, in that case, he had better return whence he came, explaining, at the same time, the bearing of the decree of the recent council upon the situation. Not feeling himself as yet so secure upon his throne that he could afford to dispense with Anselm's counsel and countenance, Henry adopted a temporising policy. Anselm received restitution by deed, with warranty of quiet possession, of the temporalities of the See of Canterbury, such as they had been in the times of Edward the Confessor and William the Conqueror,[2] on the understanding that the question of investiture and homage should be adjourned until Easter, so that Henry might try the effect of an appeal to the Pope.

In the meantime, Gerard, Bishop of Hereford, was translated to the See of York, vacant by the death of Archbishop Thomas on 18 November. Some of the

[1] Henricus Dei gratia Rex Anglorum omnibus hominibus, baronibus, fidelibus suis tam Francigenis quam Anglicis salutem. Sciatis me Dei misericordia communi consilio baronum Regni Angliæ eiusdem Regni Regem coronatum esse: quod Regnum oppressum erat iniustis exactionibus. Ego respectu Dei et amore quem erga vos omnes habeo sanctam Dei Ecclesiam in primis liberam facio: ita quod nec vendam nec in firmam ponam, nec mortuo archiepiscopo, sen episcopo, sive abbate aliquid inde accipiam de dominio Ecclesiae vel de hominibus ejus donec successor in eam ingrediatur. (Harl. MS. 458 f. 1.)

[2] RYMER, ed. Clarke, i. 9.

vacant abbacies had already been filled, and others were filled before the end of the year. William Giffard had also been elected to the See of Winchester, but had not as yet been consecrated; and Anselm, of course, now declined to consecrate him while as yet uncertain of his own status in the realm.

During the winter, however, Anselm's attention was engaged by a matter much more interesting, if of less intrinsic importance, than the question of investiture and homage. Henry was by birth an Englishman, was perhaps not without English sympathies, was at any rate astute enough to appreciate the political value of an English wife; and in the seclusion of Romsey Abbey, wearing a nun's veil, under the tutelage of her somewhat rigorous aunt Christina, a fair English princess, as intelligent as fair, and as learned as intelligent, Edith, daughter of Malcolm III. of Scotland, by Margaret, sister of Edgar the Atheling, and grandniece of Edward the Confessor, was languishing her young life away for want of a husband. Henry was minded to wed her, sounded her inclination, and found it by no means adverse. In short, all that stood in the way of the match was the law of the Church, which claimed the lady as the bride of Christ. In this emergency Edith laid aside her veil, quitted the convent, and laid in general terms the state of the case before Anselm. At first, under the impression that she had taken the vow, he bade her return to the convent; but on learning that she had never made any profession, or felt any inclination towards the conventual life, that she had assumed the veil solely at the bidding of her aunt, who had deemed it necessary for the protection of her honour, during the license of the preceding reign, he convened at Lambeth a council of clergy and laity, before whom he laid the entire case in due form, with the result that the Lady Edith was set free to follow the bent of her natural inclinations. In this he did but follow a precedent set by Lanfranc; but he thereby earned the enduring gratitude of the future queen. The way thus cleared, the marriage was hurried on, the rite being performed by Anselm in Westminster Abbey, on 11 November, 1100, seven weeks after his return to England. Queen Edith, better known in history by her more imposing name Matilda, amply vindicated the wisdom of Henry's choice. Devoted to her husband, and—notwithstanding her early aversion to the life of the cloister—to the Church, to God, and good works, she won golden opinions of her warm-hearted subjects, who loved to call her the good Queen Maud; nor was ever daughter more attached to father than she to the aged, infirm, and careworn churchman, to whom she owed her all too brief portion of earthly felicity.[1]

[1] She died on 1 May, 1118, and was buried in Westminster Abbey.

CHAPTER XVII.

RETURN OF DUKE ROBERT—HENRY'S CROWN SAVED BY ANSELM—HENRY'S GRATITUDE

THE winter of 1100 was probably spent by Anselm in giving final shape to his treatise on the Procession of the Holy Spirit; in composing, for the behoof of Bishop Waleran, of Naumburg, who had Greek proclivities, a brief tractate on another question much agitated by the Eastern Church—to wit, whether leavened or unleavened bread should be used in the celebration of the mass, and in quietly reorganising, so far as was practicable, the monastic life of the archdiocese, now sunk, in all probability, to much the same level of laxity from which Lanfranc had raised it. On all hands there would be abundant need for inspection, admonition, exhortation. Hence it is likely that not a few of Anselm's extant pastoral letters are to be referred to this period.

While he was thus engaged, an event occurred which brought him into sharp collision with the king. Among the abbacies filled by Henry upon his coronation was that of St. Edmund; to which, with ostentatious disregard of propriety, he had nominated Robert, son of Hugh the Wolf, who had taken the cowl at St. Evroult, probably for no better reason than that there happened to be then nothing else for him to take. His intrusion was vehemently resented by the monks of St. Edmund's, and was only made good by military force. After remonstrating in vain with Henry on this high-handed procedure, Anselm wrote to the Abbot of St. Evroult; imploring him to recall the intruder, but without success. He then laid the case before his old friend, Archbishop Bonne Ame of Rouen, who also did not see his way to interfere. So the king had his way, and the monks of St. Edmund's were fain to make the best of "the little wolf," as Anselm, with bitter pleasantry, termed the new abbot. The affair did not tend to improve Anselm's relations with Henry.

Towards the end of the year, Guy, Archbishop of Vienne, afterwards Pope Calixtus II., made his appearance in England as legate of the Holy See. He had received his commission before the death of Rufus, and it had been already determined by virtue of Anselm's return; for it was then part of the ancient privileges of the See of Canterbury that its incumbent for the time being should, while in England, have full and exclusive legatine powers as incident to his office. Guy, therefore, left the country without disclosing the object of his mission.

Easter (1101) came, but brought with it no news from Rome; and the question of investiture and homage was accordingly again adjourned. As it happened, the delay served somewhat to strengthen Anselm's hands. The year wore on, the kingdom was agitated by rumours of an imminent invasion by Duke Robert, who had returned from the Holy Land flushed with glory, and eager to pay off old scores against his brother. He had been joined by Ranulf Flambard, who had contrived to escape from the Tower, and was now roving about the Channel in command of a squadron of privateers.

In England a powerful party among the barons, disgusted with Henry's English marriage, and no doubt, also, with his abandonment of the policy of Rufus, favoured the cause of the chivalrous duke; and of their disaffection Henry was only too well aware. To confirm their wavering loyalty, he convoked the principal tenants *in capite*, and proffered them in return for a renewal of their vows of fealty a solemn pledge on his part of just and equitable government. The barons assembled, and with one accord chose Anselm to act as intermediary between them and the king.

Thus, by the time Duke Robert's galleys sighted the English coast, the aged primate, who but a year before had been an exile and a pensioner on the bounty of the foreigner, had tendered to England's king and the flower of England's nobility, in the great hall which Rufus had built by the side of the Abbey of Westminster, the oaths which made England once more one; and when the invader, easily vanquishing the fleet which Henry had hastily gathered to oppose him, made good his landing near Portsmouth, he found himself confronted by so formidable a force that he was fain to make a hasty peace.

Anselm had accompanied Henry to the field; and throughout the anxious interval, during which the king was still uncertain how far his nobles would abide by their recent vows, or desert to the enemy, he threw the whole weight of his influence on his side; so that, if Eadmer is to be trusted—and his general trustworthiness is beyond dispute—Henry owed to him his crown, if not his life.

While the issue was still undecided, Henry was profuse in protestations that in the event of success the Church should have no more loyal son, the Pope no more obedient servant, than he; and Robert had hardly reshipped his army for Normandy, and renounced his pretensions to the throne of England, when the sincerity of the king's protestations was suddenly put to the proof.

The envoys whom he had sent to Rome returned with a letter from Pope Paschal, in which a little complimentary verbiage served merely to emphasise as high-pitched an assertion of the supernatural prerogative of the Church as could have emanated from Hildebrand himself.

"Paschal, bishop, servant of the servants of God," so ran the papal missive, "to his beloved son, Henry, King of the English, health, and apostolic benediction.

The message conveyed to us through your envoys, dearest son, we have received with joy; would also that with your promises were joined obedience. You promise, indeed, by your message to accord the Holy Roman Church within your realm those rights which she had in the days of your father, at the same time exacting from her the recognition of those prerogatives which your father had in the days of our predecessors. All which, indeed, at first sight might seem only fair, but on a closer examination, with the help of the oral explanations of your envoys, revealed itself as a grave and exorbitant demand. For this is to claim, in effect, that the Roman Church should concede to you the right and power of making bishops and abbots by investiture, so that what Almighty God has ordained shall be done by Himself alone, should become a part of the royal prerogative. For the Lord saith, *I am the door. By me if any shall enter, he shall be saved.* But when kings arrogate to themselves the function of the door, it follows of a surety that those who enter the Church by them are to be accounted not shepherds, but thieves and robbers, for the same Lord saith, *Whoso entereth not by the door into the sheepfold, but climbeth into it by another way, is a thief and a robber.* Now, in sooth, if Your Grace were to ask of us some great favour which might be conceded consistently with what we owe to God, to justice, to the weal of our order, we should very gladly grant it. But this claim is so oppressive, so prejudicial, that the Catholic Church can on no account admit it. Blessed Ambrose was prepared to suffer the extremity of torture rather than concede dominion over the Church to the emperor.

Witness his reply: 'Abuse not your mind, O Emperor, with the idea that your imperial authority extends to the things which are of God. Exalt not yourself; but if you would prolong your sway, be subject unto God. For it is written, *Render to God the things that are God's, and to Caesar the things that are Caesar's.* To the emperor belongs the palace, to the priest the Church; to you the public buildings, to the priest the House of God. What have you to do with an adulteress? And an adulteress is that church which is not united in lawful wedlock with her spouse.' Mark, O King, that church is called an adulteress which is not lawfully wedded to Christ. Now every bishop is deemed the spouse of the Church. . . . If, then, you are a son of the Church, as assuredly every Catholic Christian is, suffer your mother to contract a lawful marriage, *i.e.* suffer the Church's nuptials to be duly solemnised, not by men, but by God, and Christ the God-man. . . . And herein, O King, be not carried away by any profane imagining, as if we wished in aught to derogate from your prerogative, or to amplify our own authority in the creation of bishops. Nay, rather, if henceforth for God's sake you abandon that claim which is manifestly contrary to the law of God, which neither can you enforce with God's blessing, nor we concede with safety to ourselves or yourself, we shall readily grant whatever indulgence you may hereafter crave; so only that it be in accordance with the will of God;

and shall with zeal endeavour to promote your aggrandisement. Nor deem that your power will rest on a less firm basis, if you abandon this profane usurpation. Nay, rather your dominion will then be the more secure, the more solid, the more glorious, when God shall bear sway within your realm."

And so, commending the king to the guidance of the Almighty, the Pope brought his somewhat lengthy allocution to a close.

On reading the letter, Henry determined to convince Anselm of the true value at which a Norman prince's promises should be rated. He summoned him to court, and, in the presence of the bishops and other chief magnates of the realm, bade him do him homage, and consecrate his nominees to the vacant bishoprics and abbacies, or leave the kingdom without delay. Anselm declined to do either the one thing or the other. He could not, he said, without placing himself under the ban of excommunication, violate the canons of the Council of Rome; and, instead of leaving the realm, he would return whither his duty called him, to his diocese, there to remain until he was carried thence by force.

By this answer Henry was no little disconcerted. He was not as yet prepared to proceed to extremities against the man who had so recently saved his throne, and whose immense influence with his subjects might still be of use to him. Doubtless, also, Matilda's intercession on behalf of the refractory prelate counted for something. So Anselm was suffered to return to Canterbury and remain there in peace, while Henry's thoughts turned once more towards Rome. Perhaps, after all, he mused, if the case were restated, were solemnly argued before the Pope, some compromise might yet be arrived at. He would sound Anselm on the matter. So he wrote, inviting him to Winchester to talk the affair over amicably. To Winchester, accordingly, Anselm went, and readily assented to the proposal which the king, with the concurrence of his council, then made. Henry was to nominate three commissioners, and Anselm other two, and the five were to proceed together to Rome, and lay before the Pope the precise state of the case; to wit, that, unless he receded from his position, Anselm would certainly be remitted to exile. The envoys on the part of the king were Gerard, the new Archbishop of York, who had not as yet received his pallium, Herbert Losinga, Bishop of Norwich, and Robert, Bishop of Chester; Anselm chose for his representatives two monks, Baldwin of Le Bec, and Alexander, of Christ Church, Canterbury. The envoys carried with them an instalment of Peter-pence, and two letters from the king, one a formal application for the archbishop's pallium, the other an unequivocal and unconditional declaration of war *à outrance* in the matter of investitures and homage. Anselm also wrote to the Pontiff, explaining how he came to be represented in the embassy, and adding his testimony in favour of his brother of York, as a good and loyal churchman, in all respects worthy of the pallium.

It is needless to follow them to Rome. Suffice it to say that, except in the matter of the pallium, the mission proved a failure; that on the return of the envoys with the letter containing the Pope's definitive "*Non possumus,*" in the summer of 1102, Henry summoned Anselm to a council at London, and, ignoring the letter, required him point-blank to concede the entire question at issue or quit the realm; that Anselm thereupon demanded that the letter be read; that this the king obstinately refused, but suffered the companion letter to Anselm to be read; and that, as no means could be devised of evading its plain purport, the Archbishop of York, and his worthy *confrères* of Norwich and Chester, trumped up a lame story to the effect that the Pope had confided to them privately, by word of mouth, that it was only meant for show, and that Henry need not fear excommunication if he disregarded its contents. However transparent the duplicity of the envoys, it admitted of no immediate answer. It was in vain to urge that the papal missive spoke for itself when an Archbishop of York pledged his word that it was a mere nullity, on the strength of what had passed at an alleged private interview with the Pope. Anselm was, therefore, compelled to remit the cause once more to Rome; in the meantime, if the king chose to grant investitures, he would neither consecrate nor excommunicate the recipients. Exultant at the success of his chicane, Henry at once gave the See of Salisbury to one of his clerks named Roger, and that of Hereford to another Roger, his larderer. The larderer, dying soon afterwards, was succeeded by Reinelm, another of the royal clerks. The king now found it convenient to ignore the understanding recently arrived at, and required Anselm to consecrate these worthy persons, together with William Giffard, Bishop-elect of Winchester. The latter, it will be remembered, had been elected during Anselm's exile, but had neither consented to the election nor received investiture. On this account Anselm was not unwilling to consecrate him. The other two he, of course, declined to consecrate. Henry, however, insisted that all should be consecrated or none, and instructed the subservient Archbishop of York to perform the function, only to find himself baffled by the sudden penitence of Reinelm, who returned the ring and crosier by which he had been invested, and the constancy of William Giffard, whom neither bribes nor menaces could induce to submit to consecration without Anselm's consent. Reinelm was accordingly banished the court, and Giffard the kingdom, to find an asylum with Duke Robert in Normandy.

Meanwhile Anselm succeeded in obtaining from the king one important concession — leave to hold, at London, a convocation of clergy and laity to take in hand, in earnest, the long-delayed, and now terribly serious business of ecclesiastical reform.

At this convocation several salutary things were done. Simony was formally condemned, and Guy, Abbot of Pershore, Wimund, Abbot of Tavistock, Ealdwin, Abbot of Ramsey, were deprived for that offence, while the election of some abbots, as yet not consecrated, was avoided on the same ground. The "little wolf" was also happily ousted from St. Edmund's Abbey. Canons were also passed disqualifying bishops for holding secular courts, and regulating their dress and company, prohibiting the farming of the office of archdeacon, or the holding of that office by persons not in deacon's orders, enjoining celibacy and enforcing continence on the secular clergy, and strengthening the bonds of discipline within the cloister. Severe penalties were also enacted against all, whether clergy or laity, who should be found guilty of the hideous vice which had been so flagrant during the reign, and under the countenance, of the late king. Such, in substance, were the canons passed by the Council of London in the autumn of 1102, "which," says Eadmer, with characteristic sententious brevity, "had not been held many days before it made many transgressors in every rank of life."

CHAPTER XVIII.

THE DEADLOCK CONTINUES—ANSELM, AT HENRY'S REQUEST, UNDERTAKES A MISSION TO ROME

ON behalf of the exiled bishops, and especially of William Giffard, Anselm used his best endeavours with the king, but without success. Meanwhile the deadlock, of course, continued, until Henry, to whom it proved as little satisfactory as to Anselm, made, in mid-Lent, 1103, a pretext for visiting Canterbury, and re-opened negotiations with the primate; not obscurely hinting that were the question of his customary rights not speedily settled to his mind, unpleasant consequences would ensue.

The Pope's answer to the childish story fabricated by the Archbishop of York was, at that very time, in Anselm's possession. The seal had not, as yet, been broken, and he begged the king to let the document be opened and read.

Henry, however, had no faith in parchment. He would not even look at the letter.

"Enough of these circuitous procedures," he broke out, losing, for the moment, his self-restraint; "I demand a final determination of the cause. What have I to do with the Pope in a matter which concerns my own rights? The prerogatives which my predecessors had in this realm, the same are mine.

If any man seek to deprive me of them, let whoso loves me know for certain that that man is my enemy."

Anselm quietly replied that he had no desire to deprive the king of aught that was his; but that, not even to save his life, would he concur in the contravention of the decrees which he had heard pronounced in the Council of Rome, unless the same Holy See, from which they derived their binding authority, should issue a decree annulling the interdicts by which they were sanctioned.

Again and again Henry returned to the charge, to find the primate inflexible as adamant.

Meanwhile the protraction of the negotiations, which probably lasted some days, gave rise to rumours, speculation, and excited gossip of all kinds, so that the public mind became gravely disquieted, and the Church betook herself to prayer.

Suddenly Henry changed his tone. Convinced at last that menace was unavailing, he became conciliatory. Anselm, he urged, in a tone of entreaty—Anselm would at least go to Rome, and arrange matters, if possible, with the Pope.

Anselm, of course, did not anticipate any good result from such a mission, and probably saw, clearly enough, that the king was now chiefly concerned to remove him from the country, without taking the unpopular course of openly banishing him. He therefore proposed that the matter should be held over until Easter; then, if the bishops and magnates of the realm in council assembled concurred with the king in advising the mission, he was ready to undertake it; and, when Easter came, the unanimous vote of the council was that he should do so. He had, therefore, no option but to accept; which he did in the following terms:

"Since you are of one mind that I should go, I, though weak in body, and on the verge of old age, will not shrink from the journey, but will go whithersoever you advise, as God, the end of all, may grant me strength. But if so be that I make my way to the Apostolic Father, be assured that neither at my request, nor by my advice, will he do aught that may impair either the freedom of the churches or my honour."

The council answered, "Our lord the king will send with you his legate to make known to the Pontiff his petitions, and the concernment of the realm in these matters; your part will be merely to attest the truth of what he may say."

"What I have said I have said," rejoined Anselm; "nor, by the mercy of God, shall I be found to contradict anyone who speaks the truth."

So matters rested until the Easter celebrations were over. Then Anselm hurried his departure from a land in which, indeed, there was no longer any inducement to tarry; in which he could not even consecrate a bishop without rendering himself liable to excommunication; in which he found himself deserted by those who should have supported him, and surrounded by suspicion and intrigue, so that he dared not even open the Pope's letter lest he should find himself taxed with tampering with its contents; in which, in short, his presence was powerless for good, and a source of perpetual suffering to himself. Four days at Canterbury sufficed to make the necessary preparations for the long and hazardous journey which was before him; then taking an affectionate farewell of his faithful monks, he embarked, accompanied by Eadmer and Alexander, and on 27 April, landed at Wissant. He travelled through Normandy, and made his first considerable halt at Le Bec, renewing old friendships, reviving memories of the past, the sweeter for the suffering which had intervened. There he broke the seal of the Pope's letter, and found that it not only contained a categorical and indignant denial of the Archbishop of York's story, but placed him and his colleagues in infamy under excommunication, together with all bishops who had received consecration or investiture, pending the appeal to the Holy See. It was now more than ever evident that the mission on which he was engaged could come to nothing, and that he must make up his mind to another more or less prolonged exile. The prospect was probably not unwelcome; for the situation in England had become intolerable, and the battle of the Church could as well be fought in Rome, or Lyon, or Le Bec, as at Canterbury or Westminster. In the meantime, there was nothing for it but to possess his soul in patience, until the tedious farce of the mission was played out.

From Le Bec he journeyed by easy stages to Chartres, where he found an old friend and *alumnus* of Le Bec, in Bishop Yves, who had fought his own battle for the Church, not without suffering and eventual triumph.[1]

[1] Yves had been translated from the Abbey of St. Quentin to the See of Chartres by Pope Urban, in place of the simoniacal prelate Godfrey, in 1090; but had no little trouble with his metropolitan, Richer, Archbishop of Sens, who declined to recognise him, wrote him abusive letters, and even cited him for heresy before the Council of Etampes, in 1091. Yves appealed to the Pope, who exonerated him from the charge, and

There also he found Beauclerc's sister, the widowed Countess Adela of Blois, a devout woman, and his good friend, as will appear in the sequel. His stay at Chartres, however, was but brief. The summer heats were this year unusually severe, not only in Italy, but throughout the continent; and, by Yves' advice, Anselm, now, it must be remembered, an aged and infirm man, returned to await the autumn in the cooler air of Le Bec. From Le Bec he wrote to both Henry and Matilda, praying the one to spare the Canterbury estates, and the other to exert all her influence with her husband in behalf of the Church.[1]

By mid-August he was again on the road, and in the autumn he reached Rome. On his arrival, Paschal bade him rest a day or two at the Vatican; he then received him with all honour, and assigned him the rooms in the Lateran which had been placed at his disposal by Urban.

At Rome Anselm found the royal envoy; who proved to be our old acquaintance, William of Warelwast, busily occupied in making interest for his master in the papal court. A day was soon fixed for hearing the appeal; and Anselm listened in silence and apparent indifference while the voluble and plausible clerk magnified the dignity and munificence of the King of England, and more than hinted that the Pope would do well to conciliate his favour, while yet there was time. Paschal also allowed him to run on in this strain, until, encouraged by some signs of sympathy on the part of

confirmed him in his see. His spirited conduct in refusing to assist at the marriage of Philip I. with Bertrade, wife of Fulk, Count of Anjou amply justified Urban's choice. (Ritzke, *De Ivone Episcopo Carnotensi*, Wratislaviae.)

[1] *Epp.* iii. 79, 81.

some of the audience, he called them to witness that, be the result what it might, his lord, the King of the English, would as soon part with his kingdom as with the right of investiture. Then the Pope broke silence:

"If, as you say," he observed with quiet emphasis, "your king would as soon lose his kingdom as forego the right of ecclesiastical investiture, understand—I say it in the presence of God—that Pope Paschal would as soon lose his head as concede it to him."

Recognising at once that the Pope meant exactly what he said, Warelwast made no further attempt to argue the appeal. Paschal, however, probably at Anselm's suggestion, saw fit to grant Henry a temporary immunity from excommunication, while subjecting thereto all clerks who should take, or had taken investiture from him. The reconciliation of such offenders with the Church was left entirely in Anselm's hands. Not long afterwards, Anselm took his leave of the Pope; from whom he received with his blessing a letter, confirming to him and his successors in the See of Canterbury in perpetuity, primatial authority throughout the British Isles no less plenary than had been accorded by Gregory I. to St. Augustine.

The date of this letter, 17 November, 1103, is probably that of Anselm's departure from Rome, for he was at Lyon before Christmas. He travelled under an escort furnished by the Countess Matilda, the staunch ally in old days of both Urban and Hildebrand, now an aged woman, whose thoughts were turning towards the cloister. On his journey, or more probably from Lyon, Anselm wrote her the following eminently characteristic letter:[1]

[1] *Epp.* iv. 37.

ST. ANSELM OF CANTERBURY

"Anselm, servant of the Church of Canterbury, to his Lady and Mother in God, the Countess Matilda, uninterrupted and prolonged enjoyment of happiness in this present life, and perpetual bliss in that which is to come.

"I would thank Your Highness, but cannot find words for the purpose worthy of your merit. For, in truth, that not once only, but several times, God has through your instrumentality delivered me out of the hand of my enemies, who were waiting to take me, I acknowledge as a very great obligation. But when I consider the way in which it was done, your benignity, piety, motherly affection towards me, I perceive that it is quite beyond my power to thank you worthily. For I cannot forget the anxious prayers and entreaties with which, by my brother and son, Alexander, you besought me on no account to expose my person to peril, and the zeal with which you commanded your servants to take no less, nay, if possible, more care of my person than of your own, and to conduct me to a place of security by a circuitous and safe, rather than by a direct and hazardous route. Which they have faithfully done, understanding such to be your will. The desire of my heart, indeed, is not wanting to the utterance of my gratitude, but words and pen are inadequate to express what my heart feels. As, then, I cannot, I pray God that He will reward you, and defending you from all your enemies, temporal and spiritual, bring you to blessed and eternal security. I am ever mindful of your holy desire, with which your heart yearns towards the contempt of the world; but therewith conflicts the holy affection which you bear towards Mother Church, and which she cannot spare. Wherein it is manifest that your piety is in either way pleasing to God, and therefore you ought quietly to await some certain sign of God's will, and sustain with patience and good hope the burden which you bear in His service. This, however, I take upon myself to advise, that if in the meantime, which God avert, you should discover yourself to be in imminent danger of death, you should give yourself entirely to God before leaving this life, and to that end should have ever ready at hand a secret veil. Be my words as they may, this is my prayer, this the desire of my heart, that God should commit you to no other than His own disposal and guidance. Your Highness sent me word by my son, Alexander aforesaid, that the prayers or meditations which I have composed, and which I thought you had, you have not; and therefore I send them to you. May Almighty God ever guide and guard you with His blessing."

CHAPTER XIX.

ANOTHER TERM OF EXILE AT LYON—THE BEGINNING OF THE END

ANSELM travelled by Florence and Piacenza, and at the latter place was joined by William of Warelwast, who accompanied him across the Mont Cenis, and as far as Lyon. There the Saint halted for Christmas; and, as he took leave of Warelwast, who was bound in hot haste for the north, he learned from him that his stay might be protracted at his pleasure.

"I had thought," said the Norman significantly, "that our cause would have had another issue at Rome, and therefore I deferred until now communicating to you a message with which my lord charged me for you. Now, as I am in haste to depart, I will no longer keep it secret. He says then, that he will welcome your return to England, if you come back prepared to shew yourself such in all respects towards him as your predecessors were towards his predecessors."

"You have no more to say?" said Anselm.

"I speak to a man of sense. I have no more to say," replied the other.

"I know what you mean," rejoined Anselm; "I understand."

EXILE AT LYON

Thus Anselm entered on his second period of exile. He resumed his former place in the household of Archbishop Hugh, and lost no time in making his intentions clear to Henry in the following letter:

"To his revered Lord, Henry, King of the English, Anselm, Archbishop of Canterbury, his faithful service and prayers.

"Although you may learn through William of Warelwast what we did at Rome, yet I will briefly set forth so much as relates to myself. I came to Rome, I explained to the Pope the reason wherefor I had come; he replied that he was determined on no account to depart from the decrees of his predecessors, and moreover he enjoined me to have no communion with those who should receive investiture of churches from your hands after notice of this prohibition, unless they should do penance, and surrender what they had received, and therewith all thought of reinstatement. He also forbade me to hold communion with the bishops who had consecrated such persons, unless they submitted themselves to the jurisdiction of the Apostolic See. Of all this William aforesaid may, if he will, be witness. Which William, after we had severally left Rome, admonished me on your part, reminding me of the love and goodwill which you have ever borne towards me, that I should so order myself as that I might return to England on the same footing on which my predecessor stood with your father; in which case you would treat me in the same honourable and liberal spirit in which your father had treated my predecessor. Wherefrom I gathered that unless I was prepared so to order myself, you did not desire my return to England. For your love and goodwill I thank you. But assume the same relations with you which my predecessor had with your father, I cannot; for I can neither do you homage, nor by reason of the prohibition aforesaid made in my hearing, hold communion with those who have received investiture of churches from your hands. Wherefore I pray you, if it please you, to let me know your will whether it be possible for me to return to England on the terms I have indicated, with your peace and in the plenitude of the authority which belongs to my office. For I am ready, to the extent of my powers and skill, faithfully and in all due subjection to your authority to discharge the trust committed to me by the will of God in your behalf, and that of your people. But if it shall not please you to receive me on these terms, I suppose that any loss of souls that may result will not be imputable to my fault.

"May God Almighty so reign in your heart as that you may reign for ever in His grace."

This letter Anselm took the precaution to draught in triplicate. The original he of course sent direct to the king. Of the two copies one went with his seal to his faithful friend Gundulf, Bishop of Rochester, that in the not unlikely event of the authenticity of the original being disputed, the means might be at hand of attesting it. Gundulf was to shew it to William of Warelwast and Ernulf, Prior of Christ Church, Canterbury, but to none other until the king had seen the original. Then he was to shew it to the bishops. The other copy was transmitted to Ernulf with instructions to keep it secret until the king had shewn his hand, when it was to be forthwith published. By these means Anselm hoped to defeat the chicane which he had too good reason to anticipate.[1]

Meanwhile William of Warelwast sped northward bearing the following letter from the Pope to the king:

[1] *Epp.* iv. 34, 40.

"Paschal, bishop, servant of the servants of God, to the illustrious and glorious King of the English, Henry, health and apostolical benediction.

"By the letter which you lately sent us through your confidential agent, and our beloved son William, the clerk, we were apprised both of your well-being and of the happy successes which the Divine benignity has accorded you by the overthrow of your enemies. We learned, moreover, that your desires had been gratified by your noble and religious consort giving birth to a male child. And overjoyed as we are by the news, we think the occasion opportune to inculcate upon you, with some earnestness, the precepts and the will of God; seeing that it is now manifest to you in how extraordinary a degree you are indebted to the favour of God. We also would fain unite our own goodwill towards you with the Divine favour, but are distressed that you seem to demand from us what we by no means can grant. For were we to give our consent or permission to the granting of investitures by Your Excellency, the danger would, without doubt, be enormous both to us and to you. In which matter we would have you consider what you would lose by not granting them, or gain by granting them. For, in making this prohibition, we neither exact from the churches a more strict obedience, nor obtain for ourselves an ampler freedom, nor seek to derogate in aught from your rightful power or authority, but only that the wrath of God to youward may be lessened, and that so all your affairs may prosper. For the Lord saith, *I will honour those who honour me. But those who contemn me shall be of no reputation.* You will say, however, *This is part of my prerogative.* Nay, not so; it belongs not to earthly sovereignty, imperial or royal, but to God. His alone it is, who said, *I am the Door.* Wherefore in His name, whose this office is, I call upon you to surrender it to Him. To Him resign it, to whose love you owe all that is yours. As for us, why should we oppose your will, close the avenues to your grace, were it not that we know that to concur with you in this matter were to resist the will, to forfeit the grace, of

God? Why should we deny to you aught that might rightly be conceded to mortal man, seeing the extraordinary favours which we have received from you? Consider, dearest Son, whether it redound to your honour or dishonour, that on this account the wisest and most devout of the Gallican bishops, Anselm, Bishop of Canterbury, fears to adhere to you, to abide in your kingdom. What will they, with whom your reputation has hitherto stood so high, think of you, say of you, when this fame is bruited abroad far and wide? Why, the very men who, in your presence, applaud your exorbitant claims, will of a surety be the most strenuous in denouncing them when they have left your presence. Back, then, dearest Son, back to your own heart; for God's sake, and His mercy, and for the love of the Only-begotten, recall your pastor, we pray you, recall your father. And if, what we do not anticipate, when you have abandoned the claim to grant investitures, he should shew himself severe towards you in any respect, we, so far as may consist with the will of God, will incline him to your will. Of you we ask only that you should set yourself and your kingdom free from the stain of his banishment. This done, then whatever you may crave of us, though it be weighty, so only it may be conceded without offence to God, you shall assuredly obtain; and with the Lord's help we will be mindful to pray to Him for you, and, by the merits of the holy apostles, will procure absolution from sin, and indulgence for you and your consort. Your son also, whom your noble and glorious consort has borne you, to whom, as we have heard, you have given the name of your illustrious father, William, we will cherish with such assiduity that whoso shall wrong him, it shall be as if he had wronged the Roman Church. The course which you propose to adopt in regard to these matters for the honour of God and the glory of His Church, we beg you to communicate to us, without delay, through the medium of such legates whose accuracy may be relied upon by us and you.

"Given at the Lateran, 23 Nov."

On receipt of this letter, followed at no great interval by that of Anselm, Henry's first thought was how to gain time. Anselm was now aged, and worn by vigils, austerities, anxieties. His life might drop at any moment, and then a more pliable primate might surely be found. He must, therefore, be kept where he was until that auspicious event should happen.

So he sent Anselm, in the first instance, what appears (for the letter is lost) to have been nothing more than a formal ratification of Warelwast's message; then after a considerable interval he wrote to him, briefly indeed, but in the suavest possible terms, regretting that they should still be separated—there was no mortal man whom he would so gladly have in his dominions as Anselm, if Anselm would but consent to his terms—intimating that he was about to send yet another embassy to Rome, in the hope of at length arranging matters with the Pope, and in the meantime making Anselm an allowance out of the Canterbury revenues, a delicate hint that they were to be confiscated.[1]

Nor was it long before a Canterbury monk brought tidings of the sequestration of the entire temporalities of the see. Then followed doleful accounts of the sacrilege and rapine that stalked abroad throughout the province, mixed with bitter reproaches, natural enough in men unversed in State secrets, that Anselm should in such a crisis desert the Church of God. To the monks Anselm replied in a long and confidential letter, setting forth the true state of the case; to the king somewhat briefly, and in a tone designed to prepare the royal mind for excommunication.

Meanwhile Queen Matilda was busy attempting to

[1] This letter is in Anselm's correspondence, *Epp.* iii. 94.

mediate between Anselm and the king. To Anselm she addressed the following moving appeal:

"To the truly exalted Lord and Father, Anselm, by the grace of God, Archbishop of Canterbury, Matilda, Queen of the English, his lowly handmaid, the tribute of her most devoted service.

"Lord, Father, holy and compassionate, convert, I pray you, my lamentation into joy, and clothe me once more with happiness. Lo! my Lord, your humble handmaid prostrates herself before the knees of your mercy, and stretches forth her suppliant hands to you, soliciting the tender regard of your wonted benignity.

"Come, my Lord, come, and visit your servant; come, I say, my Father, and let my groans cease, my tears be wiped away, my grief be assuaged, my lamentation have an end, the desire of my heart be satisfied, my prayers answered. But, you will say, I am withheld by law, fast bound in the fetters of certain canons, decrees of my elders, which I dare not transgress. Nay but, bethink you, Father, of the Apostle of the Gentiles, the vessel of election, how, though he strove might and main for the abrogation of the law, yet he did not scruple to sacrifice in the Temple, lest he should give offence to those of the circumcision who believed; how, though he condemned circumcision, he yet circumcised Timothy, that he might become all things to all men. How, then, should his disciple be blameworthy, if as a son of mercy he exposed himself to the risk of death for the redemption of those in bondage. You see your brothers, servants with you of the same Master; you see the people of your Lord suffering shipwreck, tottering now on the very verge of ruin, and you succour them not; you hold not out to them the right hand; you brave not the struggle. Was not the Apostle ready to pray that he might be accursed from Christ for the sake of his brethren?

"So, my good Lord and devout Father, moderate this your severity, and soften, forgive me for so saying, your iron heart.

Come and visit your people, and, among them, your handmaid, who, with all her heart, yearns after you. Find out a way in which you, our shepherd, may advance without offence, and yet the prerogatives of the Crown be respected. Or if no such compromise is possible, come, then, at least, as a father to your daughter, as a lord to your handmaid, and teach her how she should act. Come to her before she leaves the world, for should it so chance that I should die without seeing you—I speak as a sinful woman—I fear lest, even in that land of living delights, I should be cut off from all occasion of rejoicing. You, indeed, are my joy, my hope, my refuge. Without you my soul is like an arid desert; wherefore to you have I stretched forth my hands that you may sprinkle its waste places with the oil of exultation, and drench it with the dew of eternal sweetness. If, however, neither my tears nor my uttered prayers avail to move you, I will lay aside my regal dignity, divest myself of the insignia of my rank, and scorning guards and diadem, and spurning purple and fine linen, will in tribulation of heart make my way to you. The ground you have trodden I will embrace; your feet I will kiss; nor shall Giezi, though he come, separate me from you till the longing of my heart is satisfied. The peace of God which passeth all understanding keep your heart and mind, and fill your soul with the abundance of compassion."[1]

We have not Anselm's answer to the well-meant but misconceived exhortations of the warm-hearted queen; but, from their subsequent correspondence, it is manifest that he satisfied her of his inability to comply with her wishes, and showed her that her duty lay in remaining at court and using her influence in favour of the Church, rather than in making a romantic pilgrimage to Lyon. But in this enterprise she had another and a stronger man than Henry to reckon with; for the mantle of Ranulf Flambard had fallen upon one, who, if less

[1] This letter is also in Anselm's correspondence, *Epp.* iii. 93.

unscrupulous, was no less resolute than he. This was Robert de Beaumont, Count of Meulan, the *doyen* of the Norman noblesse, who had now gained a complete ascendancy over the king. Starker knight never brandished battle-axe, and at the council board he was as sagacious and as resolute as he was gallant in the field. Nearly forty years before his had been the arm that clove the way through the English stockade at Senlac, and his prowess had been rewarded with many a broad acre in the midland shires. On the continent he had succeeded to the important fiefs of Pont Audemer, Beaumont (now Beaumont le Roger), Meulan, the key of the Vexin, and Brionne sur Rille. He had rendered Rufus signal service in his campaigns in Normandy, Maine, and France. He had adhered steadfastly to Henry during the anxious time which immediately succeeded his coronation. To Anselm he was well known, was indeed one of his earliest acquaintances in those northern parts, and had been foiled by him in a certain not very creditable design he had once entertained upon the *seigneury* of Le Bec. He was now a gaunt, ascetic man, no friend to the gluttonous Saxon; a Norman of Normans, not undevout, but somewhat jealous of the priesthood, and especially of the Papacy. He had consistently supported the royal prerogative, both at Rockingham and at Winchester, and he was now determined that the battle should be fought out to the end. Under such conditions, Matilda's mediation, of course, came to nothing; and the king's new mission to Rome, which, after due procrastination, was at length got under weigh, was only intended to prolong the suspense.

Anselm, meanwhile, had his trusty agent, Baldwin,

at Rome, invested with plenary power to represent him in the Papal presence, and had commissioned John, Bishop of Tusculum, and another John, a cardinal, to add their instances to those of Baldwin in his behalf. Their representations of the need of prompt action were reinforced by urgent letters from the Queen of England and the Countess of Tuscany; yet unaccountably the Pope stayed his hand. He seemed to have abandoned Anselm to his fate. Yet, though sick at heart with hope deferred, the heroic primate strove manfully to sustain, by his animating letters, the fainting courage of his suffering children in England; nor faltered for an instant in his resolution, or lost his habitual serenity of tone.

So month after month wore away; and the spring of 1105 found Anselm still at Lyon, when, like a bolt from the blue, came the following letter from Paschal:

"Paschal, bishop, servant of the servants of God, to our venerable Brother Anselm, Archbishop of Canterbury, health and apostolical benediction.

"By the wrong done to you, the members of the Church suffer no little, since, as saith the Apostle, if one member suffer, the other members suffer with it. For, though we are separated from you in bodily presence, yet we are one, having one and the same head. For your wrongs, your repulses, are to us as our own. It also gravely distresses us that the realm of England should be deprived of your pious care. For sheep left without a shepherd the wolf devours and scatters. Hence we are solicitous to compass your return by all means in our power. Wherefore, in a council lately holden, it has been decreed, with the common consent of our brethren in the episcopate, that the advisers of the king, by whom he is impelled upon his evil course in the matter of investitures, and those who have received investiture from him, should be excommunicated ; because they attempt to change the freedom of the Church into bondage. Which sentence we, under the guidance of the Holy Spirit, have promulgated against the Count of Meulan and his accomplices, and confirm the same, under the guidance of the same Holy Spirit, against those who have received investiture from the king. The king's sentence has been delayed by reason that he ought to have sent us his envoys at Easter of last year.

"Given at the Lateran, 26 March."[1]

The blow had fallen tardily, but it had fallen ; and it was proof that Anselm was not deserted. Hope revived, and he determined to draw nearer the scene of action.

[1] The last clause is somewhat obscure. The royal envoys had been expected about Easter, 1104, but had not made their appearance.

CHAPTER XX.

PEACE AT LAST

THE scene shifts, as the novelists say, to Normandy, where Henry was now engaged in a somewhat squalid kind of crusade against Duke Robert. That gallant and adventurous, but prodigal and luxurious prince, had mismanaged matters sadly in the duchy—had, in fact, allowed it to lapse into chronic anarchy, and in its desperate condition Henry had discerned not merely the opportunity of extending his dominion under pretext of restoring order to a distracted land, but also the means of strengthening his hands against the Church. The Pope would think twice—nay, thrice—so doubtless he reasoned, before excommunicating the conqueror of Normandy, the champion of its suffering Church. So Holy Week, 1105, found him at Barfleur, surrounded by his long-haired knights; and on Holy Saturday, in the little church at Carentan, Bishop Serlo of Séez witnessed his solemn vow to give peace to the Norman Church—nay, saw him kneel, and after him the flower of his chivalry, while a common pair of scissors, deftly manipulated by the episcopal fingers, set the seal on their sincerity, by relieving them of their redundant locks.

His enterprise thus blessed by Holy Church, Henry had opened the campaign with vigour. From Holy

Week to Whitsuntide is no long interval, but it sufficed for the burning of Bayeux, the reduction of Caen, and the investment of Falaise. Falaise, however, held out stoutly; and Henry was still before its walls when couriers arrived from his sister Adela, Countess of Blois, with tidings which caused him no little disquietude—to wit, that he must prepare for excommunication.

On leaving Lyon, Anselm had set his face towards Reims; halting, however, at La Charité sur Loire, he had learned that the Countess Adela, whose spiritual director he had been, and to whom he was much beholden for pecuniary aid during both his present and his former exile, was dangerously ill in her castle at Blois, and craved a visit from him. Such a request was by no means to be denied, and Anselm accordingly hastened to Blois. There he had found the countess convalescent, but at her instance had tarried some days in the castle, and in the course of conversation had disclosed to her the object of his northward journey. The time had come, he had frankly told her, when the wrong which, now for two years and more, her brother had done to God in his person, must be avenged by excommunication. Much distressed, the countess had at once assumed the office of mediatrix, had accompanied him to Chartres, and thence had sent forward her couriers to Falaise, to acquaint her brother with the posture of affairs.

To be excommunicated just at the time when, to his own profit, he was playing the part of devout son of the Church, was by no means to Henry's mind. Moreover, the Church had undeniably gained of late in prestige and power. He had before his eyes the example of his brother, Philip of France, who, after struggling for ten years against the papal anathema, had been reduced at last to make public submission to the Church with bare feet and bowed head, at the recent Council of Paris (2 Dec., 1104). Nay, a greater potentate than Philip, even he who had once wielded the whole might of the Holy Roman Empire, and had wrestled mightily, and at last not unsuccessfully, with Gregory VII., even he now cowered beneath Paschal's excommunication; and, shunned as a leper by his prelates, his nobles, his very son—that younger son, Henry, to whom he had given Conrad's birthright—sat moodily at Mainz, musing what the end might be. At such a juncture, the very suspicion of impending excommunication could not fail to disconcert all Henry's plans; the thing itself might cost him his crown.

It was evidently time to adopt a conciliatory attitude. He, therefore, gathered his barons together, and, with their concurrence, replied to his sister's message by inviting her to bring Anselm with her into Normandy, and condescending to hint that an interview with him might have the happiest results.

So at Laigle, half-way between Falaise and Chartres, the king, on 22 July, met the countess and the archbishop. What passed at that interview we know not in detail, but the upshot was, on Henry's part, nothing less than unconditional surrender. Without, apparently, stipulation of any kind he gave Anselm restitution of the temporalities, and restored him to his favour. Then emerged the awkward question—which, in his haste to make peace, the king had ignored—of the position of those clerks who had received investiture from him during Anselm's exile. What would be Anselm's attitude towards them in the event of his return to England?

They were one and all excommunicate. But Henry could not, in honour, desert them. Anselm, he urged, must restore them to communion. But this, of course, Anselm could not promise on his own responsibility. So, without breach of amity, it was arranged that he should remain on the continent until the Pope's decision could be obtained. Some days later Anselm, who from first to last was treated by Henry with every show of distinction, left Laigle for Le Bec, there to await the return of the envoys who were to proceed to Rome.

With due dispatch, it would have been possible to obtain the Pope's decision in less than six months; in point of fact, it took a full year to do so, for, though Henry was as good as his word in the matter of the Canterbury estates, which he at once released from sequestration, he was by no means disposed to accelerate a final settlement of the dispute. Delay, delay, delay, that was the keynote of his ecclesiastical policy. Several weeks, therefore, passed before he so much as notified to Anselm, who, in the meantime, had shifted his quarters to Reims, the name of the envoy, our old friend William of Warelwast, whom he had chosen to represent him at the Curia. When he did so, he suggested that Anselm should nominate Baldwin to accompany him, but fixed no date for their departure. In reply, Anselm pointedly drew attention to this omission, adding that if the king's envoy were not on his way to Rome before Christmas, his own would certainly leave without him.

This had the desired effect, and by Christmas Warelwast and Baldwin were actually on their way to Rome.

Meanwhile Henry, having failed to complete the subjugation of Normandy, had returned to England to raise funds for a new campaign. His fiscal methods, and their effect upon the country, are described by Eadmer, from the report of eye-witnesses, with unusual vivacity.

"The tax-gatherers," he says, "had respect neither for religion nor for humanity, but levied an oppressive and exorbitant contribution from all by barbarous means. Those who had nothing to give were either turned out of their humble dwellings, or, their house doors torn from their hinges and taken away, were left entirely unprotected against violence, or were reduced to total penury by the confiscation of their paltry belongings, or were, in other ways, subjected to extreme and cruel hardship. Against others, who seemed to have something to lose, novel accusations were devised, and, as they dared not plead their cause against the king, they witnessed with heavy hearts the confiscation of their goods. Some will, perhaps, think these matters the less worthy of remark because they were not peculiar to Henry's reign, but many similar things had been done in his brother's time, to say nothing of his father. But they seemed the more grievous and less tolerable, because much less was now raised from a people already exhausted by spoliation. Moreover, at the Council of London, as we said above, celibacy and continence were enjoined upon all the priests and canons of England, many of whom had transgressed this decree during Anselm's exile, either keeping their women, or, at least, resuming intercourse with them. This offence the king would not suffer to go unpunished, but bade his agents implead the accused, and take money from them in expiation of their wrong-doing. But, as many of them turned out to be innocent of the offence, the funds which it was sought in this way to raise for the use of the king proved less abundant than the tax-gatherers had anticipated. So, changing their methods, and condemning the innocent with the guilty, they laid every parish church under contribution, and held it to ransom in a fixed sum for the parson who ministered in it. Lamentable scenes ensued. While the storm of exaction raged most fiercely, and some, who either had nothing to give, or, to manifest their execration of unheard-of injustice, refused to give anything for such a purpose, were insulted, arrested, thrown into prison, tortured, it chanced that the king himself came to London. Upon which occasion, as he was passing to his palace, some priests, to the number, it is said, of nearly two hundred, barefooted, but wearing their albs and sacerdotal stoles, presented themselves before him, with one voice imploring him to have mercy upon them. But he, preoccupied, as happens, with a multiplicity of cares, was in no way moved to pity by their prayers, nor even deigned to accord them the honour of an answer of any kind; but, treating them as men entirely without religion, ordered them to be summarily removed from his presence. Overwhelmed with confusion, they had recourse to the queen, whom they besought to intercede with the king on their behalf. She, it is said, was moved to tears by pity, but refrained, through fear, from intercession."

Henry's usurpation of jurisdiction in ecclesiastical cases did not, of course, pass without protest on Anselm's part; and equally, of course, the protest was unavailing. The gravity of the situation, however, brought at last even his suffragans to his side, as appears from the following letter:

"To their Father, dearly beloved, Anselm, Archbishop of Canterbury: Gerard, Archbishop of York; Robert, Bishop of Chester; Herbert, Bishop of Norwich; Ralph, Bishop of Chichester; Samson, Bishop of Worcester; and William, Bishop-elect of Winchester, greeting.

"We have endured, hoping for peace, and it has receded farther from us; we have looked for good things, and our anxiety has increased. The ways of Sion lament because the uncircumcised tread them. The temple mourns because the laity have broken into the holy of holies, and invaded the very altar. Arise, as did of old the aged Mattathias; you have in your sons the valour of Judas, the strenuousness of Jonathan, the wisdom of Simon. They, with you, will fight the battle of the Lord; and, if before us you should be gathered to your fathers, we will receive from your hand the heritage of your labour. But now is no time for delay. Why tarry you in a foreign land while your sheep perish without a shepherd? No longer will God hold you excused; for not only are we ready to follow, but, if you so bid, to go before you. Come, then, to us—come quickly; or bid us, or some of us, come to you, lest, while we are separated from you, the counsels of those who seek their own should deflect you from the straight course. For ourselves, in this matter, we seek not our own, but the things of God."

To this Anselm replied as follows:

"Anselm, Archbishop of Canterbury, to his friends and brethren in the episcopate, whose letter he has received, greeting.

"I condole and sympathise with you in the tribulations which you and the Church of England endure; but at present I cannot come to your aid, as I, no less than you, desire; because I cannot tell what may be the scope and extent of my power until, through our envoys, whose early return from Rome I now anticipate, I learn what they have been able to effect with the Pope. Good, nevertheless, it is, and grateful to me that, at length, you recognise the pass to which your long-suffering, to use a mild term, has brought you, and that you promise me your aid in what is not my cause, but God's, and invite me to come to you without delay. For, though I cannot so do, because the king will not have me in England, unless I disobey the Pope's mandate in order to obey his will, and I am not yet certain what my powers are, as I have said; yet I rejoice by reason of the good will and constancy, worthy of your episcopal office, which you promise, and the exhortation wherewith you exhort me. But as to your suggestion that I should summon some of you to me, lest, while we are parted from one another, my judgment should be perverted by those who seek their own interest, I conceive that there is no present occasion so to do. For I trust in God that no one will be able to divert my mind from the truth, so far as I know it; and that God will soon shew me what to do; which I will then, as soon as may be, notify to you. How to act in the meantime your own wisdom may suffice to instruct you: one thing only I say, that I, as I know my own conscience and have hope in God, would not, to ransom my life, give countenance or furtherance to the injustice which, I hear, has recently been decreed against the Church of England. Farewell."

This letter was probably written at Rouen, where Anselm awaited the return of the envoy from Rome. His old friend, Archbishop Bonne Ame, had, by some breaches of discipline, incurred suspension from office, and Anselm had availed himself of the opportunity afforded by the despatch of the envoys to intercede on his behalf with the Pope. Hence it was that the papal letter which set Anselm free to return to England, also detained him a while longer in Normandy, by remitting to him the decision of Bonne Ame's case. The letter which was read by William of Warelwast to a synod at Rouen, in the summer of 1106, was as follows:

"Paschal, bishop, servant of the servants of God, to his venerable Brother Anselm, Bishop of Canterbury, greeting and apostolical benediction.

"Since Almighty God has deigned to incline the heart of the English King towards obedience to the Apostolic See, we give thanks for His mercy to the same Lord, in whose hand are the hearts of men. This, without doubt, we impute to the influence of your love, and the importunity of your prayers, that in this respect the Divine compassion should have regard to that people which is the object of your solicitude. Our conduct in so far condescending towards the king and those who seem to be guilty, know to be prompted by compassion, and a desire to place ourselves in a position to raise the prostrate. For none by extending his hand towards the fallen will ever raise him so long as he himself stands erect, but he must first bend towards him. For the rest, though bending seems to tend in the direction of a fall, yet it does not lose the quality of uprightness. Accordingly we release you, Brother in Christ most venerable and dear, from the scope of the canon, or, as you conceive it, excommunication decreed by our predecessor, Pope Urban, of holy memory, against investitures and homage. Those who have received investiture, or consecrated those who have done so, or done homage, having made such satisfaction as we notify to you by the joint envoys, William and Baldwin, men faithful and veracious, receive, the Lord helping you. You have our authority to consecrate them, or to demit their consecration to such as you may appoint, unless you should find in them some other sufficient reason for excluding them from the sacred ministry. For the rest, excommunicate the Abbot of Ely, as long as he shall presume to hold the abbacy into which, in contempt of our prohibition pronounced in his hearing, he has presumed to intrude himself by a new investiture. But such as hereafter shall receive preferments without investiture, even though they do homage to the king, let them by no means on that account be refused consecration, until, by the grace of Almighty God, the king, his heart at length softened by the gentle rain of your admonitions, may consent to forego this ceremony. Towards the bishops who brought back, as you know, a false report of our words, we feel no slight resentment, not only because they did us wrong, but also because they deceived not a few simple folk, and urged the king on a course of action at variance with the tender regard due to the Apostolic See. Wherefore, the Lord being our helper, we will not suffer their crime to go unpunished. Yet, because our son, the king, is more than ordinarily instant with us on their behalf, even to them you will not refuse communion, until they receive our precept to repair to us. The king and his consort, and the nobles who at our instance have laboured, and still strive to labour in the interest of the Church about the king, whose names you will learn from William of Warelwast, you will absolve, according to our promise, from their penances and sins. And now, since Almighty God has vouchsafed to us to effect so great a reform in the realm of England, to His glory and that of His Church, be it your care for the future to bear yourself towards the king and his nobles with such gentleness, discretion, wisdom, and foresight, that what still remains to reform may, with the help of God, be reformed by your zeal and solicitude. In which undertaking know that our support is with you in such sense that what you shall loose we will loose, and what you shall bind we will bind. The case of the Bishop of Rouen, and the inhibition justly laid upon him, we have committed to your decision. Whatever indulgence you may allow him we allow. God keep you safe, our Brother, for many years to come.

"Given 23 March."

This letter, it is to be observed, bates not a jot of the papal claim in the matter of investiture: it merely empowers Anselm to make the best of a bad situation by dealing gently with existing offenders, and to tolerate homage for the future, provided it be not coupled with investiture. Meanwhile, Anselm and the papal party at court are to labour incessantly to procure the entire emancipation of the Church.

This timely irenicon not only smoothed the way for Anselm's return to England, but, by the substantial concession made in regard to homage, laid the basis for a durable settlement of a dispute of which both king and Pontiff were now heartily weary. Henry sent Warelwast to Anselm, inviting him, in handsome terms, no longer to delay his return. He started accordingly, but fell ill at Jumièges, and was compelled to return to Le Bec. There he grew worse, and lay for some time between life and death. The grave news brought from Henry the following letter, which bears apparent traces of Matilda's inspiration:

> "Henry, by the grace of God, King of the English, to Anselm, Archbishop of Canterbury, his dearest Father, greeting and amity.
>
> "Know, kind Father, that your bodily suffering and infirmity occasions me the extreme grief which it ought. And know, also, that, had I not awaited your return, I should now have been in Normandy. For delighted had I been, could I have found you in my country before leaving it; now, however, I make my prayer to you, as a son to a father, that you be more indulgent to the flesh for a while, and macerate not your body, as you are wont. I also will and enjoin that you exercise the same authority throughout my Norman possessions as on your own estates, and glad shall I be if you will do so. Await me now in Normandy, for I am about to cross.
>
> "Witness, WALDERIC, at Windsor."[1]

In the course of a month Anselm was sufficiently recovered to return from Jumièges to Le Bec, but only to suffer an alarming relapse. Hearing that he was at the point of death, Henry, now in Normandy, hurried to Le Bec to receive his parting benediction; but the danger was past when he arrived, and on the Feast of the Assumption (15 August) he heard the still feeble, but convalescent, primate say mass in the abbey church. After the office, the negotiations suspended at Laigle

[1] From Anselm's correspondence, *Epp.* iv. 75.

were resumed with the happiest results. The king shewed himself fully disposed to reciprocate the conciliatory attitude adopted by the Pope. He definitively renounced the policy of pillage, and made the Church of God free throughout the length and breadth of England. The work of that day was to Anselm the best of all restoratives, and after a fortnight's repose he was able to face the fatigues of the journey to England. So, taking with him his old and dear friend, Boso, with whom he was wont to say he would rather live in a desert than without him in a palace, he crossed from Wissant to Dover early in September. At Dover he was met, amid the universal and jubilant acclaim of high and low, by Queen Matilda, who, with every mark of filial piety, attended him to Canterbury. There, in due time, he received from Henry a letter announcing the signal victory of Tinchebrai, gained on 28 September, the fortieth anniversary of the Conqueror's landing at Pevensey. This success, which the king piously ascribed to the Divine favour, and the faithful were not slow to connect with the primate's return to England, completed the subjugation of Normandy.

CHAPTER XXI.

THE CONCORDAT—LAST FRUIT FROM AN OLD TREE—THE END

AT Eastertide, 1107, Henry celebrated at London, with no small pomp and circumstance, his triumph over his brother. In his capacity of first grandee of the realm, Anselm was fain to assist at the tedious ceremonies, but at their close he gladly sought relief in the quietude of St. Edmund's Abbey. His stay there was protracted by an attack of fever until Whitsuntide, and a convocation which was to have been then holden was postponed to allow time for his complete recovery. It assembled on 1 August "in the palace of the king, at London," by which our informant, Eadmer, probably intends Westminster Hall, as the Tower of London does not appear to have been as yet used as a royal residence. Though it sat for but three days, it was no ordinary convocation, but a council of the principal notables of the realm in Church and State, the king himself presiding. Anselm, still barely convalescent, absented himself during the first two days, which were spent in discussing the terms of the concordat arranged at Laigle; nor did they pass without severe scrutiny by the still strong and numerous antipapal party.

Henry, however, was faithful to his royal word;

and on the third day, in Anselm's presence, formally renounced the right of investiture; upon which Anselm, with equal solemnity, gave his assurance that homage done by a spiritual person upon his election to an office in the Church, should thenceforth be no bar to his consecration.

To this arrangement, ratified by the general consent of the council, effect was at once given by the institution of bishops (without investiture by ring and crosier) to most of the sees then vacant in England, and some Norman sees.

A week later—viz. on Sunday, 11 August—the metropolitan Church of Canterbury was gladdened by the novel sight of the consecration by the primate, assisted by the Archbishop of York, and six suffragans, of no fewer than five bishops-elect, to wit, William Giffard, Roger the Chancellor, William of Warelwast, Reinelm, and Urban, to their respective sees of Winchester, Salisbury, Exeter, Hereford, and Glamorgan.

By the concordat thus ratified and sealed, and which governed, so far as law could govern, the collation of ecclesiastical offices, the Church, for all that has been written to the contrary, was a substantial gainer. In the article of investiture, the question of principle, which in matters spiritual is always the question of substance, her victory was complete; while the homage which she consented to tolerate was probably, from the first, in the form defined in the reign of Henry II. at the Council of Clarendon, *i.e.* was accompanied by express reservation of the rights of the spirituality. Probably, also, it did not, as it certainly did not when Littleton wrote his classical treatise on Tenures, involve the humiliating *intromissio manuum*, whereby a lay homager made himself the man of his feudal lord. And if the king retained a prepotent voice in the election of the archbishops, bishops, and mitred abbots, it must be remembered that from first to last of the controversy the question of freedom of election had not been mooted.

It was the day of small things; the emancipation of the Church, as events were soon to prove, was far from complete; but the true measure of her gain is the magnitude of the evil which she averted; and that was nothing less than the total forfeiture of her existence as a spiritual power. Thus the victory rested with her, and that victory was emphatically won by Anselm.

It is no disparagement of either Urban or Paschal, whose energies were absorbed by the mightier and more momentous contest with the emperor, to say that but for the indomitable tenacity with which, through fourteen years of persecution, exile, isolation, he maintained their standard in the North, the twelfth century would have seen the Church in England effectually reduced to the position of a royal peculiar, and the spiritual heritage of our race squandered upon the minions of a feudal court.

We English, having been from time immemorial a stiff-necked, restless, fighting folk, are very proud of the native vigour, the high courage, the resolute independence of spirit, which have prompted so many of our race in every age to rough-hew their own destiny according to their own heart's desire; bidding defiance to all human authority, whether political, social, intellectual, or spiritual, in the constitution of which they had not their voice or vote; resisting every encroachment upon their rights with the same obstinate determination as if the fate of the nation was at stake; of all this we are proud, and justly proud; for it has made and kept us at once free, progressive, and conservative, has wrung for us from Nature her most jealously-guarded secrets, stretched our dominion to the ends of the earth, and whitened every land with the bones of our adventurers. Not ignobly, then, do we boast of this temper of high self-reliance, of sober self-respect, which is the dominant note of our national character. May it ever so continue to be. But, perhaps, we are too apt to forget that there are interests higher even than the maintenance of individual freedom, of national integrity, the conciliation of order and progress, the exploration of Nature, the foundation and sway of empires; and that to safeguard them are needed men of another mould, men whose eyes are ever set on that which by most of us is ignored, or, at best, but fitfully regarded, men who hold firm as seeing the invisible; who, lacking, perhaps, the incentives to heroic action, draw from absorption in a spiritual ideal a constancy more than heroic; and who thus, from conflicts not of their seeking, sustained by a strength not their own, emerge, at length, spent, perhaps, and suffering, broken, it may be, but triumphant. Of such was Anselm of Canterbury; and should the time ever come when the memory and example of men of his type, whatever forms they thought in, whatever cause they fought in, shall cease to be treasured by us among our most sacred heirlooms; then, no matter how strong our arm, how vast our material resources, how exuberant our intellectual life, the hour of our decadence will have struck.

THE CONCORDAT

The brief remainder of Anselm's days was spent in comparative tranquillity. Not only the king, but the Count of Meulan, was now in a measure won over to his side. So, though he still retained his influence with the king, and used it to prevent the preferment of Englishmen to offices in the Church, he offered no opposition to the several reforms which Anselm had more especially at heart. Of these, one was the protection of the people against the depredations of the purveyors to the court. A royal progress in those days was almost as disastrous an event as the march of an invading army. Not content with making the necessary requisitions, the purveyors, aided by the wilder sort of the cavaliers, levied indiscriminate and exorbitant toll on high and low, rich and poor, and took a savage delight in destroying, before the eyes of the unhappy owners, whatsoever they could not profitably use, or conveniently carry away. And to these invasions of proprietary rights were added the violations of the domestic sanctities, usual upon the sack of a town. For the repression of these disorders, Henry passed a severe law, making the offenders liable to the loss of eyes, hands, or feet, or other mutilation, according to the gravity of their misdeeds.

Another reform concerned the currency, which had become seriously depreciated by the issue of false coinage by private minters. It was accordingly enacted that whoso should make, or knowingly take such coins should lose his sight.

It remained to deal with the ever-recrudescent scandal of clerical incontinence. For this purpose, Anselm held at London, at Whitsuntide, 1108, a great council of clergy and laity, which Henry dignified with his presence, and by which various stringent canons were passed.

Meanwhile, Anselm lost his old and tried friend, Gundulf, Bishop of Rochester, who, after a period of gradual, almost insensible decline, passed peacefully away on 8 March, 1108, with the words of the fifteenth verse of the seventy-ninth Psalm upon his lips: "Deus virtutum convertere; respice de coelo, et vide, et visita vineam istam" (Ps. lxxx. 14, 15 in the English version). Anselm, summoned hastily from Canterbury, arrived at Rochester in time to preside at the obsequies. Gundulf had designated as his successor one of his own monks, Ralph, Abbot of Séez, whom Anselm afterwards (9 August), consecrated at Canterbury, not perhaps without a presentiment that, as the event proved, at no distant date, his own mantle would fall upon Ralph's shoulders.

The death of Gerard, the mendacious Archbishop of York, followed hard upon that of Gundulf, and the new Archbishop-elect, Thomas, son of Samson, Bishop of Worcester,[1] proved a thorn in Anselm's side. Jealous of the primacy of Canterbury, and instigated by Ranulf Flambard, whom Henry had weakly forgiven, and reinstated in the See of Durham, Thomas applied at Rome for the pallium, without waiting for consecration by Anselm; and there were even rumours that he entertained the extravagant idea of himself consecrating a Durham monk, named Thurgod, to the vacant See of St. Andrew's.

By the canon law Thomas was bound to present himself at Canterbury for consecration within three months of his election. The canonical time, however,

[1] Thomas was born in wedlock before Samson received holy orders.

slipped by, and the archbishop-elect did not make his appearance, Anselm accordingly wrote to him, requiring his presence at Canterbury not later than the 6th of September, and peremptorily forbidding him to consecrate Thurgod. To Anselm's brief and business-like missive, Thomas returned a lengthy and evasive reply, alleging what was, doubtless, not without a substratum of truth, that the mendacious Gerard had also proved the rapacious Gerard, and had left the See of York so impoverished, that even the means of transit to Canterbury were hardly to be come by. That he had sent to Rome for the pallium he acknowledged, but averred that he had done so by the authority of the king. The rumours about the intended consecration of Thurgod were unfounded. For his attendance at Canterbury he craved some further grace.

Anselm replied briefly as before, fixing 27 September for his appearance at Canterbury, and warning him that the application for the pallium could not but be fruitless, as the sacred stole was never conferred before consecration. He then wrote to the Pope, apprising him of Thomas's uncanonical behaviour. His letter had the desired effect, and the archbishop-elect's suit made no progress at Rome.

Meanwhile, however, Thomas still neglected to put in an appearance at Canterbury, expecting, no doubt, that the primate, whose life was now visibly ebbing away, would either give up the contest, or be removed by the hand of death. So he pursued his miserable tactics until Anselm, his patience at last fairly exhausted, laid him under interdict. This proved to be his last official act of importance, and the now dying primate bequeathed the dispute—which the reader, who is now probably heartily sick of it, will be relieved to learn was eventually decided in favour of the See of Canterbury—to his successor, Archbishop Ralph.

Ever since Anselm's return to England, it had been apparent to close observers that his end was near; but though prostrated from time to time by severe illness, he had rallied as if by miracle, and thrown himself with renewed ardour into the discharge of his multifarious and onerous duties. Nay, amidst them all he had found time and strength to wrestle with those knottiest of all the knotty problems of metaphysical theology, which are implicit in the relations of sin and grace, freewill and foreknowledge; and if his *Tractatus de Concordia Praescientiae et Praedestinationis nec non gratiae Dei cum Libero Arbitrio*, in which this last effort of his genius is enshrined, fails to afford a complete solution of questions which are perhaps beyond the reach of human thought, that is rather to be imputed to the topic itself than to the decline of his powers.

Into the labyrinthine mazes of this question it would be presumptuous to enter here. The essential moments of Anselm's thought are, however, as follows. Strictly speaking, God neither *fore*knows nor *fore*ordains, but only knows and ordains, since all things are eternally equipresent to Him. It is only because what to us is future is to Him eternally present, that by a convenient license of speech He is said to *fore*know and *fore*ordain. Moreover, as His essence is absolutely simple, His knowing and ordaining are one. But His ordaining is both positive and negative, *i.e.* what is good He ordains positively, and what He ordains positively is good; on the other hand, moral evil is only negatively ordained, *i.e.* permitted by Him. Indeed, as we saw in the dialogues, *De Casu Diaboli* and *De Libero Arbitrio*, moral evil is itself nothing positive, but a mere defect, a want of correspondence with the positive will of God; and free will does not necessarily involve the power of choosing between good and evil (otherwise God, who cannot sin, would not be free), but is the power of persevering in righteousness for its own sake (potestas servandi rectitudinem propter ipsam rectitudinem); and though in man impaired by the Fall, so that, without the grace of God, he cannot, without difficulty, persevere in righteousness for its own sake; yet it remains in him in such measure as to render him responsible for his lapses, though impotent to restore himself. For his redemption from sin, therefore, man is absolutely dependent upon the grace of God. Nay, his very freedom is itself but that same grace. For as a creature he has nothing positive of himself, and therefore even that freedom which is called natural is really a grace. Alike then for his natural virtue, as for his supernatural holiness, man is entirely beholden to God.

And hence arises the antinomy of which, in this treatise, Anselm seeks the solution. For, as God is omniscient, and man absolutely dependent upon Him, his behaviour, under the influence of the Divine grace, must be known to, and thus ordained by, God from all eternity. In what sense then can he be held responsible for his acts? If not only his probation, but the issue of his probation, was foreknown and predetermined, "lucis ante originem," is not the probation thereby robbed of all reality? Is not man a puppet in the hands of an inscrutable stage-manager, who, by the fine fibres of motive, guides him to a goal, which, whether for good or for evil, he can neither seek nor avoid.

The solution of this formidable antinomy Anselm seeks in a distinction between sequent and antecedent necessity. Whatever is, or is to be, is necessary in the sense that it is ordained of God (sequent necessity); but not all things are necessary in the sense that they are products of constraining force (antecedent necessity).

That which, in the case of human volition, God foreknows, is simply how man will freely act. The apparent repugnance between the Divine foreknowledge and human freedom, is due to a mere confusion of sequent with antecedent necessity. But on a topic of such difficulty, Anselm had best be allowed to speak for himself.

"The foreknowledge of God," he says, "and free will seem to be repugnant, because what God foresees must of necessity come to pass, and what is done by free will comes to be by no necessity; but if they are repugnant, it is impossible that the foreknowledge of God, which embraces all futurity, should consist with aught being done by free will. But if it be shown that there is no such impossibility, the apparent repugnance is altogether removed. Let us assume, then, the co-existence of the foreknowledge of God, by which the necessity of future events appears to be determined, and the freedom of the will, by which many things are believed to be done without any necessity; and let us see whether it be impossible for them to consist. Now, it is the mark of an impossibility that it should give rise to another impossibility; for that is plainly impossible which, being assumed, another impossibility follows. But whatever is to be without necessity, that very thing God foresees, since He foresees all futurity; and what God foresees, that of necessity must come to be, as it is foreseen. It is necessary, therefore, that there should be something which is to be without necessity. Whoso, then, rightly understands the matter, will by no means find the foreknowledge of God, which determines necessity, repugnant to the freedom of will, which excludes necessity; since it is both necessary that God foresee what is to be, and true that part of what He foresees is to be without any necessity. But you will say, 'This does not relieve me of the necessity of sinning or not sinning, since God foresees that I shall sin or not sin; and, therefore, it is necessary that I should sin if I sin, or not sin if I do not sin.' To which I reply, You ought not to say, 'God foresees that I shall sin or not sin' without qualification, but 'God foresees that I shall sin or not sin *without necessity*'; and so it follows that, whether you sin or do not sin, in either case it will be without necessity, because God foresees that that which is to be will be without necessity. You see, then, that it is not impossible that the foreknowledge of God, by virtue of which the future events, which He foreknows, are said to be of necessity, should consist with the freedom of the will, by virtue of which many things are done without necessity. For, were it impossible, some other impossibility would follow from it; but hence arises no impossibility.

"Perhaps you will say, 'Not as yet, however, do you release my soul from the constraint of necessity, when you say that it is necessary that I should sin or not sin without necessity, because this is what God foresees; for necessity seems to have in it the ring of constraint or restraint. Wherefore, if it is necessary for me to sin voluntarily, I understand thereby that it is by some occult force that, if I sin, I am constrained to the sinful act of will, or, if I sin not, am restrained therefrom. So that, whether I sin or sin not, it seems to be equally of necessity.'

"I answer, You must know, then, that we often describe as being of necessity that which is under the constraint of no force whatever, and as of necessity not being that which is prevented from being by no restraint. For we say it is necessary that God should be immortal, and it is necessary that God should not be unjust, not because any force constrains Him to be immortal or restrains Him from being unjust, but because nothing can make Him mortal or unjust.

And so, if I say it is necessary that you should sin or sin not by your own mere will, as God foresees; it is not to be understood that the volition which will not be is by any force restrained from being, or that the volition which will be is by any force constrained to be; for, in foreseeing that something is to be by mere volition, God foresees this very thing, that the will is not compelled or restrained by anything but itself, and that so what is done voluntarily is done freely.

"Let this once be thoroughly understood, and I think it will appear that there is no incompatibility between the foreknowledge of God and the freedom of the will. In fine, if one considers the proper meaning of the word itself, by the very fact that a thing is said to be foreseen it is affirmed that it will be; for nothing but what will be is foreseen, since knowledge is only of truth. Wherefore, when I say whatsoever God foresees, that must of necessity come to pass; it is the same as if I said, If it will be, it will of necessity be; but by this necessity nothing is either constrained to be, or restrained from being. For it is because the existence of the thing is posited that it is said of necessity to be, or because its non-existence is posited that it is said of necessity not to be, not because necessity constrains it to be, or restrains it from being. For this necessity signifies nothing more than that what will be cannot at the same time not be."

This doctrine of the twofold nature of necessity, derived by Anselm from Boethius, *De Consolat. Phil.* v. §§ 4, 6,[1] affords, perhaps, the nearest approach to a

[1] Cf. Dante, *Parad.* c. xvii. 37–42, where "necessità" stands for "antecedent necessity," and "contingenza" for "sequent necessity."

La contingenza, che fuor del quaderno
    Della vostra materia non si stende,
    Tutta è dipinta nel cospetto eterno.
Necessità però quindi non prende,
    Se non come dal viso in che si specchia,
    Nave che per corrente giù discende.

Contingency in matter close confined,
    Your coarse corporeal sense may not transcend,
    Yet all is imaged in the eternal mind;
Nor to necessity doth thereby bend:
    No more than ship is wafted by the sight
    Which mirrors how she down the stream doth tend.

solution of which this transcendently mysterious problem admits.

And yet, it may be urged, is it not, after all, true that God's perfect prevision, and, therefore permissive predestination of human action, must, in some measure, limit human freedom? As little, it may be replied, as a license to travel a certain road, which, of course, carries with it an implicit prohibition of deviation, imposes upon the grantee the obligation of travelling. If he travel, he must travel by the prescribed route; but it is open to him to travel or not as he pleases.

But to this comes the inevitable rejoinder that it is known to God from all eternity, not only by what route the traveller will travel, but whether he will travel or no.

To say, with Anselm, that what God ordains is just that man shall freely fare upon his predestined course, may be all that there is to be said; but it certainly leaves the relation of the Divine and the human will shrouded in impenetrable mystery.[1]

Hardly had Anselm's spirit emerged from the dark and cavernous recesses of speculation, into which we have just cast a shy glance, than it winged its ecstatic flight straight for the empyrean, seeking its own source in the Source of all light. In other words, he began to meditate a treatise on the origin of the soul.

But while the mind remained strong and keen as ever, the fleshly tenement was swiftly wasting away; eating became almost an impossibility, and by the spring of 1109 he was too weak to walk or even stand.

[1] A concise and luminous account of the later history and present position of this still vexed question will be found in F. Bernard Boedder's *Natural Theology* (Stonyhurst Series of Manuals of Catholic Philosophy).

He was then at Canterbury, and being unable any longer to say mass, had himself carried daily into his chapel to hear it. On Palm Sunday, 18 April, one of the clergy, noting his extreme weakness, said to him, "Lord and Father, as far as we can see, you are about to leave this world for the Easter court of your Lord." He replied, "And, indeed, if it be His will, I shall gladly obey it; but should He rather will that I remain with you yet so long a time as that I may solve a problem which I am turning over in my mind, as to the origin of the soul, I should welcome the delay, because I know not whether, when I am gone, there will be anyone left to solve it."[1]

From that hour he sank painlessly and peacefully. Speechless, but still conscious, he made his last sign of the cross on the following Tuesday evening, in answer to the Bishop of Rochester's whispered request for his blessing on those who stood by, and the rest of his spiritual children, the king and queen and royal family, and the people of England. At matins one of the brothers read to him the gospel of the day,[2] the gospel of the Passion according to St. Luke. When he came to the words: "Vos autem estis qui permansistis mecum in tentationibus meis. Et ego dispono vobis, sicut disposuit mihi Pater meus regnum, ut edatis et bibatis super mensam meam in regno meo"—"Ye are they which have continued with me in my temptations. And I appoint unto you a kingdom, even as my Father appointed unto me, that ye may eat and

[1] He was doubtless feeling his way towards a reconciliation of creationism with the transmission of original sin. *Cf. De Concept Virgin.* c. xxiv. *et seq.*

[2] Wednesday in Holy Week.

drink at my table in my kingdom"—Anselm began to draw breath more slowly. Then, seeing that the hour of his passing was at hand, they raised him from the bed and stretched him on the floor, where the freshly-strewn ashes traced the emblem of his faith and hope, the ensign of his warfare and victory. And so they watched and listened, while the night wore on, and the breathing grew fainter and more faint, until, towards daybreak, it was manifest that Anselm had solved the problem of the origin of the soul.

On the morrow, the saint's mortal remains, washed with loving care, and anointed with the holy chrism, were laid to rest in the nave of the cathedral, next the tomb of Lanfranc.[1]

[1] Thence they were soon afterwards removed to the chapel of SS. Peter and Paul on the south side of the chancel, where they are still supposed to rest. Relics of him were, perhaps still are, venerated at Antwerp, Cologne, Bologna, and Prague. GERVASE OF CANTERBURY (Rolls Ser.), i. 15. Bollandists' *Acta Sanct. April.* (ed. 1866) ii. 862.

APPENDIX

CONTAINING CERTAIN MIRACULOUS INCIDENTS

Attested by Eadmer in his *De Vita Anselmi* and supplementary *Descriptio Miraculorum Gloriosi Patris Anselmi.*

A LIFE of St. Anselm would hardly be complete without some notice of the principal miraculous phenomena recorded by Eadmer in connection with his death; and for obvious reasons Eadmer had best be allowed to tell his own tale; which is as follows:—

"There was a monk of Canterbury, by name Helias, honourably distinguished by the purity of his morals and the simplicity and innocence of his life. One night, about three months before the death of Father Anselm, this man saw himself in a vision standing in the oratory alone, his mind bent, as God prompted him, on prayer. While thus engaged he looked, and lo! Father Anselm lay in prayer in front of the tomb of St. Dunstan. And as Anselm prayed, Helias observed that the upper part or roof of the tomb moved, and gradually shifted from its place. And when Anselm, disturbed by the movement, rose up from praying, he saw Blessed Dunstan in the tomb gradually raise himself towards a sitting posture; but he was impeded by the roof of the tomb, which had not yet so far receded as to allow him room to sit upright. Anselm put forth all his strength to force the mass out of his way, but in vain. He therefore beckoned to Helias, who was standing some way off, to come near, that by their joint efforts they might effect what his own unaided strength could not. He came, and where the one had failed the two succeeded. And so the obstacle being removed, the most holy father sat upright, and turning towards Anselm, said to him, 'Dearest friend, know that I have heard your prayers,' and extending his right hand, he offered him a golden ring, saying, 'Be this a sign unto you that I have spoken truth.' And when Anselm stretched forth his hand to take the ring, Blessed Dunstan withdrew his hand, and said to him, 'This time you shall not have the ring; but I will keep it, and you shall receive it from the hand of the Lord on the fourth day before Easter.' This vision the same brother Helias related to me [Eadmer] while we were gossiping on the following day; but I, desiring the life rather than the death of my master, did not then think of interpreting it in the manner in which it afterwards came true. But when the day had come, the event itself proved what the vision had portended in a figure; for, in truth, it was at the dawn of that day that the father was taken from this life." (*Descript. Mirac.*)

. . . .

"There was a man not too well provided with worldly goods, but abounding above the common measure, as he had power, in zeal for the service of Christ, who, when Father Anselm was dying, lay himself at Canterbury dying of a grievous disease. And lo! while he was thought to be already loosed from the body, in the hour when that glorious servant of the Lord departed this life, a young man of noble mien appeared to him, and asked him what ailed him. He answered, 'I die, as you see, and do you ask what ails me?' He rejoined, 'The father of this city and of this whole country is even now hastening to God, that he may exchange the world for eternal life, and shall you die? By no means. Nay, rather arise whole, and glorify God the Father that does this work in you, and glorifies your father aforesaid eternally in recompense of his merits.' And so, to the amazement of all those who had gathered for his funeral, the man recovered, and they ask, How came it that he was so suddenly restored to health?

Whereupon he told them distinctly what he had seen, what he had heard, what he had learned concerning Father Anselm's glorification. And so, leaving him, they hurry to the Church of our Lord the Saviour, and find it even as they had heard; to wit, that the said chosen vessel of the Lord had just been translated from this life." (*Ibid.*)

. . . .

"After the ritual washing of Anselm's body, his steward, Baldwin, of whom frequent mention has been made heretofore, prayed that the face of the deceased father might be anointed with an unguent, of which, the bulk of it being lost, all that remained was a very small quantity in a little vase; hoping and earnestly desiring that by that means it might be preserved ever so little longer from corruption. We acquiesced, embracing his proposal. So the bishop took the vase containing the liquid in hand, and for the purpose of anointing the face of the deceased, thrust his finger into the vase until it touched the bottom; then, drawing it out, and finding the top of it hardly moistened, thought the ointment would by no means suffice to anoint the face. He therefore ordered the unguent which was kept in the greater church, for the purpose of making the chrism, to be brought; being desirous that both Anselm's head and his right hand, with which he had said and written many good and divine things, might be honoured with such anointing. In all this I was with the bishop, and assisted him in the function. I thrust my finger after him into the vase containing the unguent, and drew it out as little, or perhaps less moist than his. I accordingly asked the bishop to invert the vase over the palm of my hand, to see if perchance a drop or so would run out of it; he assented; and forthwith, to the amazement of all, the liquid gushed forth in a copious stream, covering my hand and overflowing. The same thing was repeated again and again—many times, in fact. In short, an all but empty vase furnished such a plentiful supply of unguent, that, without recourse to the vase belonging to the church, we anointed not only the head and hands, but the arms and chest, the feet, and in fine, Anselm's entire body, not once only, but several times. He was then dressed in the sacred vestments proper to his office of chief pontiff, and carried with due reverence into the oratory.

"On the following day, while he was being committed to the tomb, it was discovered that the sarcophagus, which some days before had been made ready for him, was indeed of the right length and breadth, but was a great deal too shallow. Whereat we were disconcerted, being by no means able to endure the idea that he should sustain any injury by the pressure of the upper stone. And while the minds of most fluctuated to and fro, some suggesting this, some the other solution of the difficulty, one of the closely-packed crowd of brothers who stood around took the crosier of the Bishop of Rochester, who presided at the funeral ceremony, and extending it over the body of the father, began to wave it to and fro transversely to the sarcophagus; whereupon he found, to our great wonder, that it rose above the body on every side." (*De Vita Anselmi*, ii. §§ 67–68.)

"A nobleman, a stout soldier, known in many parts of England, Humfrey by name, being stricken with a very grievous disease, to wit, that which some call dropsy, and despaired of by the physicians, lay, as was thought, at the point of death. He had been known to Anselm, and had taken note of the many signs of his sanctity. So, prostrated by his malady, he ever had him on his lips, ever prayed, nothing doubting that, for the sake of his merits and prayers, God would be propitious to him. One of his old friends, named Haimo, was a monk of Christ Church, Canterbury. So he sent messengers to the prior of the monastery, and sought and obtained permission for Haimo to come to him; thinking that it would be some relief to him in both body and soul, if in his last moments he might have the solace of his company, and that of the brother who would attend him. The brother came, and brought with him Father Anselm's girdle. For he was my nephew, being my sister's son, and had the girdle from me in his custody. He, seeing the man, by reason of the aggravated character of his disorder, swollen in every part of his body, and to such a degree that all who saw him thought him ready to burst, gave him the girdle, telling him whose it was, and from whom he had received it. He gave a groan, and calling to mind the sanctity of the blessed father, and first praying devoutly that, for the sake of his merits, God would graciously have mercy upon him, took the girdle, kissed it, and disposed it about his person, its ends hardly meeting, by reason of his extreme distension. So he kept it on him a short while, and lo! strange to tell, little by little his body began to diminish in bulk, until the ends of the girdle overlapped for a little distance, fully the length of a man's foot; which he perceiving, straightway passed the girdle to and fro over his swollen limbs, and at its touch the exorbitant swelling which had invaded them vanished entirely and at once. Nor did the abundance of evil humour, which was the cause of the swelling, find its way out by any channel, which may, perhaps, cause you even more surprise, but perished by resolution into nothing.

"So the man recovered, and some days afterwards came to Canterbury, and presented himself at the tomb of the father to give thanks there, and told the whole story in the assembly of the brethren, and besought and obtained their thanksgivings to God, and His blessed servant on his behalf. I confess that hearing these things gave me great joy. And, turning to the man, I said, 'The girdle belongs to us: be so good as to restore it, as is fitting.' To which he answered, 'I know, I know that it is as you say. But be assured that you will recover it most speedily by coming to my house for it.' I assented; and some days later, necessary business intervening, I went thither, and received the girdle from him. At his request, however, I cut a strip from it—very narrow, but the full length of the girdle, and left it with him; and so we parted. His health gave us no more concern until, after a considerable interval of time, we heard at Canterbury that he had been seized with his old complaint, and was in grievous suffering. I therefore went to him, but found him free from the alleged malady. So, wondering whether I had come thither on a false report, I asked him whether he had really been ill, as we had heard. Upon which he avowed that he had been ill, and, in answer to my further enquiries, told the manner of his recovery. He said that, overcome by extreme suffering, he called to remembrance what he had gone through before, and how he had been cured, and bethought him that though he had not the entire girdle, which had been the means of his recovery, yet he whose it was might, perhaps, if he would, cure him by the part of it which he had as well as by the whole. 'In which hope,' he said, 'I disposed the strip which you gave me about my person, and straightway, as you see, I was restored to health.'

. . . .

"After this, when, on the petition of Alexander, King of the Scots, I had been translated to the pontificate of St. Andrew's in Scotland, and, having spent some time there, had become known to the natives of that country, and was well received by them; it chanced that a matron of a noble English family, and well approved on all hands in the Christian religion, Eastrildis by name, suffered from a grievous bodily disease, and to such a degree that whoever visited her testified that she had nothing to anticipate but death. She had heard the fame of the sanctity of Father Anselm, and being then more fully instructed therein by me—for she took great delight in hearing of the virtues of others—notwithstanding her desire was rather to be loosed from the body and be with Christ, yet she permitted the girdle of the father, concerning which I have recorded certain matters above, to be placed around her. Which done, she at once began to mend, and after a few days was completely restored to health, to the amazement of all. This I witnessed, being present, and for the favour thus vouchsafed, not I alone, but also many with me, with great joy gave praise and thanks to God.

"Later on, when the zeal of the fear of God, and solicitude for the salvation of my soul, compelled me to leave Scotland suddenly, and return to the Mother-church of all Britain—the

Church, I mean, of Canterbury, which had nurtured me from infancy—to seek counsel concerning those things which lay heavy on my soul, I came thither, but found there nothing of which I had come in search. For, in truth, Archbishop Ralph was ill; nor did health return to him, so long as he remained in the present life. At this time the hearts of many were afflicted with poignant grief, on account of one of the brethren, who had been taken with a sharp attack of fever; for he was a young man, and, by the tokens of goodness which he displayed, gave certain promise of a life fruitful to the Church of God. He then, as his malady increased in severity, being all but despaired of by himself and others, turned himself by all ways to God, and was solicitous, as far as he might, to remove every hindrance to the passage of his soul. We were with him, earnestly seconding his prayers. While thus engaged, we bethink us of the great favours which Blessed Anselm used to procure for his children; which leads us to speak of the wonders which, after his removal from the world, he wrought by his girdle. Then, without delay, at the request of the sick man, I brought the girdle, which was fastened about his neck. The same hour the fever subsided, nor did it again attack him.

"So the brother recovered, and we all gave thanks to God the Saviour for his recovery through His faithful servant. But enough of this; for were I to record, one by one, all the wonders which have been wrought by means of that girdle, without doubt I should be burdensome to all my readers. For it is the regular practice for all men who are in any manner sick, and especially for women in danger by travail, to have recourse to the girdle with a devout intention, relying with a firm hope on their release from peril by its timely use. Nor have we hitherto heard of any being disappointed in their hope—of those, that is to say, of whose sincerity in having recourse to the girdle for their relief in full faith, we have no reason to doubt.

"One other case, however, I can by no means persuade myself to pass over, the case of one of the brethren of Christ Church, Canterbury, who was grievously afflicted with a tumourous growth, in the shape of a large and smoothly-rounded sphere beneath his navel, but who was completely restored to his former health; the pain, which had reached his heart, subsiding at once at the touch of the girdle, and the swelling soon afterwards entirely disappearing." (*Descript. Mirac.*)

NOTE.—Though Anselm was thus early invested with the aureole of the saint, the process preliminary to his canonisation, committed to the care of Becket by Alexander III. in 1163, was abandoned in consequence of the subsequent troubles; nor was it revived until 1494, and then, in the irony of fate, by Alexander VI. of evil memory. Whether it resulted in a decree does not appear; but Anselm belongs to the number of those Blessed Doctors whom the ancient and universal consent of the Church has canonised. His feast, 21 April, was raised from a semi-double to a double by Clement XI. in 1720. *Materials for the History of Thomas Becket* (Rolls Ser.) v. 35; Wilkins' *Concilia*, iii. 641; *Bullar. Clement. XI.*, 8 Feb. 1720.

INDEX

ST. ANSELM OF CANTERBURY

INDEX

INDEX

INDEX

INDEX